DAISY
HAS
AUTISM

AARON J. WRIGHT

Cover Design by JudithSDesign & Creativity | www.judithsdesign.com

Editing, Interior Design, Publishing | Janet Angelo | INDIEGO PUBLISHING
www.indiegopublishing.com

Publisher's Cataloging-in-Publication Data
Names: Wright, Aaron J., 1975- author.
Title: Daisy has autism / Aaron J. Wright.
Description: [FL] : IndieGo Publishing, 2019. | Summary: This work of creative
    non-fiction recounts the struggles faced by the parents of an autistic daughter
    as they try to get the school system to provide special education services.
Identifiers: LCCN 2018967807 | ISBN 9781946824318 (hardcover) | ISBN
    9781946824356 (pbk.) | ISBN 9781946824363 (ebook)
Subjects: LCSH: Parents of autistic children — California — Biography. | Special
    education — Parent participation. | Children with disabilities — Services for.
    | BISAC: FAMILY & RELATIONSHIPS / Autism Spectrum Disorders.
    | EDUCATION / Special Education / General. | BIOGRAPHY &
    AUTOBIOGRAPHY / People with Disabilities.
Classification: LCC RJ506.A9 W75 2019 (print) | LCC RJ506.A9 (ebook)
    | DDC 371.9 W — dc23
LC record available at https://lccn.loc.gov/2018967807

For anyone who departed for Italy but touched down in Holland . . . especially for Stacia and Max.

"Let there be light."

Genesis 1:3, and the motto of the University of California

Sunflowers

Annual rites break the soil
Curious craning heads and necks rock to and fro
Sunrise becomes sunset, in time lapse

Blissful weeds, growing too fast

With beaming faces, they pose for photos
We all frolic among them
Bees buzz them in a cacophony of laughter

Wonder's prized youth with heart shapes worn as sleeves
Summer and promise are intoxicating
Fireworks kiss them in the dark, like teenagers

Fleeting as high school love, only heartache lasts

Heads heavy with the burden of tomorrow
Setting cede to circumstance, bowing in deference
They wilt and sunburn without water or shade

Dehydrated, their sweetness taken for another's honeypot
Colorless stick figures stand erect – rattling like snakes
No longer adored, skeletal and gaunt

Awaiting desiccation's perfection, the cameras are long gone

They stand in line together, in shameful defiance
Only in the memory of summer's last kiss do they capitulate
Genocide comes as summer goes, when no one's watching

The farmer smiles – a new brag-worthy crop will come again next year.

Daisy

Has

Autism

Between Turtle Rock and Apple Hill

"We are born believing. A man bears beliefs as a tree bears apples."

— Ralph Waldo Emerson

"Are we sure this is a good idea?" I glanced over at Annie as we drove Highway 50 through the rolling foothills east of Sacramento toward Lake Tahoe.

"We will find out," Annie said. "We all need to get out of Davis; besides, it's only one night of car camping – nothing super serious. There's s'mores for the kids and wine for the adults."

I tilted the rearview mirror down to look in the back seat. Charlie had his earbuds in and was lip-syncing as he gazed out the window. Magda too, had her earbuds in, but it was hard to tell because she had pulled her hoodie over her head and her hat brim down over her face. Her arms were folded into one another, protecting her abdomen. She was rejecting the changing world around her.

"I just don't know." I saw Daisy's head pop up from the back seat. She panted and flapped her ears.

"This will be a great time for you and Charlie to take a hike together or find someplace to fish," Annie said. "I think he would appreciate a little alone time with you. I worry that since she is the focus of so much of our attention, he's a little neglected."

"Who picked Turtle Rock Park?" I asked.

"Feather, of course. She says it's beautiful. It was this or someplace called Lake Comanche."

"Where is that?"

"I have no idea," she said.

As we left Placerville, an incredible sound of tearing metal erupted from within the car, and my seat began to rock. I instinctively let off the accelerator and looked at the instrument cluster. As abruptly as it had started, the noise stopped. The oil pressure was fine, the battery was fully charged, and the motor was still running.

"Did we hit something?" I asked, turning to Annie. "All the instruments say the car is okay."

"I didn't see anything. Should we pull over?" Annie glanced at me with concern.

Daisy popped her head between the front seats and flapped her ears in distress.

The grating sound returned, and this time I knew it was the banshee behind me. I slowed and pulled off the highway into the parking lot of the Red Apple Cafe. Magda continued to shriek and kick. I lunged forward as both feet struck the driver's seat with full force. When I spun around, I saw Charlie rip the white ear buds from Magda's ears and rapidly replace them with his own, and with that, the turbulence in the car ceased. Blissful silence descended.

"What did you just do?" Annie asked.

"She twists and bites her ear buds," Charlie said, "and it breaks them. Then she has a fit and thinks that her iPod is broken, when it's not. It's just the ear buds. I gave her mine."

Annie and I stared at each other, not knowing how to respond.

"Are we in Markleeville?" Charlie asked.

"No, not yet," I said. "I think we are still in El Dorado County. This is Apple Hill."

"Why?" asked Charlie.

"They grow a lot of apples here."

"No, why El Dorado?" Charlie clarified.

"I think it means something like made of gold. They found a lot of gold here during the gold rush."

"What do you guys want to talk about?" Charlie said, catching us off guard with this sudden change of subject.

"I don't know. What do you want to talk about?" Annie asked quizzically.

"What do you guys talk about in the front seat?" Charlie said. "You are always talking about Magda."

"Well, I was going to ask your mother how you knew to do what you just did with the ear buds," I replied.

"I don't know. It happens a lot." Charlie shrugged.

*   *   *

At four-thirty in the morning, Magda had still yet to fall asleep, and we had exhausted the strategies given to us by her therapists. She was kicking the sides of the tent and moaning. Every five to ten minutes she cycled back into sobbing then screaming, "I want to go home! This is not my bed!"

The picture calendar and sequencing we had laid out for Magda prior to leaving on this camping trip had evaporated into the arid mountain air. Even with weeks of preparation, the right layering to her bedding, her quilted comforter, her fleece princess blanket, her weighted blanket, and her Daisy dog – Turtle Rock Park was not her bedroom. Resistance to change seemed hell-bent on destroying any new experiences she might have, and by five-thirty in the morning, we were apologizing for waking the other families. By six, we were driving back down the hill toward home. Daisy and Magda were the only two who stayed awake with me the whole way back.

"I hope next year's teacher gets it," Annie mumbled as I pulled into our East Davis manor.

Sandy

"If the doors of perception were cleansed, everything would appear to man as it is: Infinite."

— William Blake

Six years earlier...

Like a lot of our college classmates, Annie and I left Davis, California, in the late nineties with University of California degrees in hand, ready to explore the blank slate of possibility. We landed in Oakland, Annie's hometown. Infinite possibility yielded to reality for me when I awakened to the fact that an undergraduate degree confers more debt than workplace preparedness. That reality also fed the blossoming notion that a solid friendship could mean much more, so Annie and I worked our way through graduate degrees in teaching and nursing respectively. Then, together as a unit, we sought what could be possible in a life together.

When we returned to Davis a little over five years later, we did so as a married couple with our two-year-old son Charlie toddling in tow. The move back was a milestone for us, one driven by the desire to no longer save quarters for the laundry, to sleep without traffic's constant rumble, and to find local parks where children and junkies didn't covet the same hiding spots. We felt compelled to find a place where Charlie could explore his own possibilities, and as part of that, go to a good public school. Our collegiate memories of Davis were rose-colored. The streets were safe, the sidewalks were smooth and wide, the schools were renowned.

And then, as if by serendipity, it happened. I found a job in neighboring Sacramento, and shortly thereafter, the drafty white tract house with blue trim two houses down from the corner of Pear Street and Spellman Drive in Davis would become our first home. As our realtor promised, it was only a stone's throw from Putah Creek Elementary. (Putah Creek, which once ran through Davis, is the Green River that John Fogerty sang about in the eponymous Credence Clearwater Revival song.)

As the campus that a century ago used to be UC Berkeley's agriculture school grew, the town that was Davisville became an exceptional place to live and learn. Annie and I wanted the same thing that has drawn people to Davis for a century. We wanted to live in a town where forward thinking people had converted a campus farm into a top public university and then generations later converted traditional elementary schools into centers for language immersion and alternative choices in education. Davis seemed idyllic.

Our first home, the El Dorado model of the tract homes built in the Sixties, was well worn. The three tiny bedrooms, the one common bathroom, galley kitchen, and the small dining area large enough for a card table had seen more renters than owners, and the volume of foot traffic showed. We set about patching its cracks as soon as we moved in.

One home improvement that Annie and I had always wanted was a dog. Annie had never had a dog. Charlie hadn't either. I wanted their first dog to be special. You never forget your first dog, just like you never forget your first house. I was biased, having grown up in a home with Golden Retrievers. They were all goofy smiles and wet noses when you wanted it and warm nuzzles when you needed it. On the other hand, they are a heartbreak breed; questionable breeding practices have made them prone to vascular and organ cancers. Annie, being her own person, often equivocated on what kind of dog she wanted. Goldens were high on her list, but one day in May before we moved to Davis, without clear rationale, she decided on a Black Lab.

That was all I needed. On one of many trips back to Davis, I stopped, as I frequently did, at the Yolo County Sheriff's facility in Woodland, which also housed the county's animal services. It is a nondescript cluster of metastasizing buildings mostly dedicated to tending California's only drought tolerant and sustainable crop: inmates. Regardless, I was drawn to it almost weekly.

When I pulled into the parking lot this time, the patchy and cracked asphalt was vacant as usual, except for the mid-80s Toyota Corolla I had seen there many times parked under a shade tree. Its flaking faded silver paint coordinated perfectly with the cracked back window that had been repaired with a multitude of quirky bumper stickers:

Dog is my copilot

Visualize whirled peas

Subvert the Dominant Paradigm

Who saved who?

Cure ignorance, not autism

Beyond the decals, I could see that the upholstery and armrests had been all but destroyed. The exposed and aged orange foam had been worn into a thin powder from the repeated passage of animal carriers. A haphazard arrangement of stringy towels lined the back dash. Sitting shotgun were three 55-lb. bags of Costco brand dog food. The floorboard was crammed with blue bottles of orange-capped laundry detergent.

I moved through the open chain-link gate that guarded the breezeway between the animal services office and the kennels. As always, I complied with the posted sign to check in at the main desk before looking at the animals. It was 11:12 a.m., July 12, 2005, and I checked the box "Just Browsing." The uninterested officer behind the chest-high desk gave me a familiar smile. I left the office through another metal security door, held my breath through a "sanitizing" anteroom, and pressed onward to the kennels.

The main housing wing for the dogs was composed of two adjoining and identical rectangular rooms. The far room was locked and for strays only. The room in which I stood was only for adoptable dogs. The wall tiles looked like bits of mustard left outside of the cap to desiccate. The air was stale and the light from the florescent tubes in the ceiling was glaringly unnatural.

The concrete floor was sloped toward washes in the middle and edges of the room to facilitate a daily hosing, an ingenuity that was no doubt hard on the dogs. Chain-link gates offered me the prohibited chance to push a couple fingers through to give the dogs a head scratch, and the clear plastic information pouches wire-tied to the gates told me only the most basic information about each occupant's true self.

Chihuahuas and Pit Bulls disproportionately dominated the cellblock. The occasional indeterminate mix burst forth in exuberance as I approached. Whatever their breed, they all quieted when I turned my attention from their paperwork to them. Most sat quiet and still, eyes trained on me, awaiting my next cue. Some were reluctant, others excited. All were ready to follow me out.

Past the first aisle of dogs and rounding the back wall toward the second, I spotted her, or rather her rump. She was facing the rear of her cage and seemed featureless under the artificial light. With her ears dangling forward, she was prying loose a tennis ball from under a section of chain-link. The ball was stuck, and she was a moving a blob of ink. Her haunches heaved left and right, her rear paws skidding sideways as her otter's tail yanked her body around. When she finally turned my way, she stared beyond me and barked continually.

It was a fearful, confused bark, unsure and remote, a bark I would come to know as her only bark. I kneeled down in front of her. The barking became staccato then falsetto. Her front paws danced off the floor, her rear almost touched the concrete, and she peed. She made no eye contact.

I whispered soothingly and pushed my palm against the galvanized metal. She immediately nosed and licked my hand, then dove back to pry her ball loose with no success.

I stood up and reached for her descriptive pouch: Female – Intact. Labrador. Owner night deposit/abandon. Age – approx. 10 months. Vaccines – Distemper, Rabies, Parvo, Bordetella. No Cats.

I turned to walk toward the office, and when I did, I nearly knocked someone over. It was her car in the lot, and she hadn't displaced personal hygiene in her rescue efforts, as I had prematurely judged. Her long wavy salt and pepper hair was freshly showered and tucked back in a low ponytail. Her thinly lined face was softened with her circular framed glasses. She wore a yellow SPCA polo shirt and faded blue jeans.

She smiled at me, a warm, welcoming smile.

"Do you want to take her out?" she asked.

"Sure."

"Okay. My name is Anjou. I'll be right back." She turned on the toes of her red Converse and disappeared behind a steel door, emerging moments later with a frayed nylon leash and a key to the side yard.

As Anjou opened the cage, the black mass took notice again and began to bark, but relented as she was leashed. Her head low and darting back and forth, she pulled Anjou through the kennels to the meet-and-greet yard space outside.

"She's all yours. I'll come back for you in ten or fifteen." Anjou handed me the leash.

She strode back inside and closed the gate behind her. As I stood holding the leash for the first time, I smiled. I was going to have a dog in my life again. It felt good. The possibility I held in my hand stopped just off the concrete walkway, unsure of what might come next. She crouched full bellied on the pea gravel that composed the small and fragmented outdoor enclosure. With a panting whimper, she glanced back at the door.

"Okay, let's see who you are," I said under my breath.

I bent over and ran my thumb over her head, from the depression between her eyes to the prominence on the back of her skull. Her mouth remained open but her panting slowed as she closed her eyes. I reached back and rocked her loose scruff back and forth, and then I pushed the pin to release the leash clasp.

Rocks sprayed as she bolted. She fastidiously marked in all four corners of our enclosure. I took up position on a wooden picnic table and watched.

Her coat shimmered sunlight, and as I gazed at her, I noticed that her blocky head and parallel snout formed a perfect pear.

She tipped her head downward as she trotted around in search of a treasure of smells, stopping here and there to snort and root. Her ribs were obvious; she was about fifteen pounds shy of perfect. Her lack of girth accentuated a sturdy skull and low-set black velvet ears.

She didn't pay too much attention to me, happy for this reprieve.

I called Annie and explained where I was. "Do you want to meet her?" I asked.

"No, I trust you, as long as she is good with kids."

"Let me try some things with her," I said. "Hold on a moment." I laid my phone on the bench.

The dog trotted past me, and I pulled her tail. She was unfazed. I scuffled my feet in the gravel, and she returned to investigate. I grabbed her webbed forepaw. No response. I got down on my hands and knees and pulled her ears. I shoved my hand in her mouth and I poked at her face. She was unperturbed.

I picked up my phone. "I think she'll be fine with Charlie."

As I ended the call with Annie, Anjou returned.

"Well, what do you think?"

"She's gorgeous," I said, and attempted to snap a couple of photos with my lousy flip phone camera, all pixelated black streaks.

"Is this the kind of dog you're looking for?"

I told Anjou about our house, Annie, and Charlie. I talked to her about our hour-long after-dinner walks, and expressed my own desires to have a companion for dog parks and fetch.

Anjou smiled. "She'll be perfect."

Anjou leashed the dog and started to walk her back into the shelter, but stopped short. She turned to face me. "What would you see as a justifiable cause for bringing her back?" she asked.

Perplexed, I couldn't help but do the canine head tilt.

She persisted. "Is there anything this dog could do that would make you surrender her back to the shelter?" Her face straightened. "People return dogs all the time, and I don't think any dog should have to go through that twice."

"No...I don't think so..."

I had never considered this contingency; returning an animal wasn't in my repertoire.

"I suppose if she bit my wife or son," I finally said.

The smile returned. "Good. Perfect. Let's get to the paperwork."

We returned to the kennels, and the wriggling black mass immediately went back to her tennis ball problem. Anjou led me into her office where I was handed a short stack of requisite forms. Anjou also explained that cats and dogs could not be released until they had been spayed or neutered. The bureaucratic business of the adoption made me feel strangely uncomfortable, as if taking a dog into my home and family was a cold, perfunctory business deal, not an act of love, acceptance and welcome.

Written across the top of the adoption paperwork in the tight and slanted cursive that is only still used by my parents' generation was the dog's name: Sandy. It didn't make sense to me. The sand was always blond in the beaches in my mind. That was all I could think of as I repeatedly wrote my name and address on half a dozen forms. Black sands conjured images of Humboldt County's Lost Coast, shale shattered from time and pressure into infinitesimal pieces. If this dog was broken or fragmented, I wanted that to be behind her. Besides, we had named her before she was even born.

After I had signed my paperwork and cut a check, Anjou handed me Yolo County's dog owner manual. "You will get a call from the vet in Davis tomorrow after Sandy's spay," she explained. "Do you have any questions?"

I thumbed through the generic information on housebreaking, crate training, and nuisance barking. "Why was she abandoned?" I asked.

"Lots of duck hunters around here get these dogs for Christmas. Too often the dogs are gun-shy, and they just dump them."

"The thought of dumping a dog would never occur to me," I said.

"Me neither," Anjou said.

I stood up from my chair and reached to shake her hand. She ignored it and responded with an awkward grinning hug.

Driving home, I passed dozens of cars parked along the side of County Road 102, their occupants mingling about in the bright bursts of yellow sunflower fields, smiling with cameras in hand. I too was smiling. I felt like I was nine years old and turning ten tomorrow. Back in our El Dorado, I told Annie and Charlie all about my experience. I showed them the blurry photos and some of the black double-coated fur that still clung to my pant leg. To our most common Davis home, we were adding America's most common dog, and had given her the most common canine name: Daisy.

We all found sleep elusive that night.

Expectations

"My goal in life is to be as good a person as my dog thinks I am."

— Unknown

The next day we busied ourselves with activities in anticipation of the call from the vet. Anjou had estimated that Daisy's spay would be done before the clinic opened to regular customers, and they would be calling me sometime before lunch to come pick her up. To me that meant she could be ready any time after they opened at eight, and we had nothing prepared for a new dog.

Petco was on the opposite side of town. Despite its distance from our house and congestion from the nearby students, we went there often because the SPCA held adoption events in the parking lot every Saturday.

Charlie began to recognize the mini-mall as the place where the three tile mosaic pigs in front of Peet's Coffee went to celebrate with their Navajo Nachos after outwitting the big "wolf" sitting inside the window of the Dos Coyotes Border Cafe.

With Charlie's enthusiastic assistance, we picked out a crate, food bowls, chew toys, training treats, a black leather leash, and a blue nylon collar. I also paid for a $5 token to put in the machine by the front door where I typed in Sandy's new name, Daisy, and our phone number. It whirred and hummed, and an etched aluminum dog bone clinked into a receptacle. Charlie danced. I did too, having pinched my fingers trying to get the tag onto the collar.

As an afterthought, I ducked into the Big 5 sporting goods store for two tubes of the cheapest tennis balls I could find. Later, when we returned home, I lined the back seat of my car with the new smells of our old blankets and the old smells of Daisy's green dish towel that Anjou said would be comforting to Daisy, and would help her transition into her new life with our family.

Charlie was napping, so I went to get Daisy alone. I was filled with anticipation.

The receptionist at the desk in the Davis Manor Center's veterinary office smiled as she stood and reached for Daisy's brand new collar and leash as I handed them to her. She then disappeared behind a wooden solid-core door and promptly returned with a slow and sloppy dog.

I had packed and prepared for an infant, and I was getting a drugged-out teenager.

"Dr. Clementine says she doesn't need a neck cone. Just try to keep her from licking her belly. She didn't have breakfast, but I would wait until dinner to feed her." She attempted to brush Daisy's dark fur off of her white polyester pants. "Call if you see any signs of infection." She handed me Daisy's leash.

"Nothing to sign?"

"Nope, the county took care of it."

Daisy wobbled with me over the linoleum to the double glass exit doors. Davis' midsummer sun was baking the concrete sidewalk and liquefying the adjacent asphalt. Daisy stopped and refused to walk any further. Her head rocked side to side. I paused with her, unsure of what was happening. I watched her wanting to resume her stride, but her body refused. I picked her up under her chest and haunches like a forklift and carried her to the car. She lay still in the back seat, her head pushed sideways into her green towel displacing her lip upward against the back seat. Her eyes remained partially open as she battled the anesthesia on the short trip home.

When I got home and opened the car door, Daisy didn't move, so I carried her to the front door. I managed to free one hand to knock, and when Annie opened the door, she and Charlie squealed with delight. I set Daisy down and gently guided her into the entry, where she promptly vomited.

I watched her all afternoon waiting for her to move. She lay curled in a C shape with her jaw flat on the floor between her front paws. Occasionally she lifted her head and licked the air in an attempt to cure her dry mouth. She slept for hours while I read my new *Idiot's Guide to Positive Dog Training*. It was an impulse buy at the checkout counter.

It wasn't long before I traded my book to play Thomas the Train with Charlie. I could tell it was taking extraordinary effort on his part not to drive Thomas and his friends over Daisy, but he knew the rules we had rehearsed. He kept his impulses in check with my promise that the dog would be a better playmate in the morning. Still, some of Charlie's trains decided to garage by Daisy's hindquarters that afternoon.

The moment we sat down to eat dinner, Daisy roused. Her nametag on her collar jingled as she shook off the effects of her drug-induced slumber. She stood still smacking her lips and looking thoroughly unsure of herself and her new surroundings. I opened the door between the kitchen and garage, sure that she would need to pee after an hours-long nap. She stretched a back leg and lumbered out, her nails click-clacking over the tile. I followed her and led her out the garage side door to our narrow side yard. Daisy squatted and peed on the hard soil. I congratulated her enthusiastically like a good idiot was supposed to. She then slumped down against the house, obstructing the musty breeze that emanated from the crawlspace vent.

Annie beckoned me inside through the window above our kitchen table. "Just leave her food and water outside for a while, and come in and eat."

I obliged.

Daisy awoke after dinner and thundered around the yard. She found a branch that had fallen from the pecan tree in our backyard, and decided it was just the thing to play with. She grumbled under her breath as she trotted, head tilted with a backward glance as she dragged her first new toy around between the back and side yards in a continuous loop. I held Charlie up to the window to watch, and he was so delighted that his uncontrollable laughter ended in a bout of hiccups. Finally, Daisy disappeared from view followed by a loud bang as she slammed into the back of the kitchen door with her prize.

Charlie and I laughed.

"Time for a walk!" Annie announced.

Annie readied a fidgeting Charlie into his stroller as I went out to the backyard to get Daisy for our first family walk. As I would soon find, Annie had the easier job. I stepped outside and breathed in the cool evening breeze from the Sacramento-San Joaquin Delta, new leash in hand. Daisy seemed to barely sense my presence. She never darted, but she never looked my way, moving to each new area of interest while keeping at least ten feet of space between us. Only the repeated screeching of a squirrel high up on the power lines distracted her enough so that I managed to click the lead onto her new collar.

When I gently moved then tugged in the direction of the side gate, I was met with cogwheel rigidity. For reasons unclear to me, she finally relented. I made sure to lead Daisy through the redwood gate, not the other way around. I had heard that it was important for me to take the lead.

Daisy was a yo-yo on the leash. She moved independent of the direction that Annie, Charlie, and I were traveling. She had little regard for our presence as she caromed off my knee across Charlie's stroller and cut through Annie's legs. She kept her head down sucking in the scents of the sidewalks, lawns, and sewer drains. She frothed and drooled, and only paused long enough to urinate, then cough, gag, and dry heave. I stopped frequently, unsure if her upset stomach was from the continual tension on the lead or the inhalation of a noxious odor.

"Labs are easy to train, right?" Annie's question dangled in midair.

"I think so," I said, trying to remain positive. "Well, she is still technically a puppy and has a lot of energy. Let's walk farther and see if we can't drain her out a little so she will sleep tonight."

By the time we reached the end of a shaded path that would loop us back to our home on the other side of Pole Line, Daisy's panting was feverish, and all she could do to cope was spin in circles. Thankfully, her shadow headed east, away from her gaze, and no longer confused her.

On the way back, Annie walked with Charlie on the sidewalk. Daisy and I kept to the street where there were fewer lawns and hydrants. When we returned home, Annie and I were tired. Daisy was not. Rather than helping to calm her, the walk seemed to energize her. She was a like a wild Mustang. Her forepaws shadowboxed the air as I made her wait outside the fence before I returned to lead her through the gate. She broke ahead of me and immediately peed in the same spot she had that afternoon. I couldn't fathom how she had any urine left, but I congratulated her nonetheless. She then gracelessly pounced on her pecan branch completely unaware of my presence and praise.

I contemplated not letting her in the house and bedding her in the garage that night, but my mind flashed back to the floors of the shelter and the endless hours of solitary confinement she must have endured there. I questioned whether she was even conscious of my existence, the companionship I could provide, and if she would find comfort in our home. If she was in fact aware of us, she had no idea how to relate. I stood inside the kitchen with the door open and called for her to come. Either she didn't hear me or she hadn't learned her new name yet, but she finally saw the open door and nearly tripped as she plowed past me into the house.

Daisy rooted through the house like a pig in search of truffles. I kept a distance, but watched as she loped from room to room in a disorganized manner, her head down and her tail up, repeating her inspection several times.

She bounded into the bathroom where Annie was bathing Charlie and skidded on the tile floor in an attempt to stop, but her lack of mass prevented her from tipping over the edge of the tub and joining Charlie. She pulled her head away from the water and looked at Charlie then at the water then back at Charlie. She licked his face three times and retreated from the bathroom. Charlie was delighted.

* * *

In the summer, when the Pacific pushes cool humid air across the confluence of the Sacramento and San Joaquin rivers, the nighttime temperatures sometimes drop to the low sixties, even if it has been in the hundreds all afternoon. The delta breeze is the northern valley's natural air conditioner. In Davis, if you own an older home, you also own a whole-house fan, which is nothing more than a boxed fan bolted into the ceiling. When you turn it on at night, hinged flaps open, and the newly revealed oversized blades pull the chilled outside air through your open windows into your house. But more significantly, it blows the super-heated air out of your attic. So, if you close your windows by nine in the morning, after running your whole-house fan all night, your house will stay relatively cool until about three or four in the afternoon, even if your walls have little in the way of R-value insulation.

The fan generated a white noise that Annie and I pretended was the ocean. As the louvers and belts realigned themselves with the influx of air, we imagined it was the sound of gulls and herons crying overhead.

To keep the motor singing peacefully, we had to open all six of our windows at night. Any fewer and screens became asthmatic as the house rattled.

I had gone to bed by ten that night, and by eleven, I awoke to the sound of unfamiliar sea birds slapping their wings and sneaker waves crashing.

My thoughts raced as my foggy brain came awake. *Daisy must be licking her incision!* I jumped out of bed to check on her.

The hardwood was cold and unforgiving on my bare feet. When I rushed into Daisy's room, I saw that her tongue was not lapping at her belly, as I had feared. She was grooming her front paws with a metronomic wet smack. Infinite cycles of inter-digital cleansing and violent head shakes to flap her ears clean were only briefly punctuated by the drive to circle in place and moan while readjusting her bedding. My presence briefly startled her from her ritual, as if I had hit her internal pause button, but as I stood confused at the threshold, she again hit play. Her pattern repeated ad infinitum.

"Ignore her," Annie said as I crawled back into bed, her face buried in her pillow.

"She has to stop at some point," I mumbled.

She didn't stop. She couldn't stop. It seemed as if an internal compulsion was forcing her to recollect and organize the day's scents. It was a self-soothing mechanism, but not for Annie and me. Any semblance to our peaceful beach sounds had mutated into a dripping faucet. Daisy was a slowly leaking toilet whose tank filled every thirty minutes.

I had to be at work by six, and I was up and grooming myself by a quarter to five. By then, Daisy had taken notice of the water running in the bathroom sink as I prepared to shave. I heard her panting and rocking in her crate, so I opened her enclosure to let her out, thinking I could keep her from waking Annie and Charlie if I gave her some freedom. She sprinted out wildly crashing into walls, chairs, and cabinets. I managed to lead her out through the garage to the side yard. The moment she squatted to pee, I saw our next-door neighbor, Ms. Calamondin, return home from her graveyard-shift job stocking shelves at the Costco in Woodland. Daisy barked at her in high-pitched rapid succession, her hackles flared.

I confronted her with a loud "Ahht!" She stopped, continued to urinate, then rolled onto her back, her fur still raised. Belly up, she continued to bark, but muted.

When I came back inside, I apologized to Annie for waking her and Charlie, who stood clinging to her leg while she braced herself against the kitchen counter. She was filling a teapot with her free hand.

"It's fine. I was awake getting kicked in the bladder anyway." She moved her hand to her growing belly and rubbed. "This one hardly ever moves, so I should be happy she's kicking."

"Daisy is kind of a mess," I said. "She needs to be walked, but I can't do it until I get home tonight. She is really anxious and fearful — hyperactive, even."

As if on cue, Daisy slammed into the back door.

I let her in to eat, and she coursed around the house from this to that, seemingly unaware of our presence. The marimbas played as I filled her stainless food dish with kibble. There was no response, no interest. Daisy was a pinball. As she bounced off the bumpers of chairs and deflected off the flippers of furniture, she came to rest, tilted, in the middle of the kitchen floor, her body tense and coiled. Annie and I stood waiting for the plunger to be drawn back and Daisy to be set in motion again. Sure enough, with her mouth drawn tightly, her ears pricked, and her eyes darting, she did just that, her toenails clattering against the grout lines as they searched for purchase on the kitchen tile.

Before Annie and I could react, Charlie wrapped himself around Daisy's barrel chest and squeezed. At that moment, Charlie gave Daisy what she had been searching for since she arrived in our home. Her ears dropped. Her eyebrows fell. Her panting stopped. Her features softened.

I called Annie several times from work that day to see how everyone was faring.

"She seems very sweet, but anywhere she goes, she runs," Annie said. "I've had to keep her outside most of the day, which I feel terrible about, but she keeps knocking Charlie over. And, her spinning and flapping hasn't been too kind to the lamps."

"I'm sorry." It was all I could say. "I will walk her when I get home. Hopefully that will help." I was unconsciously rubbing the tension in my shoulder.

"I think she is going to need more than walks," Annie said. "She doesn't sleep or nap at all. She is in perpetual motion."

"I know, but we have to start somewhere. I've already called the vet's office for a checkup. I read online that hyperactivity could be the result of a metabolic problem, and her ear flapping and constant licking could be an infection or parasites."

I could hear Annie's silence.

Gaslighting

*"Autists are the ultimate square pegs, and the problem
with pounding a square peg into a round hole is not that the
hammering is hard work. It's that you're destroying the peg."*

— Paul Collins

By the end of the first couple weeks with Daisy, Annie and I were frazzled. Daisy still seemed unaware of our presence in the house. She was an up-all-night newborn and a toddling, childproofing nightmare during the day. Walking her was like walking a sidewinder snake. The overall vector sum of the movement was in one direction, but her body took a circuitous path. The lack of sleep pushed Annie and me to being short with each other. Our exhaustion had also begun to feed questions about bringing a dog into our home in the middle of Annie's pregnancy. I knew we needed help; we wouldn't be able to fix this problem by reading a few dog-training books.

I hadn't paid much attention to the Pets Veterinary office the day I picked Daisy up from her spay, probably because I never paid much attention to the Davis Manor Shopping Center even though the whole place had been painted in lime and tangerine hues with lemon highlights. Pets Veterinary sat wedged between a vacuum repair shop and a coin operated laundry in the newly dubbed "Popsicle mall."

A perfume of medicated shampoos and sanitizing solutions greeted us at the door, carried us through the waiting room, and followed us into an examination stall. I tried to explain to Dr. Clara Clementine that bringing a dog into our household had not been as seamless as it was supposed to be. She placated me by nodding her head as she palpated Daisy's underbelly. Dr. Clementine was exceptionally short and round, preferring to examine Daisy on the floor rather than the stainless steel exam table in the center of the cramped room. As if it would easily peel away from her body, her embroidered and starched lab coat breathed in and out as she darted around Daisy.

The only way Daisy would hold still is if I put her head in my armpit and wrapped my arms around her chest. "She violates the laws of conservation of energy and mass," I said half joking. "She really doesn't eat, and she is constantly vigilant. She rarely sleeps at night and never naps during the day, yet according to your scale, she has put on weight since we brought her home. I don't know how that is possible."

"What training techniques have you used with her?" She unplugged one ear of her stethoscope long enough to look up to see if I would answer truthfully.

"Positive reinforcement, I suppose," I answered referring to my Idiot's guide as support. "It just seems that a lot, if not all of those strategies, don't work for her. She won't even take treats."

"Uh huh." Dr. Clementine pried my elbows up as she checked Daisy's ears. "Dogs won't eat when they're stressed," she said talking into Daisy's ear as I stared down at the top of her waxy and deeply orange hair. "When she is less hyper, try higher value treats like liver."

"Why is she so stressed all the time?" I asked. I didn't allow the doctor to answer. "We took her to my friend Frank's house to play with his dog Berdoo. Daisy acted like she was the only one there. I thought most dogs enjoyed playing with other dogs."

Frank had been my roommate during our freshman year at UC Davis. He too had moved back to Davis after finding his purpose elsewhere. Just married, his dog, a one-year-old handsome Saint Bernard, had been his engagement present. Frank and I had reconnected and were bonding over dogs, married life, and non-student life in Davis.

"Daisy was completely non-responsive to his play-bows and belly-ups," I offered, hoping this information would be helpful. "All she did was run up and down the back fence line for at least an hour."

"We will run some tests for mites, worms, thyroid disease, kidney and liver problems," the flitting doctor proclaimed. "Some Labs are just hyper – they need an outlet. She may not even be purely Lab. There may be something else in there." She paused and met my eyes. "Get a Kong and put a mix of wet and dry dog food in it, and then freeze it. It helps focus them during feeding. It takes them longer to eat. Get her socialized. Find other dog friends. Take her to a dog park."

"I guess what I'm saying is that I don't think she learns like other dogs do. I don't think she even knows who I am."

Dr. Clementine sighed. "Look, this dog is nearly a year old. It could be six-week puppy syndrome. She could have been weaned too early. She could have been rejected by her mother, or she could have been abused. Dogs have a critical period of socialization after they have been weaned, which you missed because you adopted her after that." She paused. "Maybe this is the wrong dog for you and your family. That's okay. It happens sometimes. There are many breed-specific rescue groups around Sacramento. I can give you a list."

"What?" I narrowed my eyes and pulled my chin into my neck. "I'm not here to complain about my dog so I can offload her. I'm here for help. We are invested in this dog, not just any dog. I'm not taking her back to Macy's because she didn't fit."

"I get it. I'm sorry. We can start prescription antipsychotic and anxiolytic medications if you would like, or there are herbal alternative agents you can use like valerian, ginger, or chamomile."

I didn't respond. I didn't know how. I stared at the grid lines in the linoleum floor tile. Her suggestions didn't feel right to me, nor would they to Annie.

She took my silence as hesitation. "If you're reluctant to go down the medicinal route, and you're willing to commit to her, I would buy these books and find someone to come into your house to train her, or send her to a board and train." She penned a list of book names and authors. "Regular obedience classes probably won't work for you."

She looked up. "I've heard good things about the Drop the Leash Canine Academy in Woodland. It's no frills, but it is effective." Without waiting for my response, she added it to her list. "And it's probably your best choice, if she is really as bad as you say she is."

It was all so much to take in, I just sat there mute.

"Don't worry, most Labs calm down by age two. I'll call you with the results by the end of the week." She turned to leave. "She is a beautiful dog. Bye, cutie," she said to Daisy, and air-kissed her as she closed the door.

* * *

The Drop the Leash Canine Academy website was slow to load, and when it did, the backdrop was grainy and unfocused. The owner had attempted to replicate the viral photo of a row of trained German Shepherds sitting off leash as a cat saunters by. Instead, four Shiba Inu sat foxlike with ears pricked and tails curled while a tabby, striking a pose similar to Maneki-neko, sat cleaning her face in front of them. The white About Us tab, nearly hidden in the mass of light-colored fur in the photo, directed me to a separate page about the owner, Gavin Amador.

Amador's thumbnail mug shot was of equal quality to his backdrop. His mission statement was outlined around him in three Comic Sans lines of Haiku.

Dog will learn respect
Man and dog learn discipline
Peace at home always

The FAQs list was equally difficult to find, but at least it was more informative. After a $900 three-week Basic Dog Boot Camp, Daisy should come home knowing how to walk on a leash and follow eight specific commands: come, sit, stay, down, off, load (getting into car), potty (on command), and look.

I called the number listed in the Contact Us section, and our conversation was brief and to the point. I did my best to summarize Daisy's behavior and our wishes for her. I was met with echolalia.

"She is very hyperactive and scared," I said.

"Hyperactive, scared," Gavin repeated with gravel in his throat.

"We want her to be obedient."

"Be obedient."

"We want to be able to walk with her on a leash comfortably."

"Walk – comfortably." He coughed.

"We want her to be peaceful and calm, and socialized."

"Calm, socialized," he mumbled.

At first, I thought maybe he was writing down everything I said, but as our conversation progressed, I felt like maybe he was riffling through his mail, paying his bills, or throwing darts. In any event, I didn't give it much thought as I penciled in my tour of his facility with Daisy and the accompanying intake interview for noon the next day. I could make better sense of him in person, I thought.

I hung up the phone and looked at Annie. She just closed her eyes and nodded.

* * *

The Drop the Leash Canine Academy had taken over a converted single story business complex on the east side of Woodland. The tongue and groove address sign out front was the color of the famous split pea soup from Santa Nella.

His office was a kiln. Daisy panted and bounced. Gavin Amador was unfazed and paid no attention to our disorganized black mass, or the heat.

He took Daisy's leash and handed it to a young man wearing a green jumpsuit. I assumed it was his son.

"She is in good hands," he said as they left through a door behind his steel desk, which had clearly seen a lot of use over the years. He pulled a single sheet of paper from the bottom right drawer, and sat in the creaky office chair. "Fill this out." He handed me the form.

I sat opposite Gavin penning our contact information and Daisy's veterinary history, or lack thereof, as his interrogation began.

He pointed at my chest. "What do *you* want this dog to do?"

I was taken aback by his abrupt approach. "I don't think it is as much about a specific task," I floundered. How best to explain why I was there? "Annie and I want her to be comfortable, peaceful, and calm. Daisy is agitated all the time. I've never encountered a dog like her before, and I'm familiar with how to handle dogs. That's why I'm here."

I removed my sweating arm from his paper questionnaire and handed it to him.

"Go on," he said.

I described the difficulties we were having with Daisy, her compulsions, tics, and ability to be completely out-of-sync with everything around her. I repeated what I had told Dr. Clementine – that it seemed like Daisy didn't learn the same way other dogs did, which mainly involved interacting with their human companions and trainers. His blank stare told me he was bored or listening, I wasn't sure which, so I emphasized Daisy's inability to read the social cues of people and other dogs.

"Do you hunt?" he interrupted.

I paused, confused, beads of sweat coalescing along my forehead into droplets no longer immune to gravity. "No, I don't." I wiped my brow with the back of my hand. "I'm not sure what that has to do with…"

"Labs hunt," he mumbled.

The heat in the room was adding to my confusion. I wanted to ask for my dog back, and return to Dr. Clementine to ask her what she was thinking by sending me here, but I'd come this far, so I plodded on.

I shared with Gavin what I thought was a funny anecdote about Daisy and the tennis ball cans.

"Somehow she had managed to pop open the vacuum sealed lid and had lined up all six balls at the foot of the washing machine. When I found her, she didn't seem intent on playing with them as much as keeping them in a straight line."

I described how, if I took one out of line and bounced it or threw it to her, she immediately returned it to its original position, seemingly unconcerned with my attempt to interact with her, and unable to handle the change in the ball's proper position. It was as if the balls were animate, not I.

"A dog's life is a task," he said. "A failure of the dog is a failure of the owner." He set a 6 mm Allen wrench he had been spinning like a helicopter in his hands on top of a worn VHS copy of a movie starring Ingrid Bergman. He then pressed his hands together as if praying.

"If your dog does not live in a home of discipline, she will have a disordered adjustment to her life." His voice deepened. "If you continue to enable her hyperactivity, she will become oppositional and defiant to you." His index finger again shot in my direction. My eyes refocused from his face to his short and pitted fingernail. His knuckles were knobby and arthritic.

I sat there in silence with my mediocrity and shoulders sinking into the foam-backed chair, directing my stare to my own hands. I nodded, accepting his blame.

When I felt brave enough to meet his eyes, I asked, "How do I provide the structure she needs? What tasks do I give her? How do I engage her?"

"I will show you after she has completed basic training with me. We need to separate her from the bad habits you have made at home."

He stood and showed me to the door. And that was it. I left without my dog.

* * *

The peace that was so elusive with Daisy's presence was now uncomfortably loud in her absence. The sound of Charlie thrusting his toys across the hardwood floor echoed Daisy's bursts of exuberance. The cyclic spray of the dishwasher reverberated Daisy's own cleaning ritual. Only the whole-house fan breathed easily. Annie, Charlie, and I tried as best we could to return to our normal daily routines, but it was difficult.

Two days after Daisy's departure Dr. Clementine phoned to let us know that all of Daisy's tests had returned "within normal limits," and to tell us there was "nothing wrong" with her. I thanked her but politely told her I disagreed.

Invisible Disability

"The fight is never about grapes or lettuce.
It is always about people."

— Cesar Chavez

Annie and I found some of Dr. Clementine's recommended reading list at the public library. However, I could find no discussions about mental health problems in dogs. The topics only covered the inherited problems of purebreds such as hip dysplasia, deafness, and splenic hemangiosarcomas, a condition my first Golden Retriever had. Many pointed fingers at artificial selection, backyard breeding, and puppy mills as causative. Online I was able to find brief affirmations that dogs did in fact suffer from conditions such as depression and obsessive-compulsive disorder, yet none of the resources offered any real solutions.

In an effort not to dwell on the mounting guilt we felt about leaving Daisy at Gavin Amador's boot camp, Annie and I reflexively returned to our home improvement projects. The atmospheric high pressure ridge that had been sitting over most of northern California since May that year had moved east toward the Four Corners, and we got a taste of late September in August. Anxious to take advantage of the cooler days, Annie wanted to plant shade trees in our barren front yard. It was becoming increasingly difficult for Annie to get around, but she was still instinctually trying to nest.

We scoured the *Sunset Western Garden Book* and the internet for the most regionally appropriate, low maintenance, and best-looking street trees. As we sat and read, Annie's silence told me she felt unsure about putting our dog in someone else's hands. Annie had few tells, but silence was one of them. Early on in our relationship, I had learned to be wary of silence. Silence was this woman's word for a thousand things: anger, concentration, sadness, guilt, fear, patience, retribution, to name a few. Annie was in the silence of believing we had made a mistake, not just about Gavin Amador and his academy but about adopting Daisy.

"Let's plant fruit trees instead." I tossed the Sunset guide on the coffee table to relieve the dead air of silence.

"What?" Annie said half listening as she thumbed through her book.

"Come on, fruit trees can provide shade and food. Besides, they'll be beautiful in the spring. Who gives a crap about fall foliage? This isn't Oakland, let alone Vermont."

Annie finally managed a grin.

"I'm pretty sure there is a city ordinance requiring us to plant fruit trees in our front yards," I teased.

Charlie tossed aside his picture book about caterpillars and apples, mimicking my gesture and siding with me.

"Have you finally decided to go full-Davis?" Annie asked.

"Next thing you know, I might be attaching a milk crate to my bike and building a chicken coop." I shrugged my shoulders and pointed at Charlie. "Why not pears? Charlie likes them."

Charlie yelled, "Pears! Pear Street, Pears!"

Annie's lower lip protruded. Her head bobbed in agreement.

* * *

Our neighbor Mari Calamondin sat on her rickety lawn chair in the middle of her driveway sifting through the *Enterprise*. The newspaper had landed there, and so had she.

Mari was first to welcome us to the neighborhood. She did so with a pistachio bundt cake and a copy of the Pear Street emergency phone tree. Mariposa, as she had been christened, had at least two vices that Annie and I knew of. Her most obvious was her infatuation with the *Enterprise*, Davis' only daily paper. Front to back, nothing escaped her eye. Reading it seemed to cause her physical distress, yet she persisted.

"The definition of an addiction," Mari would say. She waffled between denial and acceptance.

The aluminum frame of her chair scratched and creaked as she stood up and refolded her paper. Her arms were short stalks with wing-like appendages exaggerated by her ribbed tank top. Standing erect, she was slender yet cylindrical.

She had been obsessing over someone's bent in an op-ed. "Did you see my letter last week?" She flitted toward us proudly.

Mari frequently wrote opinion pieces under her nom de plume, Tae Ng-Kabayo. She said it meant "shit of the horse" according to Google Translate. She told us this every time she was published, laughing and snorting, finding more humor in pulling what she thought was a fast one on everyone rather than in the actual content of her commentary. Her latest tart missive was aimed at the rumors of developing the agricultural land around the old Hunt-Wesson tomato cannery into tract housing.

I smiled. "I did read that one – well written."

If Mari had a second vice, it was that she was a bit of a neighborhood know-it-all, with constant feelers out for gossip.

"Where's Daisy?" she asked.

I gave her the brief rundown of our last few weeks as Annie struggled to buckle a fussing Charlie into his car seat.

"Don't worry about her," she said. "She is so pretty, and you are great with her. She'll be just fine. We had a crazy dog when I was growing up. It was totally a puppy phase thing. They grow out of it." She waved a dismissive hand.

"I hope so. Well, we're off to get a couple new pear trees for the front yard." The car chimed as I put the keys into the ignition.

"Ooh, those won't do well here at all," she said coming to Annie's window as I closed my door. She was sweetly fragrant. "This soil is like cement, and it pushes their roots up to the surface. Besides, fire blight is rampant in Davis."

"What's fire blight?"

"It's awful. Your trees will be going along just fine, then out of the blue they start burning black, withering and dying. You have to be vigilant and prune it away before it kills the whole tree. It's not worth trying to grow pear trees in Davis – it just won't work. You will spend more time fighting the disease than enjoying any fruit. Get your pears from the grocery store – it's less work." She rapped the top of the car to drive her point home.

I thanked her for her horticultural insights and pulled away.

* * *

"We usually only sell fruit trees in the winter as bare root," said the pleasant and bushy mustachioed man in the orange smock. The name FRED was neatly penned in permanent black ink on his nametag. "But we do sell some potted five-gallon ones throughout the year." He pointed toward the back of the lot in the area cordoned off by wheelbarrows, injection molded sheds, and interlocking steel racks of chicken and steer manure.

"Hey, what about a plum or nectarine?" Annie asked.

"Too messy."

We both kept digging.

"An apple?" I posed.

"Maybe . . . what kind?"

"Wait, I found one . . . nope, found two," I announced. "Moonglow, early large pear, fire blight resistant, relatively free of grit cells, requires a pollinator, ripens in mid-August, 700 chill hours." I paused. "Moonglow – that sounds like a good hippie Whole Earth Festival-attending Davisite tree."

"Daisy!" Charlie shrieked in excitement.

Annie and I both stopped and looked up.

"No buddy, that's not her." I sprang toward Charlie who was already trotting with arms outstretched toward a black Lab perusing the perennials. The dog didn't flinch, nor did the man I assumed was its owner, a middle-aged man wearing khakis and a tucked-in navy polo, and holding the loose leash. The dog was striking and unfazed in his orange vest.

"This is Sammy. He's learning how to be a guide dog," the man said as he took a knee next to Charlie.

Charlie wasn't too far off in his assessment of the dog. Sammy did show a strong physical resemblance to Daisy, but his temperament, mood, and affect were noticeably different. This dog was amenable, compliant, and deferential. He understood intention and movement. His sensory input was organized and stratified, and he adapted to change without any overt physical response.

"We have a Black Lab as well," I said.

Sammy's nose made one arching evaluation of Charlie then refocused on his handler. Charlie stopped reaching toward the dog, mostly because he was confused. He looked at Annie and me, unsure of why some dogs were not just for playing, or that dogs could have jobs. He was flatly befuddled that all dogs weren't exuberant like Daisy.

"Aren't Labs great?" The man smiled. "Their ability to tolerate stress, their desire and ability to learn. Easy to train these guys."

Annie and I smiled in uncomfortable agreement and glanced at each other.

"Charlie, okay, come on buddy," I said. "Sammy is working right now. We have some work to do too. Can you say goodbye to Sammy?"

"Goodbye, Sammy. Daisy is crazy," Charlie divulged as he willfully turned and headed back toward the trees without any doubt that what he had said was simply the truth.

Annie and I smiled again, waved, and trotted off after our little whistleblower.

"Can you imagine Daisy as a guide dog for the blind?" I mumbled as we drove out of the parking lot onto Main Street.

"It would be a blood bath," Annie said with a distant smile, and shook her head at the mere thought of the devastation that would ensue.

Inclusion

*"Cautious, careful people, always casting about to preserve their
reputations . . . can never effect a reform."*

— Susan B. Anthony

D aisy's stint at boot camp was up the next day, and for the last three
weeks, I'd had daily visions of her drilling, weaving pylons, and
sitting at attention. With one word from Gavin and me by proxy, Daisy
would be heeling, staying, and taking leisurely after-dinner strolls. She
would be the navigator, with Annie and me in the back seat and Charlie
the bombardier. With the window down, she would breathe in the sights
and smells of the passing scenery on our way to hike Stebbins Cold
Canyon.

In my mind, wherever we went, Daisy was with us. Daisy was going
to help our life look like a Subaru commercial.

Back home, Charlie and I dug two holes in our front yard and we planted our trees offset from the walkway that led from the driveway, through the front yard, and to the front door in an attempt to improve privacy and maximize our view of their spring blooms.

Charlie and I stood hands on hips as Annie inspected how our plantings framed the front of the house and our newly painted front door. The door was the most solid thing in the house, and certainly the most ornate. Annie had wanted a truly red door since before we were married, and so the first project we tackled after unboxing was stripping rainbow layers of lead-based paint, priming the sundried wood, and giving the front door three coats of something called Cranberry Bog.

The door felt heavy when it was opened, and it swung slowly with an arthritic draw. When the door was slammed shut, the door was quiet, but the whole house shook.

The doorbell was mounted in the center of the door and it was spring-powered. Charlie found it fascinating, probably because of the sound, but also because it was mounted at his eye level.

Daisy did not find the doorbell nearly as interesting when deliverymen and Jehovah's Witnesses paid us visits. Pressing the button activated her propensity to bark in fear and then run and hide in her crate with her face buried in her blanket. If the doorbell rang to signify package delivery, she barked long after we signed for our packages and shut the door.

Annie and I hoped that this behavior had been cured.

Every time we saw Mari, she asked how Daisy was doing at "school," partly out of concern, mostly out of curiosity. She always asked if she could help in some way, to which we always said no, but when she asked today, I asked her if she would be willing to watch Charlie while we went to pick up Daisy She eagerly agreed.

We promised Charlie lemonade. Mari promised him cookies. He was an easy sell.

As we drove to Woodland, we gazed in silence at throngs of dead sunflowers marching in lockstep in the farm fields we passed, their crisped trunks evenly spaced at branch length from each other and their crowns all sadly facing downward, as if publicly mourning the loss of something we didn't yet understand.

Gavin Amador had started to grow a goatee since I had seen him last. It was gray, uneven, and wiry. His bottom lip scratched his beard as he talked, like two wrong sides of Velcro trying to mate. He led us into his office after I introduced Annie and we exchanged pleasantries. We then passed through the door in his office where Daisy vanished nearly a month ago.

He instructed us to take a seat on a low slumped couch wrapped in a coffee-stained slipcover. We sank as we sat, releasing a sweetly astringent, naphthalene odor.

The wall opposite the couch contained a sliding glass door hidden behind gently swaying vertical blinds. They created static as they rubbed broadly across themselves like two-dozen pendulums. We could see the courtyard through the slats as they oscillated in the faint breeze.

"When Daisy comes in, you are not to move or talk to her," Gavin said, as he stood planted before us. "This is the most important part of her training. She must not see you as she saw you when you brought her here, but as how you are going to be to her now that she's been trained."

Annie's silence was quizzical.

"Do you agree?" he asked.

"Yes – sure – absolutely," we chorused.

"But when can we interact with her?" Annie requested.

"Not until instructed."

The thick plastic blinds applauded as Daisy made her entrance through the sliding door. She arrived on a pronged choke lead with Gavin's son holding the other end of the leash. She barked at Gavin in uncertainty as she pulled toward us. The change in the texture from the exposed aggregate concrete of the courtyard to the flat and uniform low nap fibers of the accountant's office, along with the sharp yank of the leash, broke her stride. Her coordination deteriorated into that of a novice firewalker. No footfall was secure. Gavin's son popped the chain that cinched her neck, but Daisy vocalized her fear and anxiety through barks that originated in her throat and never made it past her teeth. With closed lips, her jowls puffed outward in bursts of frustration and fear.

"She is left footed," said Gavin, as if that explained everything. "They are difficult to train. You will have to work twice as hard."

Annie and I looked at Gavin with questioning glances.

"Dogs who lead with their left forefoot when they walk are notoriously difficult to train," he said in answer to our unspoken question. "You will have to follow the directions that I will send home with you very carefully if you are not to fail."

We nodded in silent assent.

Gavin added, "Jackson will release her once she has sat and calmed. Again, you must not acknowledge her until I instruct you to do so."

Annie and I sat, waited, and watched, but Daisy didn't calm. She panted, whined, and spun. Her ears flapped and her head dove as she attempted to stroke her forepaws with her tongue, but the shortness of the leash prevented her from doing so. As she stood choking, she cascaded through her repertoire of coping strategies. All were failures. Jackson popped the chain. Daisy stood erect, trying desperately not to burn her feet on the proverbial bed of coals laid out before her.

Again, Jackson yanked the leash to pop the chain, and Daisy whimpered then collapsed to the floor, belly up, hyperventilating and pawing at the air.

After what felt like an eternity, but was only a few minutes of Daisy being supine, Gavin spoke.

"That is good enough. She is submissive."

Jackson reached down and unhitched the barbed collar from Daisy's neck. It unfurled as it fell open and landed with a muted thud on the carpet. Daisy sprang up and darted around the room, sucking in the smells and drooling them onto the floor. There was no visual cueing to her movement; she felt the room through her nose like a blind man casting his cane about in a manner only clear to him.

Daisy's nose finally made its way to the couch, and Annie, then me. She started at my foot and dotted moist nose prints up my leg until she wedged her head between my elbow and my chest, and tried to nuzzle between my rib spaces. Then she stopped moving. I felt her breathing slow, and her tail drooped when she was calm.

Daisy didn't move. As instructed, neither did I.

Daisy had lost her turgor, and her body had wilted since we had last seen her. Any weight she had gained with us, she had since lost. I could see her already pronounced ribs become more defined as she breathed. Her skin had loosened and her downy undercoat was coming out in clumps around her haunches. She smelled of fear. I fought the urge to stroke her and let her know that everything was okay.

We sat quiet and motionless in Gavin's office with Daisy sticking out of me like a febrile appendage. The fluorescent tubes above us flickered and tinkled, and the ballasts hummed. I looked at Annie in shared silence; this was the first time Daisy had really shown either of us any affection, let alone recognition. It may have been maladaptive, but I was overjoyed that she had taken a small step toward finding comfort in me.

"You must be firm with her." Gavin broke the peace that had settled in the room. "You must continue the routine we have started here."

"What routine?" I asked. "I understand she is difficult – trust me, that is why we came to you, but what does her being left footed mean for us?"

Annie nodded.

"Feeding time is at the same time of day, every day. She will eat at seven in the morning and at seven in the evening. I have a list of instructions and commands that you are to practice with her twice a day. These instructions are to be followed in the manner in which I instruct you today. You will give immediate rewards for success. You will implement immediate discipline for failures."

We nodded.

"And now, I will show you how to walk her on a leash." He took the leash. "You must walk the dog. Do not let the dog walk you." He wrapped the chrome prongs around Daisy's neck. "Come!" he commanded.

Daisy did not obey. Gavin popped the leash, and only then did Daisy leave the comfortable confines of my armpit.

"Follow me," he instructed us. "She should always be on your left." He held the leash short and Daisy's head up as she fought not to move in the direction he was traveling.

The vertical blinds clapped as Annie and I followed Gavin Amador and his son Jackson into the courtyard.

"Here." Gavin handed me the leash. "Walk with her, and when I say turn, you turn ninety degrees."

I complied. With Daisy's leash folded on itself several times in my left hand, I walked away from Annie.

"Don't look at her!" he yelled.

I lifted my head and stared at the black metal bars of the security gate that led to the rear training area.

"Turn right!" he barked.

I turned. Daisy did not, and my arm extended as she tried to move in our original direction.

"Yank!" he yelled.

"What?" I turned and looked at him.

"Yank," he growled. "Do not hesitate."

I pulled hard on the leash and grimaced at the brutal sound of the articulated prongs popping against each other as if I were tightening a metal zip tie around my dog's throat. Daisy yelped and her head banged against my knee as she gasped for air.

"Turn right!" he yelled.

I turned right, but again, Daisy did not follow my lead.

"Yank again!" he hollered. "Don't let her lead you – yank!"

We were now walking back toward Gavin. I struggled to maintain balance as Daisy yanked me in the direction her nose wanted her to go. The consequence of the correction didn't matter to her beyond the immediate pain. Either she was forgetting immediately thereafter, or she couldn't integrate the pain and the error as cause and effect. Either way, it didn't matter.

"When she fails — YANK!" The old man boomed.

Again, I complied. Daisy screamed.

"Left!" Gavin yelled.

I turned. Daisy did not. Again, her skull echoed as it collided with my knee. I yanked. Her shrill yelps were like the prequel to a motor vehicle collision, rubber skidding on asphalt. My shoulders cringed as I prepared for the resulting sound of shattering glass and crunching metal.

"Right!" Gavin bellowed.

I turned and readied myself to yank again, and again I had to. I could hear the other residents of the Drop the Leash Academy taking note of Daisy's anguish.

I finally made it back to where Gavin and Annie stood waiting.

"Stand completely still," Gavin instructed. "Say and do nothing until she is absolutely calm."

I stood unmoving, waiting for his next command.

Gavin handed Annie a three-page list of our homework and reviewed with her the commands we should drill with Daisy.

I was unsure what to do next, but I wanted information on what we were to do at home, so I interrupted his instructions to Annie. "Is this the routine that you have been working on for three weeks?"

"Yes," he said without turning to me. "We need to schedule your follow-up visit. Success will depend on how well you practice and work with her."

I stood confused. "If she couldn't accomplish even walking with you during this time, how am I supposed to be able to do it?"

"She walked fine with us," he bellowed, finally looking up to glare at me. "Dogs always walk differently when the owner is around. It is your attitude toward the dog and unwillingness to assert discipline that creates the problem. She does not respect you."

Dumbfounded, we followed him into his office to pay for Daisy's training and to schedule our follow-up booster session. I could tell that Annie was on the verge of tears as she wrote the check.

He cleared space on his desk to reveal his oversized calendar, and grumbled the entire time as if making excuses for the dismal "failure" we had just witnessed. "We train all dogs the exact same way. All dogs learn the same way. Only people think dogs are different because all dogs look different. This dog will be capable of so much if you just apply yourself."

I have no explanation for how Annie managed to remember to say thank you to Gavin as we wrestled with Daisy on our way to the car. Daisy collapsed onto the back seat in a malodorous mushroom cloud of fur and dander.

I cranked the engine and turned to Annie. "We came here not because we are incompetent, but because we wanted help. We are not going back for the follow-up visit."

"Uh, no, we are not," Annie said. "If this is what they did for three weeks straight, she hasn't learned anything except fear of abuse. I feel like we just assaulted her and put her in harm's way for the last three weeks. On top of it, we just paid for all of that. I'm calling the Better Business Bureau."

"I'm calling Dr. Clementine," I added.

Daisy's undercoat was two shades lighter in color and weight than her overcoat. It floated in the air like black dandelions as the breeze from the open windows blew it from the back seat to the front of the car. As we shuttled and loomed down the perpendicularly woven county roads with their soft shoulders, Daisy was unaware of the world passing by. Annie and I were silent after our initial reaction, each of us trying to wrap our minds around what had just transpired, what we needed to do next, and how we needed to help this unique dog that was now part of our family.

Arriving home, I carried Daisy's limp body to the back yard and organized the supplies to clean her. She was dead to the world, her skeletal muscles depleted of all fuel. Any energy she had left was devoted strictly to life support functions.

As I washed Gavin's boot camp out of Daisy's fur, she lurched and tried to tuck her hydrophobic head into herself, but had no energy left to mount a thoughtful defense against the garden hose. Her body finally relaxed as I covered her head and torso in a towel and hugged her dry.

I led her to the same spot in the living room I had placed her when we first brought her home from the vet. She didn't object. Her legs gave way, and the only thing preventing her from falling into the center of the earth was the inch-and-a-half strip hardwood pressing against her. I sat in front of her and stared blankly at the black hole that was her body not knowing what we should do next.

I thumbed through Gavin's instructions for dog training. . The whole document read and looked like a driver's education manual from 1952. The linotype title lettering was all capitals and in bold – BASIC DOG TRAINING – as were the accompanying instructions in a smaller all caps font. DOG TRAINING CAN BE FUN AND ENJOYABLE FOR BOTH YOU AND YOUR NEW BEST FRIEND, the instructions began. A series of sequential cartoon frames showing how to properly use different hand signals along with verbal commands for maximum compliance and reinforcement illustrated just how to properly apply the brief lesson learned above. I didn't see choking the crap out of my dog on the instructions, but maybe that paperwork came with our booster session.

I wadded the handouts between my palms into a ball of anger then pressed hard enough to return the paper to pulp.

Daisy's sleep was fitful and full of muted barks, but it was the longest Annie and I had ever seen her with her eyes closed and immobile.

"She must be hungry," I said. "Look at her. She is emaciated."

"If she wasn't eating very much when she was here, I can't imagine she was eating with them." Annie groaned in disgust. "That place was horrible."

"Maybe it is a texture or smell thing. Why don't we try some different brands of food?"

"I suppose we have to start somewhere." Annie rubbed her belly as
Magda played her stomach like bongo drums.

Charlie stayed home with Annie and Daisy while I went back to
Petco.

Sundowning

"If I'm free, it's because I'm always running."

– Jimi Hendrix

I returned home with a mixed bag of different kibble samples – chicken, salmon, sweet potato, organic grains – some cheap, and some horribly expensive.

Daisy was still asleep. Charlie had tucked her in with his favorite blanket and was using the back of her shoulders as a headrest while he read from a stack of picture books. I paused for a moment and got choked up. This was what Annie and I wanted when we talked about all of the wonderful reasons to own a dog, and this was what I remembered as a child.

I said quietly to Annie, "When Charlie is grown, and he looks back at his childhood memories, Daisy will be the standard by which he judges all other dogs. No matter how flawed we may think she is, all Charlie's brain knows about a dog comes from Daisy."

Annie nodded. "Frank called for you. He wanted to hear how Daisy was doing, so I gave him the rundown. He agrees we should call the Better Business Bureau."

"What good is that going to do?" I dismissed. "I'll call him back later."

Daisy didn't rouse until after dinner, and when she did, she announced it by bounding for the door between the kitchen and the garage. She stumbled down the stairs as I led her out.

There was no landing from the kitchen to the garage. There were no handrails. There was no object permanence to the kitchen floor as it dropped down two steps and met the sloped concrete floor below. I frequently lost my footing and rolled my ankles the first week we moved in. Thankfully, Charlie learned to navigate the stairs much more quickly than I did.

After Daisy toileted, I poured her a bowl of the food we'd been feeding her and set it on the garage floor. She was uninterested, so I pulled out one of the dog food samples from my plastic bag. It was a carrot, rice, and chicken blend. It had been molded into the shape of little stars and smelled of yeasted bread. Daisy sniffed but walked off, choosing to wander and recount the smells of the garage instead.

I opened a bag of sweet potato, barley, and pork in the shape, size, and color of peas; it emanated my great-grandmother's powdered laxative. Daisy wouldn't take that either. I then opened a bag with kibble shaped like flattened Cheerios. It was a blend of duck meat and wheat. It smelled oddly of a dry salami sandwich. Daisy took no interest.

The light had begun to wane, and I knew without having to look that the sun was beginning its daily disappearing act. During most of the day, the moving stream of light pouring from the solitary garage window onto the concrete floor acted as a sundial. The absence of a direct beam of light told me that it was the time of day when you could easily fool yourself into thinking that the dusk was dawn, and your day was just beginning rather than ending. With no direction to the transitioning light and no shadows cast, I was mildly disoriented.

Feeling as if my hypothesis of food tastes and textures was going to be disproved, I reached for the last kibble sample. It was salmon, rye, and yam. The dark brown mixture had been formed into pyramidal briquettes, and it was as rough as 120-grit sandpaper. It had the fetor of putrefied onions and asparagus. I gagged as a whiff of it emanated from the bag, so I held my breath and rubbed a piece between my thumb and forefinger at arm's length then dropped it onto the concrete floor. It tap-danced, and Daisy was immediately drawn to it. She trotted over and ate that piece, and came to the bag in my hand to investigate, shoving her face in for more. I had finally found Goldilocks' just-right porridge.

I took a piece in one hand and held it out; she took it. I took another, and she did the same. I took a third out of the bag, and held it in my fist. She mouthed at my fist with force. I didn't release it right away because I was curious to see what she would do. She backed away and barked at my hand with suspicion.

Daisy stood looking at my hand, confused. She didn't speak to me or look at me, only my hand. I sat down in front of Daisy with my two-cup bag of rancid dry dog food. I wanted to see her eyes. I wanted to have a conversation with her. I was tired of reading books. I refused to use Gavin's horrific methods. I was sure I could find out what Daisy needed, and she could find out what I needed if we could just build trust.

Like Daisy, I was confused. Never before had I been mystified by a dog. I had always intuitively known what my dog wanted, and my dogs knew how to get it from me. It was always reciprocal. But Daisy and I had been stuck at an impasse from the beginning.

"Daisy, look at me," I said, calmly holding the kibble in my closed hand.

Daisy returned nothing, not even a fleeting glance, only more mouthing at my hand.

"No." I gently pushed her muzzle with the back of my hand. "Just look at me, and you can have this."

More whimpering and two confounded barks at my hand as she spun in place.

"I know you can do it."

Her forepaws danced and her hind legs skidded on the slick concrete floor as she again nosed my hand then flapped her ears.

"No, just look at me, and this is yours."

Another bark, then she pawed at my fist.

"I promise, we can be great friends."

And there it was, brief and transitory, but her pupils hit mine. I'm sure she didn't mean to; she was looking for a key to a locked box. I don't think she expected to find it in my face. Her eyes were chocolate truffles. I dropped the kibble.

"Good girl!" I congratulated as she crunched.

She dove back at my open hand, ferreting for more. Finding nothing, she spun and flapped her ears several times. The cellophane bag crackled as I reached for more food.

"Daisy – Look."

Again nothing. Only more pining at my hand then several head flaps and two spins in place.

"Daisy – Look."

She lunged at my hand, and that time it hurt.

"Ouch!" I yelped.

She paid no attention to my complaint, but persisted at my hand. Maybe she had been taken from her litter too soon as Dr. Clementine had suggested. Everything I had read said that Labradors were a soft-mouthed breed. They are supposedly capable of carrying an egg in their mouths without breaking it. But Daisy had never learned bite inhibition from her mother or siblings, never had the opportunity, or didn't have the ability.

"No." I popped her nose with the back of my hand again.

Confused, she recoiled and stared at my right hand.

"Daisy – Look."

She whined and ran a lap around the inner circumference of the garage before returning to the enigma that was my hand.

"Daisy – Look."

Then it happened again. It was ephemeral, but my persistence was rewarded. Her irises were 40 percent cocoa and 60 percent milk solids. If I was to believe anything the books Annie and I had read, it was that one of the first events of domestication was that the dog would learn to use us as a reference.

Our simple acts of pointing, subtle eye gazes, posture and movements, the tone of our voice, were supposedly all clues to a canine detective incapable of understanding our sophisticated lexicon with its verbs, nouns, adjectives, and tenses.

It took nearly half an hour to get through the sample bag of food while Daisy and I worked the Look command. As the day finally turned dark, a moth spun pirouettes around the incandescent bulb that now set the open rafters aglow.

Even though Daisy had finished an entire bag of food, and I had repeated the same command at least a hundred times, the interval between the command and the glance didn't improve much. The exercise was time consuming, but I needed to believe it was worth it.

Daisy was fascinated by the moth and spun with it as I went inside to tell Annie I was going to take Daisy for a walk. Annie seemed equally unsure if what Daisy and I had accomplished in the garage could be considered progress or simply coincidence, but she was sure that I had just spent more time working with Daisy than Gavin or Jackson Amador had in the three weeks they'd had her.

The bench vice sat mouth agape as I threw the pronged collar into the trashcan atop my plywood workbench. The bin echoed as the metal hit bottom. I clipped Daisy's leash to her blue collar and we left out the side yard gate. Daisy pulled and yanked. She spun and whined, and stopped, squatted, and peed at nearly every corner, hydrant, and lamppost. I mimed the day's earlier courtyard exercise: left turn, right turn

– right turn, right turn, right turn – left turn, left turn, and a right turn. We weren't going anywhere, and in fact, we were going backward.

The electrified sodium vapor faces at the end of the long-necked streetlights watched me move like a bee that had just returned to the hive to tell its fellow worker bees where to find the nectar, the sweet spot. Daisy didn't speak English, she didn't speak leash, and she didn't speak bee. My left wrist, elbow, and shoulder were fatiguing. So was my will. A bat squeaked overhead in what sounded like derisive laughter at our futile dance.

I was rapidly deflating. Between the morning's experience, watching Daisy spend the afternoon in a coma, and then spending half an hour trying to get her to look at me, I could feel my constitution beginning to falter. I didn't understand how the breed of dog that Wikipedia said required fewer than five repetitions to understand a new command had created such difficulty for me. I could feel the adrenaline and cortisol weeping out of my pores. I grasped for a scapegoat: Anjou for telling me that this dog would be perfect for our family, Dr. Clementine for telling me that Daisy was "within normal limits," and Gavin Amador for taking our money and providing nothing in return.

After several minutes of walking aimlessly, Daisy snorted and dry heaved as she insisted on pulling me forward into the street at the corner of Pole Line and Loyola. I pushed the button for the crosswalk and stood anchored to the steel pole waiting for the walk signal. All I wanted at that moment was a simple sign to tell me how to walk her, a luminous LED display to show me the way. Why couldn't it be that easy? Follow the instructions, push a button, wait your turn, and voila!

The illuminated red DON'T WALK hand signal affirmed its legal obligation to keep me safe from the nonexistent traffic. I only wished Daisy could understand. The weatherproof control box next to us buzzed and clicked as its internal relays and switches changed. Finally, the little green man appeared, assuring us it was okay to cross the street.

The pain in my arm was progressing like a toothache, the dull soreness punctuated by searing stabs. As Daisy tugged and spun me through the intersection, the red hand flashed at us, and warned me that I was walking her all wrong. "Hey, whoa, you better stop, you are not doing this right!" it shouted as the flashing ceased.

This whole process felt wrong. By the time we had made it three more blocks, I had had it. Under pressure, I finally cracked.

"Goddammit!" I yelled in frustration and disgust, and I threw down the leash. It slapped like the crack of a whip against the faults in the monolithic sidewalk. "If you want to run off, go for it!"

And she did just that without looking back. Like a car that had been push started, Daisy popped the clutch and idled off in second gear. Under her own power she headed east, riding the graduated edge between the gutter and the sidewalk like it was Braille. "Ah, shit," I said under my breath. She didn't sprint away as I had predicted and prayed she wouldn't. She just motored off at a pace much more brisk than a walk, but well shy of a bolt, the fluidity of her gait only occasionally broken when a paw caught the leash dragging behind her.

"Daisy – Stop!" No response. "Daisy – Come," I said more loudly. No response. "Daisy – Look!" I bellowed to no avail. Daisy was on cruise control. Her bearings had been preprogrammed. No contingency or countermeasure would adjust her speed or purpose.

I sprinted after her, finally reaching her after another two blocks. As I ran up alongside her, she looked back at me with her chocolate truffle eyes as if I had been there all along – as if she and I did this routinely. Her trot had brought me to her heel, and in stride, I picked up her leash with my right hand, the wrong hand; she was at my right side, the wrong side. Daisy ran with a thousand yard stare, only responsive to an internal stimulus. Shell-shocked by the external demands placed on her, daring and darting cats were of no bother, hydrants had no meaning, and the commentary left at the lampposts was irrelevant.

At first I didn't understand what was happening. I was running next to Daisy and she was at my side. There was no tugging. There was no gagging. There was no tension on the leash. Even though Daisy was running, she was somehow more sedate. I didn't know what to do or what to expect next. So we just ran. We ran beyond Slide Hill Park and passed where Loyola once dead-ended in a barricade. We followed the lazy curve past Linda C. Brown Elementary, past the fortresses of homes within the Lake Alhambra Estates, until we found ourselves at the eastern city limits – and at the head of the Mace Boulevard curve.

I was panting. I had to stop. I wasn't a runner. I hadn't run that far since I was forced to in high school PE, a course I was able to stop taking after my sophomore year, a course that I had said had nothing to do with what I wanted to do with the rest of my life, like trigonometry. Daisy's easy breathing changed as I stopped. Yanked back into reality, she shot out in radii looking for the enlightened path she had just fallen from. She couldn't transition to a slower speed and couldn't adjust to my need for a break. I wiped the sweat from my face with the front of my shirt and turned around to double back.

I didn't want our progress to be hamstrung by my lack of endurance, so I pushed forward into a trot, then into a jog. Daisy followed suit. Her stride was steady and smooth, and her black leather leash hung in a low and sloppy U. By the time we made it back into the familiar facades of our neighborhood, my shins were splintering, and I could feel my toenails bleeding. I was a newborn dragon, wheezing fire and coughing smoke. At the end of our four-and-a-half-mile trip, Daisy was on a runner's high. I stood in our driveway with my head hung low beneath my knees, and gasped for air.

We both stumbled into the house. I spilled into a chair at the kitchen table. Daisy crashed wildly through the doorway, flapping and spinning around the house as I fumbled to untie my shoes. I found no blood, only blisters.

Annie came out to inspect the racket. "Are you okay?"

"Yes – I think so – can you crate her for me?" I said in fragments between rasping gasps.

"What did you do?"

"We went running." I massaged my thighs.

"Why?"

I told Annie all about it as Daisy returned to her self-stimulating and self-cleaning routine.

"I don't know how I'm going to keep this up, but I think she needs it. This was the first time in nearly two months that I felt like I was able to make any sort of connection with this dog."

"You should get some proper running shoes and socks if you're going to make a habit of this." Annie frowned at my tattered old Vans.

Daisy and I repeated our new ritual every night after dinner. It took well over a week to achieve any consistent repeatability with just getting Daisy to look at me. Every week, I tried to work in a new command from what I could remember from Gavin Amador's manual, with no learning of new instructions coming any faster from Daisy than with the original. Daisy's ability to learn put her on the opposite end of the bell curve from her Labrador kin. Her learning style more closely resembled that of the bullheaded Bulldog.

I didn't know why I felt obligated to adhere to any of Gavin's lessons. I felt no obligation to that man, but I had to believe that doing something – following some sort of plan – was better than not. A routine and schedule made more sense than not. Daisy's success with all of the other commands came no faster than any other, but my legs were learning, my lungs were learning, and my heart was learning that she belonged with us.

Dusk became the time of day that Daisy associated with dinner. Her circadian rhythm was locked with the solar cycle and the tilt of the earth. She would only break her fast between the sun and the moon. I often wondered if she would starve to death in an Alaskan summer.

Daisy completely ignored our family's social cues about eating. The clanging of pots, the slapping of food being doled out onto our plates, and the clatter of silverware during our post dinner cleaning held no temporal consequence. Our movements from food preparation in the kitchen, to eating in the dinette, to cleaning dishes in the sink paled in significance to the changing light from the western-facing windows.

Daisy had no ability to sequence and motor plan. She had created an arbitrary link between the frenzy of sunset and the stillness of dusk. As if Mother Nature had rung Pavlov's bell, she became Dustin Hoffman in *Rain Man*, anxious for Judge Wapner to appear. She circled, and fretted, and spun circles as sunset came a few minutes earlier with each autumn day.

And so, when Magdalena Mae was born at 6:32 p.m. on Wednesday, October 12, 2005, I knew that Daisy was bouncing and flapping about the house in anticipation of being fed by Mari, who had agreed to babysit Charlie and Daisy while Annie and I were at the hospital.

Fear of the Unknown

"Worry never robs tomorrow of its sorrow.
It only saps today of its joy."

— Leo Buscaglia

Understanding Daisy was easier after Magda was born. While Annie and I weren't present for Daisy's puppyhood milestones, the more time we spent with Daisy, the more we were certain that those developmental signposts were as late and uneven as Magda's. Unlike the theoretical autistic, Magda never regressed; she just never progressed like she should. Both Daisy and Magda were mostly internalizers, generally incapable of displaying the normal outward signs of distress, like barking or screaming only when in full duress. For them, adrenaline meant it was time to inhibit, not excite.

If before birth, God or Darwin had offered them the ability of flight or fight, they chose the hidden option to freeze instead. Phrases like dyspraxia, sensory integration dysfunction, and non-functional routines all began to make as much sense in the context of Magda as they did with Daisy. They both shared impairment in the organization of their movements, a disorganized response to sensory signals, and an inflexible devotion to the particular. Through our newfound vocabulary, we learned to better understand them both, or at least to be able to talk to each other about what we were seeing in them.

Before we knew anything about the direction of Magda's life, we knew that transitioning from one child to two was not a matter of simple addition. The coordination of mealtimes, bath times, nap times, and play times all required an understanding of exponents, logarithms, and the limits of calculus. The economic principal of scarcity reigned in our small home; supplying the attention that the demands of two young children required was difficult. Sleep was at a premium after Magdalena was born, and Annie and I walked like zombies through the first few months of her life.

Rarely could we deviate from our foggy routine of passing bottles in the night, handing off diaper bags during the day, and trying to give Charlie and Daisy the attention they needed and deserved. The clarity and recognition that the fatigue we were experiencing was beyond that of normal began to manifest itself just as Magda emerged from her first winter. We had just been to see Dr. Comice for Magda's well-child visit and booster vaccinations. Dr. Comice was a kind and competent man who had a gift for working with children and their parents. He had intelligent eyes and understanding hands. As a diagnostician, he was scalpel sharp. Everyone in Davis wanted him as their child's pediatrician; very few were that lucky.

He had been tracking Magda's head circumference, charting her growth, asking about rolling over, quizzing us about babbling, and trying to sort out Magda's interest in people or objects. In his calm, un-alarming way, Dr. Comice suggested that Magda should undergo some additional testing because she was "showing developmental delays," and her head was "large for her age." And so, as it was with Daisy, Magdalena underwent a battery of blood work, but Magda's included genetic testing along with a trans-fontanel ultrasound of her brain to rule out hydrocephaly. All were "normal studies."

By the end of Magda's first summer, our own realizations of our daughter's differences and Dr. Comice's concerns collided. Her fussy eating, hatred of bath time, and seemingly endless projectile vomiting no longer could be thought of as phases she might outgrow.

Magda's head was still much larger than any typical percentile ranking for her age. She wasn't yet crawling reliably or showing much interest in walking. She wasn't saying or attempting words or even waving at loved ones. If she gained the sporadic use of an age-appropriate skill like pointing, she just as quickly lost another basic skill like standing with support.

Dr. Comice thought a brain MRI prudent. His concern about her developmental delays coupled with her seemingly large head mandated that he rule out a congenital brain malformation, a cerebrovascular entanglement, or a tumor. The remainder of her non-life threatening differential diagnoses would have to take a backseat.

* * *

"How are you not worried about this MRI?" Annie whispered.

"It's after three in the morning, and I'm still awake."

"Does she have to have an IV?" she asked with trepidation.

Anne had asked me this before. I knew she wasn't hoping for a different answer; she was hoping that this wasn't real.

"She has to be sedated. She has to be still for nearly thirty minutes. She can't do that on her own." I turned on my side.

"You're not scared? The form said she could stop breathing, have brain damage, or go into cardiac arrest."

"They have to tell you all the bad things that can happen…"

"What if she has a tumor," she dared say aloud.

"Then we'll make a plan and go from there."

"How can you be so pragmatic about all of this?" Annie was no longer whispering.

"What other choice do I have?"

"Can you imagine having a child with cancer?" she asked.

"No, I cannot."

"Couldn't that be the reason she is throwing up all the time?"

"Comice said it is just reflux," I countered.

"Then why aren't the medications working?"

"He said they might not."

"Then what else could it be? Clearly there is something wrong."

"I don't know, but I can't live in the land of what could be. I have to live in the world of now."

Annie rolled toward me. We lay face to face.

"She is always crying…"

"I know."

"Are we doing something wrong? Charlie was never like this."

"No, I don't think so, and no, he wasn't. If we were doing something wrong as parents, we wouldn't be taking her to get an MRI," I said.

"It sounds ridiculous, but the only thing that gives me hope is that she seems calm and content when she is with Daisy," Annie said.

"I've noticed that too. It seems like those are the only moments when Daisy is also calm."

"I find Daisy in Magda's room all the time," Annie said.

"I've noticed that too."

"Do you think we should let Daisy sleep in her room at night?" Annie asked.

"I don't know. Maybe we should. She is up all night anyway, rattling in her crate, flapping her ears, licking."

"Magda is up all night too." She rolled onto her back and stared at the ceiling. "What are we going to do if she has a brain tumor?"

"We are going to do what we need to do . . . what we have to do."

"I'm scared." Annie began to cry.

"Everyone is," I said reaching for her hand.

Puzzled Pieces

"Consideration for others is the basis of a good life, a good society."

— Confucius

In an attempt to take our minds off of Magda's impending head scan, and worse, the possible outcome of its result, we filled every minute of our free time with activities. On the Saturday preceding her scan, we wanted to feel like normal parents, so took the kids downtown to the Davis Farmers Market. We left Daisy at home. It was less stressful that way.

On Saturday mornings in Davis, the open-air market is a nice alternative to going to the grocery store and a good place to run into friends and be social, a concept that felt remote to us after the insular lives we had led the past year.

Charlie had always liked the Farmers Market because he could ride on Fredrick the Frog, Willie the Worm, or Silvie the Cat on the Flying

Carousel of the Delta Breeze. In true Davis fashion, the merry-go-round that centers Central Park is pedal powered. As the pedals turn the chain ring, the long sloppy bicycle chain bounces in rhythm. An articulated conga line of rollers, pins, and plates dances through the mysterious box that stretches to the center of the carousel to a place hidden behind the bright hexagonal core. Hidden from public view, the rotational energy changes vectors, and the hand-carved animals attached to dangling spiraled brass poles spin clockwise.

The cost of admission, usually only a couple of dollars, was for the benefit of whatever public school had lobbied for time riding the one-of-a-kind machine. Most children loved the experience, except for those brave few wise enough to recognize that at the end of the music, they had only gone in circles, finding themselves right back where they had started.

As adults and parents, Annie and I loved the park the WPA had built for the city during the Depression. It was family friendly, spacious, and green. As a novice adult, I had a completely different view of the park. It was a place my roommate Frank and I had to traverse between campus and downtown on Thursday and Friday nights in our search of free libations and live music. The periphery of fraternities and college rentals that ringed the park meant that Central Park was never a destination – only an obstacle.

Today, as Charlie and I walked toward the buffet of stalls and merchants, we passed the century-old oak tree with its adjacent decking, I flashed back to the bloodshot memory of Frank and me parting ways on our last drunken walk together as undergrads. Now, a group of bright-eyed children stood in front of the great tree waiting inebriated with their parents' money as a clown twisted balloon animals for them and a street artist painted their faces. Charlie wanted to join them, but I convinced him to walk the length of the market with me. We zigzagged through a maze of people, inspecting the end–of-summer bounty and the colorful beginning of the fall harvest. Charlie and I started with coffee and a hot chocolate, but as we wove our way back to Annie, we landed on cinnamon rolls instead of the apples I told Annie I wanted.

When Charlie and I found Annie, she was talking to a medium height woman in a purple long-sleeved crocheted maxi-dress. Hanging beneath her black turtleneck was a silver-dollar-sized peace-emblem pendant. It waved back and forth across her chest like a hypnotist's charm as she spoke. Her wavy brunette locks were highlighted in silver. She was pointing and gesturing toward Magda, who was sitting, turned away from everyone, in a pile of woodchips under the play structure near the great oak tree. As Charlie and I walked up, I mumbled to myself, "Whoever said never trust a man in a suit had never been to Davis."

Annie saw me approach and made introductions. "Mercy, this is my husband Arthur and our son Charlie. Arthur, this is Mercy Valencia. She is a social worker for Yolo County…" Annie gave me an unsure smile.

"Hi, Arthur." Mercy's voice was born on a southern California beach, sun-kissed with a saline rasp. Not as husky or breathy as Kathleen Turner, nor as impetuous as Lindsay Lohan, but as pacifying as the Pacific. "I was just telling your wife how beautiful your daughter is."

"Absolutely, she is."

"This is my youngest daughter Gustine," she said. "She is a little older than Charlie."

Gustine planted herself about six inches from Charlie's face and grabbed his left hand. "Do you want to go play on the structure with me? I'm the cop, and you're the robber, okay?"

"Okay," Charlie said, and he handed me his cocoa and cinnamon roll and trotted off stride for stride with the older girl to play in the imaginary jail.

"I was telling Annie that I had been watching Magdalena for a while, and I noticed she isn't doing things that other one-year-olds are doing by this point. Posture. Play. Eye contact." Mercy launched into a script of what I thought was going to be more of the unsolicited parenting advice Annie and I had come to loathe.

Before I could interrupt her diatribe about developmental milestones, Mercy added, "I hope you don't mind me being intrusive, but this is what I do for a living. I'm sure that one way or another you would have made your way to me. I used to work for Orange County Health and Welfare until I moved to Davis ten years ago with my now ex-husband." She rolled her eyes. "I've been telling your wife that I can expedite the referral process for Magda."

Confused, I didn't know what to say. I looked at Annie.

"Ooh, sorry," said Mercy. "I should have said that now I work for Yolo Early Intervention Services."

"Okay," I said. "What type of referral do you mean?"

"Whatever she qualifies for – OT, PT, speech therapists. I understand that you don't have a diagnosis yet, and that's fine..." Her voice trailed. "We will have her evaluated by a group of specialists from the county. When she qualifies for services, she will be seen at least weekly, probably in a clinic setting and in your home." Her pendant danced and reflected sunlight into my eyes.

"I guess I'm still a little confused, and clearly I came to the conversation late, but—"

"Annie told me about the MRI," Mercy interjected, "and that is fine, but results or no results, you need to get Dr. Comice to write you a referral for early intervention services ASAP so that Magda can start to catch up to where she should be developmentally. I know this is a lot for most parents, and most of the time parents come to me, not the other way around. Trust me, I don't like taking unsolicited advice either, but it will the best thing for you guys as parents, and for your daughter." She said all this in a no-bullshit manner that I could finally trust.

Mercy reached out and shook both our hands firmly. "I'll be in touch. I need some lettuce." She turned and made a beeline to the lettuce stall. I went to find Charlie.

* * *

By the time we made it home, there was already an email from Mercy with a bullet point list of what Annie and I were to do next. In so many ways, running into Mercy was a blessing. Her instructions, list of consultations we needed to call, and referrals we needed to chase down gave Annie and me something to do while we waited for Magda's MRI results, which turned out to be "normal."

Two weeks after Magda's brain scan, Mercy Valencia delivered on her promise as a steady stream of rookie and veteran therapists came in and out of our house to evaluate and ultimately treat Magdalena. Everything they did with her looked like play, but oxymoronic to the term "child's play," it was anything but. For Magda, it was incredibly difficult. Annie and I stood and watched, second-guessing how we interacted and played with Magda. We often became part of the sessions themselves, learning the "right" way to engage our daughter. Having to break down what came intuitively to Charlie was cumbersome and awkward for us as we tried to engage Magda.

As simple tasks such as asking to play with a ball and sharing in a game were fractured into infinitesimally smaller subtasks, I often felt like I was standing in the garage with Daisy breaking down the most mundane activity into its most basic atomic components before being able to tie those elements back together into molecules and compounds of socially acceptable behaviors. As with Daisy, Annie and I experienced multiple failures with Magda, and found only fleeting moments of success. Being defeated by Daisy was one thing; there were television shows that reaffirmed we weren't the only ones who had a troubled relationship with their dog. But in Davis, everyone was a perfect parent, or at least that was the mask everyone wore. With Magda, Annie and I felt far from perfect.

Some families openly bragged to us about the walking and talking their children were doing, which they knew Magda simply couldn't do, while others just withdrew from events where they knew Magda would be present.

I could tell it hurt Annie more than it did me. I coped by calling them assholes, but Annie persisted in the silence of exclusion.

Our joys with Magda were never photo friendly moments as they were with Charlie. They were fleeting joys grasped in desperation when we finally had Eureka revelations of the "duh – of course that's why" kind. Joy was defined by those moments when we could find the puzzle pieces that we were sure had been mixed into another box or lost to the vacuum cleaner, joy in the moments when we remembered that puzzles are a lot easier to solve when you invite the right people to help.

Sensory Profiling

"I have great faith in fools; self-confidence, my friends call it."

— Edgar Allan Poe

By Magda's second birthday, Daisy and I were marathoners. We had to be – it helped us both to self-regulate. Life had become about the long view. Daisy needed to run as much as I did. Our mental health depended on it. If neither of us got our exercise, we both were bouncing off the walls. Six miles a day was easy, eight was better, and ten felt like a vacation.

The smaller milestones of being able to reliably sit, stay, and come for Daisy had become secondary to finding an internal regulatory state that was calm, focused, and at peace. But no matter her savant skills as a runner, Daisy still had no reliable ability to find emotional balance or to refrain from bounding into furniture, people, and closed doors – unless the world became too stimulating, and in those moments she froze or sought refuge.

Magda continued to struggle with her own internal speed as well. She had long bouts of isolating and internalizing catatonia punctuated by gleeful externalizing mania. In public, or during the increasingly rare times we had people over to visit, the commentary was always along the lines of, "Oh, she is such a calm and contented child," or, "Wow, look how happy and joyful she is. What is wrong with that?"

When Magdalena started walking at eighteen months, she seldom did. She always ran. She rarely stopped of her own accord; it usually required running into a bed, a couch, Annie, me, or Daisy. But when she did stop, it was with permanence.

Magda was often mesmerized by someplace other than where she was. Calling for her attention, looking for her eye contact, and asking her to come out from wherever her brain had hidden her, was impossible.

We went everywhere for help. Mercy Valencia, Yolo County, and Dr. Comice led us to UC Davis' Medical Investigation of Neurodevelopmental Disorders (MIND) Institute. Annie joined a local support group for parents of children with Sensory Processing Disorder, and that led us to Dr. Lucy Jane Miller's Sensory Therapies and Research (STAR) Center in Denver. As we trekked through Magda's unmapped life with our ever expanding three-ringed binders of assessments and our videos of Magda's behavior, our "duh" moments expanded. So did our repertoire of tricks to prevent and control the howling banshee that emerged when we tried to buckle her into her car seat, get her dressed, or cut her hair. We began to understand the mysticism required to resurrect her from the death that occurred at every family function, every trip to the store, and every time the phone rang.

As we navigated the seas of dyspraxia, mixed expressive-receptive language delays, regulatory disorders, and sensory processing disorder on our journey to autism with Magda, my nightstand books on canine psychology were replaced by books like Jane Ayers' *Sensory Integration and the Child*, Temple Grandin's *Thinking in Pictures*, Carol Kranowitz's *The Out-of-Sync Child*, and Stanley Greenspan's *Engaging Autism*.

Annie and I often lamented that we knew parenting was going to be hard work; we just didn't realize Magda would turn it into a career for us. We needed something akin to Gavin Amador's dog-training pamphlet with simple hand gestures and one-word commands, but none existed. And it was just as well because that didn't work for Daisy; why would it work for Magda?

With all of the cognitive testing that Magda had endured, I began to wonder if any such testing had been done with dogs. Everything I had read had defined autism's core deficit as a gap in social skills and communication. It was the working theory in most human studies, and communication certainly seemed to be where Daisy and we were failing. So I asked Google about canine social skills, and remarkably, someone had already studied this notion. I clicked on the link to a PDF of a study from the Max Planck Institute in Germany. Two researchers had tested a dog's ability to understand and use human social and communicative behaviors like gestures and pointing to locate food.

The study was simple. A treat was placed under one of two opaque cups sitting in front of a dog. A human would gesture, in some manner, to the cup with the treat. Dogs of all ages and varying levels of exposure to people were able to accomplish this task. The tests were repeated with the human using one of a variety of social cues such as glancing, nodding, pointing, or touching during each test. Across the board, the dogs were successful with several forms of human nonverbal communication. The dogs were using the convergence of canine and human social skills as one of their tools for success. I was amazed and immediately had to reproduce this study with Daisy.

Annie had no interest as she sat reading her third Dr. Seuss story to Magda and Charlie on the living room couch – it was *Horton Hears a Who*. "That's nice, honey, don't break anything," she said as I grabbed our his-and-hers coffee mugs from the cabinet above the kitchen sink. I shoved a handful of Daisy's rancid kibble into the front pocket of my Levis and sat on the kitchen floor. With my knees, shins, and ankles pressed flat against the tile, I made Daisy sit in front of me, two yards away. She could smell the kibble, and she smacked her mouth in anticipation. I hid one kibble under the cup to my right and pretended to hide one under the cup to my left.

I looked at Daisy, she looked at me, and I glanced from her to the cup with the hidden kibble several times. I then released her, and she bounded for the empty cup on the left. "Not off to a good start," I said under my breath as I set her in position again. This time I placed the treat in the cup on the left. Again, I altered my gaze from her to the cup with the treat. I released her, and again, she missed the mark. It took four attempts for her to ultimately find the prize. I repeated the exercise with her another sixteen times. She was nine for twenty, with no noticeable improvement as the tests went on. I then moved on to nodding toward the correct cup – and again, Daisy did no better than basic probability would estimate; she was eleven for twenty. With pointing, she was ten of twenty, and finally, with tapping, she was right on thirteen of twenty attempts.

According to the study, Daisy had the social communication skills of a control group wolf, an animal whose evolutionary success had nothing to do with interacting with people; they were independent problem solvers. Daisy was flummoxed by my attempted instructions. She had ultimately learned to look at me through the repetitiveness of our evening feeding ritual, but she had no clue what to do with the information my eyes provided. The look command was operant conditioning. That was it. If it held more meaning for her than that, she was incapable of expressing it.

I went back to my old pediatric nursing texts to see if the study was telling the truth when it said that human children acquire this social skill by fourteen months of age. Sure enough, interpreting an adult's gestures should be emerging by the time a child turns one and mastered by a year and a half, something lacking in Daisy – and Magda.

And then I thought *screw it*. I grabbed my coffee mugs, a handful of Cheerios, and knelt down in front of my daughter to repeat the same experiment. Looking at someone had become operant for her as well, rewarded not with kibble by her therapists but with exuberant praise in a singsong voice and goldfish crackers.

Her postural tone was poor as she sat back against the couch cushions. Annie had finished her Seuss marathon and was silently questioning what I was doing.

Magda sat immobile staring at me as well, chewing on the edge of her blanket. Magdalena has my father's eyes. She also has his furrowed brow. It is a look of concentration, protecting a mind deep in thought from the sensory information bombarding their heads and faces. With him, I could ask what he was thinking about if he didn't offer his thoughts freely. With Magda, I had no idea what was on her mind.

I put both cups on the seat cushion in front of us, three feet apart from each other. The furrow remained steadfast. Annie and Charlie watched as Magda scored just as poorly as Daisy on the first three attempts. Her eyes darted back and forth, and she seemed only capable of guessing. When I glanced at the cup with the Cheerios, she got eight of twenty. When I nodded, she got nine of twenty. When I pointed, she got twelve of twenty, but when I tapped on the cup, she aced it, twenty for twenty. Annie sat drop-jawed.

"Whoa. That is crazy," I said.

Annie nodded.

"I wonder if it is because tapping is more than just a visual stimulus," I proffered.

"Right," Annie said.

"Maybe it is the combination of watching me tap coupled with an auditory reinforcement." I felt compelled to force a hypothesis.

"I just think that the tapping forced her to look for the sound, not that you actually communicated where the Cheerios might be. She was investigating the noise." Just like that, Annie popped my hypothesis. "All of her therapists think she is hypervisual and can't filter out what is or isn't important. Everything shares equal value. Your pointing is just as important to her as the color of your shirt."

"Huh," I said, choosing a safe noncommittal response.

"Hey, professor, before you wander off, remember, we have paperwork to fill out." Annie derailed my train of thought. Every six months, or with every new provider or developmental center, we had to fill out standardized test questionnaires and pop quizzes about Magda's habits, tics, quirks, shut-downs, explosions, anorexia, gorging, bowel and bladder habits, insomnia, hypersomnia, and responses to wind, rain, and thunder. They were all trifold triplicate scrolls enumerating and scaling endless sensory and motor derangements.

Our answers were to be translated on modified Likert scales, with the subsequent data tallied as a raw score converted into standard scores, assigned a percentile rank, then reported as an "area of concern" or "not." For our part, we needed to remember that 1 meant never, 3 was sometimes, 5 denoted always, and 2 and 4 represented somewhere between the extremes but not right in the middle.

"How many of these things have we filled out in the last year, six?" I complained. "Can't we just photocopy the last one and resubmit it?"

"No. Things are always changing with Magda, and her therapists need an accurate picture of who she is now."

"I understand. I'm just tired of filling out paperwork every time we turn around. I guess I'm just tired period."

Annie forced a grin. "We all are, including your son."

"Why don't we do one on Daisy?"

Annie shook her head no. "Can we just fill them out now so we can start working on dinner, baths, bedtime…?"

"Sure." I lied. I picked up the thick stack of questions and stood in front of Annie, Charlie, Magda, and Daisy.

"How old was your dog when he or she learned to walk," I said in baritone, licking the tip of my pencil.

Annie laughed. "Um, she doesn't walk yet. She only runs."

"Mm hmm, I see." I pretended to write the answer down.

Charlie laughed.

"At what age did your dog first make eye contact with you?"

"One year old," Annie answered.

"Ooh, that doesn't sound normal," I said in my best therapist's voice.

"Now, for the next set of questions on the CBA – the Canine Behavioral Assessment – I want you to tell me if you see the behavior sometimes, always, or never."

Annie guffawed.

"Allows you to cut or trim her nails."

"Uh, never," Annie said.

"Doesn't respond to name, but hearing is fine."

"Always," Annie moaned.

"Acts in an appropriate manner around strangers."

"Never," Annie and Charlie said in unison.

"Enjoys playing in the water at bath time."

"Never," Annie and Charlie chorused.

"How often does your dog chase cats or other small animals?"

"Always," they said simultaneously.

"When the doorbell rings, how often does your dog bark, run, or hide?"

"Always!" they sang.

"Until you disassembled it," Annie added under her breath.

"How often does your dog bring you toys to play with?"

"Never," they refrained.

"How often does your dog sleep all the way through the night?"

"Never," they returned.

"How often does your dog make abnormal physical movements like shake her head or spin in circles?"

"Always," they said as Charlie developed the hiccups.

"How easily does your dog calm down after play or exercise?"

"Never," they sang.

"How often does your dog enjoy being around other dogs?"

"Never," they said, as our strophic song ended.

"Alright, let's actually fill this thing out so we can get on with things," I said trying to regain my composure.

Annie was still laughing with her hand over her mouth and Charlie was doubled over with hiccups, "Ask more <hiccup> Daddy <hiccup> ask more."

Daisy began barking in confusion and distress as Mari pull-started her weed eater next door. Magda began to cry. I shook my head as I sat down wedging myself between the armrest and Annie, dropping my head to her shoulder. We were a Simpson's couch gag but the only ones tuned in.

* * *

Charlie's hiccups returned while he watched his sister struggle to chew her plain pasta noodles. Magda's face contorted, and she shook her head as if to say no. She threw the remnants down to Daisy, who had sat waiting at Magda's side for whatever food gifts were handed down this mealtime. Her tail fluttered in excitement. Daisy mouthed the pasta and her face recoiled in an expression of "Yuck!" She thrust the food from her mouth in the same expert way she coughed out her heartworm pill. She stared at the tile floor in disgust.

Magda squealed in delight at Daisy's reaction.

"I'm glad nobody likes my cooking," Annie said.

"They both don't like it!" Charlie said with a belly laugh.

Magda contently hummed as she dipped another piece of her penne in ketchup, sucked it clean of the Heinz, and threw the pasta at Daisy's feet again. At first Daisy was thrilled, and then remembered her disgust when she tasted Magda's second offering.

Magda erupted in laughter.

"I wish she could use her words to tell us if she doesn't like the food," I whispered to Annie.

"Everyone is working on that," she said.

* * *

Later that night in bed, I reached for Annie's hand. She reflexively squeezed mine, but I knew she was asleep. Her name was stuck in my throat, pulled down by a weight in my chest tethered to my voice box. A cold torrent ran down the sides of my face, pooling in my ears before falling like water bombs onto the bed sheet.

Annie stirred. "Are you okay?"

My body tensed as I fought full convulsions. Nausea was like a noose around my neck.

"She rarely looks at me." I whispered. "I can't keep doing this. Every time we fill out one of those forms, it's like being cut all over again." My forehead began to sting. "It's exhausting being the ballast. I feel like I always have to be even keeled about this for everyone – for her, Charlie, our parents. I can't mourn this." I wiped my face with the back of my hand. "Mourn what, I don't know, because it makes it sound as if I don't love her or she is broken. But I feel like she isn't even connected to me."

"You are connected, and she is certainly connected to Daisy.

She gravitates to you because you're calm. It helps her."

"It's the things that I feel like I might lose decades from now, like walking her down the aisle, dancing the first dance."

"I know…" Annie drifted off and let go of my hand.

First Stages of Grief

"Should you shield the canyons from the windstorms, you would never see the true beauty of their carvings."

— Elisabeth Kubler-Ross

I awoke with what felt like an axe buried in my head, split down the middle, paring the two halves of my brain. Every time my head turned, the axe's handle collided with the nightstand, the wall, or the doorframe. The result in my brain was akin to what I imagine it would feel like to hold a tuning fork in my teeth and strike it repeatedly, blurring my vision, angering my amygdala. My mind felt like it had been halved. Reality was becoming absurd and inside out. My headaches were becoming more and more frequent, and I often found myself talking to myself, muttering and mumbling. It was mildly schizophrenic. Life with Daisy and Magda was becoming more and more demanding, and the individual who I thought I once was lay split like a log, waiting to be thrown onto an all-consuming fire.

"Frank must have stopped by early this morning," Annie said, walking into our bedroom with our his-and-hers cups of coffee in hand and folded papers under her left arm. "He left you this in the mailbox." She handed me a stack of several collated sheets of paper that had been folded along their long axis.

"Coffee first," I said, reaching for the mug she handed me. I was like a heroin addict; without my daily caffeine fix, I felt physically sick. Withdrawal left me feeling on edge. Double vision made my migraines worse. The years of bottomless cups of hospital grade coffee to help me survive twelve-and-a-half-hour night shifts, inconsistent breaks, and infrequent meals had left me immune to the high of caffeine.

I took a long slurp of Major Dickason's Blend and felt an immediate sense of relief.

"By the way, that headache isn't getting you out of going tonight, and that one needs to be exercised," Annie trailed as Daisy tore through the house.

My vision worsened.

The second Sunday of every month was Sensory Family Night. What began as a listserv group for parents of kids with sensory issues to ask questions and network had morphed into a monthly mandatory potluck. It was a patchwork gathering of people who potentially once had the capacity to be social, but who now contended with a kid who perceived the world and the majority of its stimuli as noxious. Unfortunately, our commonality seemed to be the only common grounds for discussion, something Annie was fine with, but I found hard to tolerate, especially if I had to go to work the next day.

I had read a story on the Yahoo! homepage that said after college, adults start rapidly losing friends. It was short and stupid, a paraphrase of something someone probably spent a fair amount of time researching – how well, I couldn't tell. I found the blurb a waste of the meager energy it took me to move the mouse and take the clickbait, yet still it annoyed me. They called it the quarter life crisis. As you age, you become stuck in a career mostly with people who have to work together, not who want to work together. And in your private life, your children's friends' parents become your only social outlet. Before you know it, those care-free days of associating with whomever you please have evaporated, never to return until you get old enough to retire, move into an assisted living facility, and then have the captive (and likely deaf) company of other people who are willing to sit around all day complaining about constipation, denture cream, and melanoma. That is if you and your marriage have survived your mid-life crisis and you don't end up poor, isolated, and alone in some state-run "skilled" nursing facility.

A lot of our college friends left Davis never to return. College was simply a developmental phase. An occasional email or text would arrive from someone we hadn't seen for five years or more, asking if we would be in town for various events: Picnic Day, UC Davis' yearly open house; the Causeway Classic, UC Davis' annual football rivalry with Sacramento State; or the Whole Earth Festival, a three-day patchouli oil-and-drum-circle-fueled flea market of expensive pottery, hand-woven hemp cloth-ing, and free awareness on the quad between the Coffee House and the Shields main library.

Before Magdalena was born, Annie and I jumped at the opportu-nity to get out of the house and relive good times with good or even questionable friends. Charlie was often in tow, and while he was fully capable of a tantrum, he could still be playful with our friends' children. Even if Charlie wasn't with us, we were completely comfortable with the knowledge that he was under the watchful eye of a teenaged babysitter or Mari. Either way, Annie and I were able to maintain some form of communication with old friends.

After Magda was born, when we received such invitations, we lied most of the time as a way to decline, and said we wouldn't be in town. It was easier. Magda couldn't tolerate babysitters, and she couldn't tol-erate restaurants. In essence, we as a family had become autistic, our social capacity functionally diminished. Our events had to be planned, discussed, and put on Magda's picture schedule as well as on her poster-sized calendar mounted next to the front door. Impromptu guests inevitably led to insomnia, and unplanned trips out of the house came with the added benefit of banshee tantrums or the opposite – complete introversion and shutdown. There could be no ambiguity in the daily routine. Spontaneity had died the day Magda stopped hitting developmental milestones.

Annie and I had met a handful of likeminded families via Charlie through the Putah Creek PTA and Davis' AYSO soccer program. But as Charlie and his friends grew, so did the activities of those parents. Potluck dinners changed to events that required reservations, corkage fees, and something less comfortable than jeans and flip-flops. Backyard cookouts graduated to overnight camping trips in the Sierras, and trips to Slide Hill Park's Manor Pool became outings to the Jelly Belly factory in Vacaville or miniature golfing in Roseville.

As Magdalena neared her third birthday, she could barely handle going to the grocery store without completely falling apart, let alone take a car trip out of town with a bunch of rowdy kids. So, much to our chagrin, we turned a lot of invitations down. We felt bad for Charlie. In a lot of ways, we became single parents living under the same roof just so he could have access to what we thought was right for him. On the nights and weekends I had Charlie, Annie had Magda. Annie would take Magda to speech and occupational therapy in Woodland, and I would take Charlie to soccer practice at Tremont Elementary. So, in addition to losing more friends than one would in a typical quarter-life crisis, we were losing time with each other. The only uniform routine Annie and I had together was organizing Magda's picture schedule for the next day's events. In a lot of ways, I needed the schedule as much as Magda, so I knew where to go with Charlie, and where I could find Annie if I needed her. The routine was turning us into roommates, leaving banal messages on the refrigerator like "dishes are done" or "don't forget trash tomorrow."

So on this day, just hearing the reminder about the dreaded monthly potluck brought out the whiner in me. "Can't we just do something together instead," I moaned as I crawled out of bed, just before Annie was completely out of the room. The caffeine had finally antagonized the addict in my head, and I was in resistance mode. I wanted comfort and solace.

"No!" boomed Annie, not turning to look back at me.

"Dammit," I mumbled to Daisy.

She flapped her ears.

We didn't talk about developmental milestones the way we did with our friends in Oakland when Charlie was younger. No one ever asked, "When did Magda rollover?" or, "When did she take her first steps?" or, "What was her first word?" The benchmarks we once celebrated and announced in mass emails and Christmas cards about Charlie were only brought up in reference to Magda to say that they had been missed or never attempted. The conversations at Sensory Family Night were all about the obstacles and stumbling blocks that prevented our kids from being like the "neurotypicals." Instead of asking when these kids did things, we asked questions about the sensory stimuli that may be responsible for preventing age appropriate changes, such as, "Is your son more smell sensitive or touch sensitive? Can your daughter handle the texture of Rice Krispies or fettuccine? Does your daughter howl when she hears fire trucks?"

These tended to be circular discussions about sensory diets that ranged from how to mitigate tactile defensiveness to how to determine whether gravitational insecurity would become a lifelong trait. Sensory families didn't ask where to get the best deals on a trip to Disneyland or when to get the cheapest flights to Hawaii; they asked where to get weighted blankets, compression clothing, and referrals to the STAR Center in Colorado and the UC Davis MIND Institute. Sensory kids need these things more than a vacation so they can feel where their bodies are in space, and sooth them from a world that seems hell bent on assaulting them.

I never mentioned that not only did my daughter experience these things, but my dog did too. Daisy didn't like the sound of zippers or impact sprinklers. It didn't seem appropriate to share that she cowered behind the couch when the compressed natural gas-propelled Unitrans and Yolobus passed our house. No one but Annie knew that the smell of jasmine made Daisy pant and drool uncontrollably, or that we had to buy her one of those compression shirts for the fourth of July, the occasional thunderstorm, and Thanksgiving dinners. A calming phenomenon we assumed was akin to Temple Grandin's hug machine. For a town with the best veterinary school on the west coast, hardly any one of the sensory families had a dog unless they had spent tens of thousands of dollars and waited a year or more to get a trained therapy dog – typically a Labrador. No one could relate to my anecdotes about Daisy. No one cared. Everyone was busy reliving the past, uncertain of the present, and petrified of what the future might hold. The answers parents sought at these potlucks took on the fierce urgency of now.

Sensory Family Night always brought me to the edge of despondence. I did not know why. I assumed it was being held captive by others' grief. Sharing someone else's pain was validating for Annie, but it further crammed me into a world of denial that Magda was different from what I was hearing.

I knew she was different from all these other children. She had to be. I needed to cling to something hopeful. Magda wasn't born from a ruptured placenta previa; she never aspirated meconium; she never needed a neonatal ICU. Magda's one- and five-minute Apgar scores were both perfect tens. Besides, we had different diagnoses than other parents, and I could see the difference in Magda's eyes. I had to believe that she would eventually be able to understand and use language to express herself. We had read to her every night, and she seemed to crave it. I could also sense the connection she had with her therapists, and of course with Daisy.

It was on nights like Sensory Sunday that I tried really hard to use the therapeutic listening skills I was taught in nursing school. "That must be very difficult for you guys," I would say with an understanding nod. "I can't imagine how that must have made you feel." But I just couldn't be engaged. *This is my day off, dammit!* I wanted to shout, but kept it in my thoughts. *Can't we do something fun? Can't we be normal?* Then I would chide myself for being insensitive, and I wondered what someone else would do if they had to listen to me complain about how difficult our life had become.

A lot of parents' stories about the obstacles they encountered in getting a diagnosis, finding a good family therapist, or dealing with the public schools in Davis seemed fantastical and without obvious logic or reasoning. Surely, normal professional people wouldn't act in ways these parents described. "Why would anyone do something like that to a child?" I would ask, half incredulous and half looking for proof that they were embellishing the story to get a reaction out of the rest of us. Everything that Annie and I had heard about Davis schools was positive, but I wasn't so naïve to believe that there couldn't be some exceptions. There were always a few bad apples among school administrators and teachers. But still, I wondered – maybe Davis parents were too militant, hovering, and overly involved in their children's lives. Helicopter parents, the older generation had branded us.

Thankfully, most of the kids or their parents couldn't handle the sensory overload of the monthly potlucks, so these gatherings tended to be smaller affairs. As much as I complained about having to go, they were not wholly awful and generally involved lots of Napa or Sonoma valley wines. Davis parents didn't drink cheap wine, and I appreciated that.

Truthfully, the biggest pain-in-the-ass part of the evenings was the food. Menus were designed around being flexible to the children's palates, not the adults, so the food was typically bland. Often the host would make requests for dry-baked chicken or some other flavorless protein, free of seasoning, and served with plain rice. A lot of families had also gone gluten and casein-free, which meant giving up two protein compounds that bloggers considered antagonists to individuals on the autism spectrum.

Every gluten-free cake I've ever eaten tasted horrible. They trick your brain like a Wayne Thiebaud painting – glossy and inviting, but they taste like acrylic and chalks. The first time I took a bite of one, I felt like the dog in the commercial eating a spoonful of peanut butter trying to clear my mouth of the adhesive paste, constantly gasping and moving my tongue in an effort to swallow. And in a casein-free home, you can't have a glass of milk to wash it down. That left me no choice but to drink wine, so I did drink, a lot – a dangerous affair on an empty stomach.

Annie knew that I often came home hungry from Sensory Sunday, so she packed her purse with snack bags of food. I wanted to think she did it all for me, but in truth it was more so that Magda wouldn't cause a scene spitting her food on the floor because the texture was wrong, the color was off, or hadn't come out of the exact same container that it normally did at home.

Tonight's dinner was at Feather and Ash Hamlin's house. Their only child, Quincy, was twelve and had been labeled everything under the sun. He had been categorized as having a pervasive developmental disorder, then a sensory processing disorder, then obsessive compulsive disorder, gender dysphoria, major depressive disorder, bipolar disorder, and ultimately a diagnosis of autism by the time he was ten. Quincy was never visible at any get-together. If a gathering was held in their home, he hid under a pile of dirty laundry in his parents' closet until everyone left. Quincy was on two different medications for seizures, a stimulant for ADHD, two antidepressants, and a tranquilizer to put him to sleep at night.

Quincy's father, Ash Hamlin, was a reserved man and often spent very little time talking with guests or his family for that matter. Impish and bespectacled, if crowds became too large for him, he retreated to an unoccupied room, the front passenger seat of his car, or the backyard, and read old cracked-spine paperback science fiction novels from the Yolo County Library discard pile. In the year I had known Ash, we may have exchanged a total of five sentences – I three and he two.

Feather, on the other hand, was verbose and opinionated. She was a slight woman who seemed to float around Sensory Sunday lecturing on a wide array of topics in her patchwork of repurposed secondhand clothes that she gave new life to after spending hours meticulously combing through the racks at the Yolo County SPCA Thrift Store. As a college student, she was what I envisioned as the prototypical Davis resident, a twice-weekly bather and an advocate for every cause.

The night we hosted Sensory Sunday, she went through all of our trash cans making lists of what we should be recycling and how food scraps mixed with yard waste would make an excellent compost for our pear trees. The next morning I found Daisy eating through a pile of composted fruit and vegetable cuttings that Feather had created in our backyard without my knowledge.

In the last few weeks, everyone in Feather's email contacts lists had received warnings about the environmental dangers of using a wood-burning fireplace for home heating. She cited particulate levels, respiratory ailments, and soot in her rationale for joining the "Don't Light Tonight" brigade for improving Yolo County's air quality.

Feather made a lot of environmental choices that she thought everyone ought to be making, and she wasn't shy about telling you that you should too. She chose to wash her clothes in her utility sink in the garage with reclaimed rainwater and hung them on sundrenched clotheslines. She chose to donate her car to KVIE in favor of biking around town to reduce her carbon footprint. She chose to paint the inside of her house purely in discarded paints. Feather believed California should restore Hetch Hetchy and Owens Valley, ban GMOs, stop importing clothes from countries that turned a blind eye to forced labor, and make it unlawful to build a new house without installing solar panels. Arguably, those are great causes, but Feather made sure you knew all about them within the first twenty minutes of meeting her.

You also quickly found out about the Yolano Union School District, the Davis Schools' parent organization, and how she and Ash had to fight to get Quincy qualified for special education, and then get speech and occupational therapy, and then get an aide, and then get a behaviorist. It was a convoluted story with more twists, kinks, and mutations than the DNA she and Ash studied and taught.

Feather was a prizefighter for special needs. In her world, there were only heroes and villains. If you stood in her way, you were just another villain she had to conquer on her way to the title match. There was no room to be a neutral third party. "You can't be neutral on a moving train," she would say, echoing Howard Zinn, or if she sensed indifference in you, she would remind you of Eldridge Cleaver's famous saying that if you are not part of the solution, you are part of the problem. Conversations with Feather about the schools in Davis were uncomfortable. At best it was like talking religion or politics in unfamiliar company, and at worst it was like listening to someone you don't know very well at work spill all the family secrets about their alcoholic parent or porn-addicted brother-in-law.

So on this Sunday morning, headache abated somewhat after making it halfway through my coffee, I turned my attention to the papers that Frank had dropped off. "Thought you might need a laugh – found this while cleaning old papers from the garage," was inked in Frank's handwriting underneath the spot where a single staple was fighting to keep its grip on the lot. As I opened the coffee ringed pages, I immediately recognized what my old friend had left me.

Frank and I had different majors, but we managed to take three courses together: Music 110A – an introduction to Beethoven, Herpetology 134 – the study of reptiles and amphibians, and Drama 10 – an introduction to acting. Beethoven was interesting, when we were awake, but often we were not. Fifty minutes in the back of a darkened music hall, shielded behind flimsy music stands, was better than any amount of NyQuil or chamomile tea.

Held in the old firehouse next to the arboretum, Drama 10 was one of Frank's favorite courses. It was there I discovered a penchant for writer's block. The collection of papers Frank had dropped off was my script from the class's final project, a play. Our final grades hinged upon a five-minute original play that had to be acted out in front of the class during finals week. Frank and I were paired together, and we had starring roles in each other's play.

Frank had named his play *Give Me the Cure* after his favorite Fugazi song. Frank made my job easy; I had no lines in his play. He had written a three-minute monologue about two high school football players. Frank's character, and only speaking part, gave a painful monologue of regret. My character, a victim of incessant teasing about his weight, articulation disorder, and lack of a girlfriend had taken his father's pistol to his head and shot himself in his football team's locker room. Frank's character longed to go back in time and tell me, lying prone and lifeless, that things would get better and that high school didn't define your life. It was cathartic for Frank; I just didn't know it at the time. When I asked him how he came up with the play, he told me it was about someone he knew in high school. Years later, it became clear that he had contemplated suicide in high school because of how out-of-place he felt.

My play wasn't as deep or layered. No big theme. No global message. In fact, mine was so unoriginal that I borrowed Frank's idea of naming it after a song. But I ultimately called it *Kings Play Chess On Funny Green Squares* after the mnemonic I used in Biology for remembering the classification of living organisms: Kingdom, Phylum, Class, Order, Genus, and Species. It sounded ominous and diabolical, but it poorly hid the shallow contrived nature of my work.

In retrospect, there had always been moments in my life that felt like a play, times when I felt placed in some manufactured space with very few props and really bad lines. Lots of clichés and bravado and rigid pre-prepared pieces of dialogue stripped of everything else in life that colors it, where the heroes are infallible and villains are pure evil – all in a theater space where I have no control over what is being said or done. I just have to do as I'm told – which was exactly how I felt about Sensory Sunday at the Hamlins'.

Hesitantly, I uncreased the fold and began to read. The title and the dramatis personae were missing, leaving the first page of lines exposed. The mere effort of reading made my headache worse, and I had to stop. I wished I could go back in time, write the play again, and put in a real effort. I couldn't believe the professor actually gave me a B+. I think she really enjoyed Frank's work, and inflated my grade by association.

My head continued to pound. I slowly made my way down the hall, feeling the walls for support. With my sense of smell heightened and my spatial awareness diminished, my nose led me toward the coffeepot in the kitchen. I poured another cup, folded the script, and threw it in the paper-only recycling bin that Feather had given us.

"Arthur!" Annie yelled. A note of alarm reverberated through my skull. "Magda!"

"Charlie! Where is your sister?" Annie was in full panic. "Magda!"

Annie tore through the house frantically. Daisy was in panic mode too. She frenetically paced and flapped her ears. Confused by the terror gripping Annie and my confusion, she barked and ran from room to room, jumping from bed to bed.

"Magda!" Annie yelled. "Where the hell is she?" she screamed.

I ran out the back door and searched the yard.

My heart was racing. My head was throbbing. "Magda!" I screamed into the emptiness of our backyard.

"There she is!" Charlie yelled from his bedroom. I sprinted back into the house and to his door. I heard Annie charging behind me.

"Look," he said, standing on his bed, pointing out his window to the front yard.

Magda was across the street and sitting in the neighbor's patch of swamp timothy. She was systematically ripping the heads off and casting them aside as if they served no purpose.

My anxiety ebbed as my fear began to flow freely.

"Oh my god! She could have been hit!" Annie flew from the room.

As Charlie and I stood watching the bizarre scene unfold, through our view framed by the window, Annie ran across the street, grabbed Magda, and pushed her into her chest.

* * *

"What is that, Daddy?" Charlie asked.

"It's a chain lock."

"What does it do?"

"It's supposed to help keep people out, but hopefully keeps your sister from walking away from the house."

"Good," he replied.

* * *

Feather had pinned me in the corner. I had forgotten one of the central tenets of nursing safety: always leave an escape path between you and the door and never put yourself in a compromising position.

She had me wedged in. I was stuck between a secondhand love seat that looked as if it had been ripped straight off the set of *Golden Girls*, replete with a cream and teal floral theme, and the prickly thorns of a potted indoor citrus tree. She had me on the ropes. I had no exit strategy. Every time I tried to bob and weave she threw me back into the corner, readjusted her mouthpiece, and resumed her assault.

"What do you mean you don't know what you're going to do? You have to go to the school district before Magda turns three. It's the rules," Feather jabbed. "Yolo County will stop paying her therapy bills after her birthday. Trust me, those aren't cheap. And just wait, they will try not to qualify her for services. They do it to everybody, and everybody just accepts what they do as normal. They figure Davis Schools are good, and school officials must know what they are talking about. But they don't." It felt as if she had landed a rapid succession of sucker punches to my gut.

Her tone dropped and her speech slowed. "And you tell them that it is wrong. Tell them you will file suit if they don't do the right thing."

Her finger now pointed into my chest.

"They are afraid of lawsuits, and they are afraid of looking bad publicly. You just have to keep threatening. They will fight tooth and nail to keep you out, and once you are in, they still won't want to help you, but it will be too late for them because you'll be in." She grinned conspiratorially. "There are laws that protect you." It was her crowning triumph.

A buzzing sound came from the kitchen.

"And just wait, they'll try to put you through one of their SSTs, or stupid stall tactics, as I call them, or even worse one of their RTIs —their infinite reasons to ignore," she added with dramatic air quotes.

"I don't think I threaten people well, and I'm not sure what an RTI is." I looked for an escape and spotted Annie coming out of the kitchen.

"Response to intervention," Feather spat. "It is unlawful to delay testing a kid for special ed once you ask for it. But they pretend like these delays are all just part of the process. They are not part of the process! They are roadblocks!"

"Feather, I think your oven timer is going off," Annie said.

"Oh, great. Thank you. I made gluten-free lava cakes for dessert." She flew from the room.

"Where have you been?" Annie whispered through gritted teeth. "We need to leave."

"You don't have to tell me twice."

"I haven't been able to find your daughter for the last half hour," she said holding the huddled mass that was Magda against her chest.

Magda had buried her face in Annie's shirt so that her eyes and ears were covered, her only stimuli the pressure of being held and the scent of Annie's chest. It was a familiar and comforting place for Magda, like Linus with his blanket.

"Where was she this time?"

"Hiding in the dryer in their garage," she said.

"It's a good thing they never use it."

"What have you been doing?" Annie pressed. "I could have used the help. Charlie took himself out back and was reading books with Ash."

"Good for him. He probably had more fun than I did. My excuse for being AWOL is that," I added in a quiet voice, nodding toward Feather in the kitchen.

Annie rolled her eyes at me.

"I'm sorry, I had no clue Magda had run off again," I pled.

"It's fine. We just need to leave." Annie threw her one free hand in the air.

"Glad to." I can't handle all this doom and gloom lecturing. It's depressing in here. Can't you feel it?"

"Well, I don't think Feather is lecturing you. She's just trying to be helpful," she said.

I had no reply.

"Lots of people here tonight are having a hard time with their kids in school," Annie added.

"I can't worry about them right now. I'm sure Charlie will run into his fair share of problems in school too." I felt selfishness scribbling in red crayon outside the lines of my face.

"Well we are going to have to worry about it sooner rather than later." Annie stared directly at me.

I grabbed Annie's purse with one hand and took Charlie's hand with the other and strode toward the front door.

"You're not leaving, are you?" Feather exclaimed as she came out of the kitchen with an oven mitt on her right hand.

I spoke before Annie could. "I'm so sorry, but we really have to. The kids are falling apart, and I have to go to work tomorrow."

"Here." Feather pushed a pink flyer into my chest. "It's spoken word night at Delta of Venus on Thursday, and I'm performing. You guys should stop by."

I always avoided the Delta of Venus as a student. If Davis ever had a counter culture, I was certain that the Delta of Venus would be their hidden lair. I had no doubt it was home to the covert meetings of the Secret Society of the Delta Smelt or the Colony of Bacterial Culture.

"Okay, we'll try, but it might be really hard." I motioned with my head toward Magda burrowed in Annie's chest.

"It's really important that we foster a community and safe space for parents like us," she said. "Even if it isn't important to you, it is important to someone else that you were there."

"Sure," I said. "I'll definitely make an effort."

"Great, I'm slated to go on at eight."

Annie and I both smiled.

"Okay, have a nice night, thanks for coming," Feather said, her tone perky and peppy.

"I have a headache again," I moaned as soon as I closed the door behind us.

"Me too."

"I hate Delta of Venus," I grumbled. "Everybody raves that the food is good, but I always feel like I'm being judged by the people who go there."

"Judge not lest ye be judged."

"Thanks." I fumbled for the car keys. "Next month, can we just have a pizza delivered from Woodstock's and tell everyone we're sick?"

"We can talk about that next month. We need to be supportive of this group." Annie struggled to strap Magda into her car seat.

"We need to be supportive of ourselves." I took the easier task of watching Charlie put himself in his booster seat.

Annie didn't respond, so I persisted. "I remember when going out meant we started the night by you holding your hair off to one side and me getting a sneak peek at the nape of your neck or the small of your back as I zipped up your dress."

"You're drunk," Annie said.

"No, unfortunately, I'm not."

Annie got behind the wheel and I strapped myself into the front passenger seat.

"The stories from these parents are awful," I said.

"There are assholes everywhere," Annie said, taking the keys from my hand and putting them in the ignition.

Magda began to cry as we pulled away. I wanted to join in.

Failure to Thrive

"Normal people have an incredible lack of empathy."

– Temple Grandin

When Daisy and I went for a run, we crossed Pole Line, ran straight east on Loyola, then curved behind Brown Elementary. From there we followed the bike path south through the tree-lined corridor that used to be the driveway to the old Mace family ranch house, over the Pelz pedestrian freeway overpass into South Davis through the neighborhoods of Native American-named streets, then across the Richards overpass and under the Richards tubular underpass into downtown. But tonight, rather than run through campus on our way back home, we stopped and stood outside the Delta of Venus, an early Davis cottage home, all stucco and windows. Out front of the non-descript façade was an ADA accessible ramp and a painted picture of Venus being born from a cup of coffee. The porch and patio dully echoed footsteps while clanging plates and clinking glasses welcomed Feather Hamlin as she stepped up to a lonely microphone and its stand. Daisy spun in circles, uncomfortable without movement. She dove her head between my calves, and like a racehorse wearing blinders, she steadied herself, snorted, and stomped. Feather's eyes met mine, and she acknowledged me with a slight nod. I smiled back.

"My name is Feather Hamlin, and this is my spoken word poem," she said in a serious tone.

"Frustrated; how does it not?

They tell you that these are home problems, not school problems. They tell you that they care, and try to convince you that they care more than you do.

'That must be awful, that must cause you such anxiety' – with downturned faces they feign empathy.

'We can't imagine how stressful your home must be' – the counselor says.

'Unfortunately, we just don't see an academic impact at school; our tests don't show it; his grades are fine' – the authoritarian principal spouts.

'All of the other children love having your son in our class – the confabulating teacher lectures.

'Have you talked to your doctor about medications? I hear they can help' – the clairvoyant director chastises.

'It's just a phase, lots of kids go through this; we need to fade his supports; he will do just fine; we see it all the time; just relax' – the flippant psychologist scolds.

But I've heard it before, and I refuse to hear it one more time. I want to scream, 'Hell no!' But that will only permanently affix the label of crazy they have already painted upon me.

So instead, I have this to say:

> Prove to me he is doing fine – because he can't complete any of his classwork and has never been able to go on a field trip.
>
> Prove to me the other children want to be his friend – because never once has he been invited to a play date or a birthday party.
>
> Prove to me that the disorientation, anorexia, anhedonia, and the insomnia aren't from one of the twenty medications I've tried with him.
>
> Prove to me his autism is a phase!
>
> You can't! Because what I have is proof. What I have is evidence. What I have is the truth, and what you have is a lie…
>
> If I can't make coffee in the morning because the smell makes his nose bleed, how does that not affect his ability to learn?
>
> If I can't clip his nails, cut his hair, and I constantly struggle to get him dressed in the morning, how does that not?
>
> If he can't tie shoes, yet the sound of Velcro tears his ears off, how does that not?
>
> If he has to eat with plastic utensils because silverware burns his tongue, how does that not?
>
> If he is twelve years old and still can't ride a bike, how does that not?
>
> If he hides in his closet during a dinner with my parents because the sight of too many people is like needles in his eyeballs, how does that not?
>
> If he can't run on the playground because he refuses to wear shoes, but standing on grass is like standing on a porcupine, and the asphalt burns like fire, how does it not?

If he goes all day without actually going to the bathroom, but spends all day asking for the potty pass, how does it not?

If we can't wrap his birthday presents because the ripping of paper tears his soul out, how does it not?

If the soft breeze from a fan cuts worse than dull scissors, how does it not?

If he has no reflexes to protect his face when he falls, how does it not?

If I am exhausted from having to provide twelve layers of support, planning, and preparation for him so that I can vacuum the house, empty the dishwasher, or turn on the oven, how does it not?

If he will barely eat at home, let alone in your cacophonous cafeteria, how does it not?

If, at the end of a school day, he won't stop crying until he falls asleep, how does it not?

When there is no difference between make believe and what is real for him, how does it not?

When I pour my heart out about my child to you, and you still won't change what you have already predetermined he doesn't need, how does it not?

So I refuse to believe that the twenty-eight creaking hard plastic chairs, the recess, the lunch, the dismissal bells, the wind against the classroom window, the worn ball bearings on the janitor's cart, the crinkling of returning homework, the sharpening of pencils, the six-hundred screaming, running, – jumping – touching, smelling other children, and the apathy of your staff does not have an educational impact.

Do I sound frustrated? How can I not?

Have you talked to your doctor about what medications you should be on? Is your autism a phase? Who will teach you how to see another's perspective?

Who will teach you how to move beyond sorting, classifying, and lining things up in a nonfunctional row?

Who will teach you how to engage in reciprocal communication?

Who will teach you how to care for others other than yourself?

Who will teach you how to share what you have?

Who will teach you how to manage yourself when this town fades its support?

Who will teach you? It might just be me.

Do I sound frustrated? How can I not?"

Feather bowed.

The audience erupted in applause. Feather again bowed her head in acceptance and appreciation. When she looked up from her bow, she once again made eye contact. I smiled and gave her a thumbs-up. Daisy and I then trotted off up B Street, past the Yolano Union School District offices, through the remnants of Old North Davis, and onward to home.

"How was that?" Annie asked as Daisy rooted and spun in the crate, rearranging her pillows and blankets, nudging the folds in the fabric until they were just so.

"Interesting, I suppose. Funny to hear the same material in a different context. She just seems so full of anger. I wonder if she ever finds peace."

As Daisy finally settled in, I could hear Annie singing "Twinkle Twinkle Little Star" to Magda as she did every night. And just as she also did every night, Annie layered Magda under her bed sheet, then her comforter, then her weighted blanket, and finally the tied-knot fleece blanket that Ms. Calamondin gave her the day we brought Magda home from the hospital.

KINGS PLAY CHESS ON FUNNY GREEN SQUARES
A THREE-ACT PLAY

Dramatis Personae:

ANNIE RUSSELL: Woman in her early to mid-thirties. Mother of two and wife to Arthur.

ARTHUR RUSSELL: Man in his early to mid-thirties. Father of two and husband to Annie.

DAISY: A black Labrador retriever.

DISTRICT OFFICIAL: Man in his late fifties. Preschool testing specialist for the special education program of the Davis branch of the Yolano Union School District.

ACT I (CHILD FIND)

SETTING: The city of Davis, California, on a spring afternoon. This scene takes place on a split stage. On stage left is the Russells' kitchen table. Arthur has just returned from a run with his dog as Annie sits organizing a three-ring binder of their daughter's therapy and medical records. Stage right remains unlit.

AT RISE: Lights up stage left. We find Annie at their kitchen table as Arthur enters through a red front door and heads to the refrigerator and removes a Mason jar of canned pears.

ARTHUR

I just got a text from Frank. He is going to the rally at the Capitol tonight to oppose the anti-gay marriage legislation. Do you want to go?

ANNIE

I don't see how she is going to qualify.

ARTHUR
(unleashes Daisy, who bolts off stage left)

What? Who? Qualify for what?

ANNIE
(pushes hands through her hair)

He said in order to qualify for special education, we have to show that she has an academic problem. Any other problems, parents are expected to manage at home.

ARTHUR

Who did you talk to? What are you talking about? I think we do manage her problems at home, don't you?

ANNIE

Some district administrator said this. I think he is the person who tests kids to see who gets into the preschool program. I'm not even sure anymore.

(pauses)

What I'm talking about is getting Magda into
special education. We've only been talking
about this for months.

ARTHUR

I'm sorry, I don't understand. Hasn't she
qualified for just about everything since
birth? She qualified for early intervention
and the regional center services. The First
Five California people won't stop sending
stuff to our house telling us how important
early academic support is. She has been
in speech therapy, occupational therapy,
behavioral therapy, and physical therapy
since she was one. How many diagnoses does
she have - eight at least? I don't get it.
Did you give him all of the reports from the
county?

ANNIE

Yes, I dropped them off at his office over four
weeks ago. He said he read them and it doesn't
matter because public schools aren't required
to listen to recommendations from private
therapists. He said he feels for us and our
situation.

ARTHUR

That's stupid.

ANNIE

I'm not saying I agree. Of course it's stupid.
But what are we supposed to do? Feather was
right.

ARTHUR

Wait a minute – is he saying that he won't test
Magda?

ANNIE

Well, no, he never actually said that. It just
felt implied that testing her was a waste of
our time and theirs.

ARTHUR

How is Magda not supposed to have academic
problems? She can't even tell us what she needs
at home. How is she supposed to ask a teacher
for help? She holds a pencil like a sword.

(makes a stabbing gesture)

How will she ever be able to learn to write?

ANNIE

(flips violently through the
binder)

He said it is really hard for young children
to qualify for special education because the
early years are mostly about finger painting and
learning how to stay in line. He said there is
limited space, and the program typically serves
very heavily impacted kids who will never be
able to survive in a normal classroom.

ARTHUR

(raises his voice)

Well, are we so sure she is going to be able to
survive a regular classroom?

ANNIE

(throws hands in the air)

If you would let me finish, he said we aren't
supposed to worry about reading or writing
until first grade. Apparently, it's not the
California standard to focus on teaching that
in preschool or even kindergarten. He said
parents in Davis are just pushy about getting
their kids ahead, and going to kindergarten is
apparently optional. In California, you aren't
required to enroll your kid in school until
they are six.

ARTHUR

I'm confused. Did he really say all this?
Everyone says if you have any concerns about
your child's development go to your doctor.
You go to your doctor and they say you really
need to go to your school. You go to your
school and they say you've been misinformed.
What kind of bullshit hot potato game is
this?

ANNIE

He said speech and OT are just related
services.

(Makes air quotes as she says
"related services")

They alone don't qualify you for special
education. And even if she qualifies, he said
sometimes kids qualify only to not qualify a
few months later.

ARTHUR

Services related to what? Related to her
disability? Related to my cousin Vinny? The
county stops paying for services at three years
old, right?

ANNIE

Lower your voice, Arthur. You're going to
startle Magda. Would you like to call him?
Maybe he is still at his desk. And yes, the
school is supposed to manage eligibility for
services at age three, so we will have to start
paying Children's Therapy Center out of pocket
if she doesn't qualify.

ARTHUR

Where is his number?

ANNIE

(removes the cordless phone from
the wall, dials, and hands the
phone to Arthur. Stage right
illuminates. A middle-aged man
is sitting at his desk sorting
papers and signing forms. He is
well dressed and sits with proper
posture. His phone rings.)

DISTRICT ADMINISTRATOR

(chews gum loudly)

Special education.

ARTHUR

Hello, my name is Arthur Russell. You just spoke
with my wife about our daughter Magdalena.

DISTRICT ADMINISTRATOR

Oh yes, how are you sir?

ARTHUR

I guess I don't understand what the rules are.
The school website says that Magda would be
tested for special education. Did you test
her?

DISTRICT ADMINISTRATOR

Anyone who suspects that a student is disabled
may request an evaluation, Mr. Russell. If you
would like your daughter evaluated, I will need
a written request. We then will respond to your
request within fifteen days. Usually a student
study team or SST is set up with parents to
determine what testing is recommended. If
testing is recommended, the district has sixty
days to perform its evaluations. If assessments
are not recommended, the SST will explain why
in writing to you.

ARTHUR

What does that mean?

> (mouths 'asshole' to Annie while
> covering the mouthpiece of the
> phone)

DISTRICT ADMINISTRATOR

It seems like every pediatrician in town sends families to me because they are worried about their little ones. The vast majority don't need special education, just a little support from their family and teacher to get their bearings.

ARTHUR

How many children do you accept into the preschool?

DISTRICT ADMINISTRATOR

Children who qualify for these services demonstrate significant delays or disabilities impacting their ability to function in a preschool program or at home, and are at risk for academic difficulties when they reach school.

ARTHUR

Magda has been getting disability services for a long time now, and —

DISTRICT ADMINISTRATOR

(cuts off Arthur)

Mr. Russell, private therapists don't understand schools and academics the way we do. We work in the schools, and we see how these issues actually play out in a classroom. Davis schools are renowned across the state for how good they are. It's why families move here. Of course your private therapists are going to continue to recommend services. They want to stay in business, don't they?

ARTHUR

These aren't private therapists. They are
contracted by the county and the state regional
center to provide services. I believe they want
what's best for my daughter, as do we.

DISTRICT ADMINISTRATOR

Oh, we couldn't agree more. Here at YUSD we
believe that our community has a responsibility
for the well-being of its members. Education
is a fundamental right. We believe strongly in
our system here. Did you know that when your
daughter enters high school here, she will have
the option to take many classes not offered
at most high schools, like Mandarin. Not only
that, but nearly fifty percent of our students
take Advanced Placement classes in high school,
giving them the opportunity to get college
credits.

ARTHUR

That's well and good, but my daughter has at
least one if not several disabilities.

DISTRICT ADMINISTRATOR

(moves papers around his desk)

Yes, Mr. Russell, I understand that. Medical
diagnoses and qualifying for special education
are two different things. Simply having a
diagnosis is not a guarantee of qualification,
or academic need for that matter. If your
daughter qualifies for services, she will no
longer receive county-based services. Services
are determined and provided by us.

ARTHUR

(places hand over the mouthpiece
and addresses Annie)

Do you really want this guy testing Magda? He
seems like a moron.

DISTRICT ADMINISTRATOR

When your child is school age, we do have
several programs like the reading room, the
SSTs I mentioned earlier, and a wonderful
program called Response to Intervention or RTI.
These are all programs aimed at supporting the
student in school.

If it makes you feel any better, I can arrange
for testing for your daughter. We are really
impacted right now, and it will take at least a
few months before I can get to her.

ARTHUR

That just doesn't seem right.

DISTRICT ADMINISTRATOR

Unfortunately, we don't include holidays and
school breaks in the time window in which
we are required to test. So these testing
windows can get really strung out. I hear
your frustration, Mr. Russell. Trust me,
this process frustrates me too. What can we
do, right? But Arthur, I also must warn you:
this testing can be really stressful on your
daughter.

ARTHUR

(shakes head)

I don't know what to say.

(Annie walks off stage left when
she hears a young child crying)

ARTHUR

(stands and moves across the
living room)

I don't want to lose the services she is
getting now. Sir, my daughter is exceptionally
smart and has adapted to what she struggles
with in what we think are amazing ways. I
guess we were thinking this would be a much
more seamless transition than what you are
describing.

DISTRICT ADMINISTRATOR

Yes, lots of kids in Davis are smart. Did you
know that our high school has a ninety-seven
percent graduation rate, and our kids typically
score 250 points higher than the national
average on their SATs?

ARTHUR

I don't think I'm being clear.

DISTRICT ADMINISTRATOR

Well, if you believe your daughter is truly
gifted, we have a wonderful gifted program in

Davis. Children can be tested to get into our self-contained gifted classes in third grade. If you want some pointers on how to prepare for those tests, you can find many helpful hints on our district website. The site covers all the tests we use and accept from outside facilities. It also has a list of activities you can do with your daughter to help maximize her test scores.

(uses computer mouse and clicks)

I can email you the link if you would like. It is actually kept under a file folder named Hidden on the external site. Of course, cutting down on TV time always helps.

ARTHUR

I'm sorry. I do not understand you completely. Is there a list of the tests used to get into special education, or instructions on how to study for them, or who we can go to privately to get the testing done?

DISTRICT ADMINISTRATOR

(removes his glasses)

No, no, no. We don't do that – that isn't how those tests work. There is a law called IDEA, and we have to follow it to a T. Mr. Russell, like I said, lots of parents have concerns about their children. They don't all need special education. Trust me, I'm a Davis parent too. We hover too much. It's a fact. Helicopter parents, every last one of us. That's why we moved here, right? God help our kids when they

grow up. They won't know how to do anything on
their own.

(forces a laugh)

ARTHUR

To be honest, from what I understand, I don't
think testing will be fruitful for Magdalena
right now. Thank you for your time.

DISTRICT ADMINISTRATOR

Well, just let us know if there is anything we
can do for you in the future. We are all about
the kids here. We are always here to help.

ARTHUR

Will do.

(Arthur   and   the   district
administrator hang up their phones.
Arthur mutters incoherently. The
district   administrator   places
a stack of papers in his waste
bin and returns to shuffling and
signing the remaining papers on
his desk. Stage right blacks
out.)

(Annie returns from stage left).

ARTHUR

We'll just figure out a way to pay privately.
The insurance has to pay for something. I want
to go with Frank to Sacramento tonight.

ANNIE

Let's see if Mari can watch the kids. I want to
go too.

(BLACKOUT)

The Bullies of Toad Hollow

"Beauty may be skin deep, but ugly goes clear to the bone."

— Red Foxx

Everybody in Davis knows about the toad tunnels, and anybody who visits Davis quickly learns. They are one of those safe topics that boyfriends can talk comfortably to their girlfriend's dad about when they come for a visit, and know that discussing the toad tunnels will fill just enough dead air before the conversation turns again.

The peaceful and sometimes flooded meadow that was the toad's habitat sat next to the city's storm water drainage pit, and was bisected by the development of a freeway overpass. The toad tunnels' importance, and ultimately determined lack thereof, is routinely reported by outside press when describing how "quirky," "odd," and "wasteful" the City of Davis can be. The ridiculousness of this debate even attracted *The Daily Show* correspondent Stephen Colbert to record a comedy bit about it.

As if no time had passed, Toad Hollow was where Frank and I picked up right where our college friendship had left off before jobs, adulthood, and marriage filled the years. Frank taught special education courses to future teachers at Sacramento State on Mondays, Wednesdays, and Fridays. So when I had a free Tuesday, Thursday, or weekend, we would meet at the dog park. He would bring Berdoo, and I would bring Daisy. Berdoo was a majestic Saint Bernard, one hundred and eighty pounds of calm. He was a descendent of the war dogs of the Roman armies, but he was as relaxed as a Hindu cow.

Berdoo was a good playmate for Daisy because he had no expectations of her. He was happy just to lounge around and watch her. He didn't antagonize her. He just let her be. He didn't try to get her to do something she was incapable of doing. He didn't run off and play with other dogs; he just sat and was patient. He waited for her to engage, not that she ever did, and that was okay with Berdoo.

By the time Annie and I moved back to Davis, Frank was married. On February 25, 2004, Frank married his partner of four years, Angelo, in San Francisco.

In college, we lived on Gilmore 2 in the Segundo dorm on campus. Frank thought our bland concrete building was the best of the lot because he was a rabid Pink Floyd fan, and on every piece of mail he sent to family and friends, he renamed his return address 201 Gilmour Hall in honor of the singer and guitarist.

Frank was an affable guy, and had an infectious grin that could tame a lion. His size was impressive, and his presence could be imposing, as was my first impression of him when he filled the doorframe of our room the day we met. Frank played on the offensive line for the UC Davis Aggie's football team.

In the first few days of school, we bonded over a love of music. He by far was more versed, and I was fine with that because I liked learning, and he liked teaching. A week after we moved in, he covered his half of the dorm room's window with a 4' by 6' *Dark Side of the Moon* poster he had picked up at Armadillo Music.

Frank was a true music aficionado. His preferences were so eclectic, from ABBA to ZZ Top to mainstream, that he often boasted he needed two Columbia House subscriptions to obtain all the music he just had to have.

In the football offseason, he dragged me everywhere. The Cactus Club in San Jose, Slim's on 11th street in San Francisco, or Old Ironsides in Sacramento were regular haunts. His favorite was 924 Gilman in Berkeley, a punk venue at the end of the East Bay that proclaimed on a sign at the door exactly what they would not tolerate: "No racism, No sexism, No homophobia, No alcohol, No fighting, No stagediving."

Frank told me he gravitated to music because of its absence in his family home in rural Madera County, the heart of California's Central Valley. When he first called me after our dorm assignments came in the mail, and told me where he lived, I said, "Where the hell is that?"

"You know, the place where the palm and the pine tree are planted right next to each other on Highway 99. It's the artificial horizontal fault line, the midpoint of the state. If you blink, you miss it. It's supposed to represent the differences between the two halves of California, southern and northern – it's a total metaphor."

* * *

On May 2, 1996, three years into our undergraduate careers and on the eve of the Whole Earth Festival, Frank fumbled and mumbled on my answering machine as he asked me to join him at a Brodys show at the G Street Pub. He rambled for a while, laundry listing why he didn't feel like going to any of the Whole Earth festivities, and then abruptly ended with, "I'm transferring to San Francisco State," before the machine beeped telling me his answer had ended.

I was shocked. I couldn't grasp why he felt he had to leave Davis, and why he never returned my call. From my perspective, life as a student in Davis was a fun experience. In the ignorance and bliss of my late teens and early twenties, I couldn't see why his perspective was so different from my own, but if I'd had my eyes open, I would have seen that the first visible fractures in what I thought was a good place to live and what was a good friendship had begun to show months and even years before.

In the spring quarter leading up to Frank's transfer from Davis, he made a conscious choice to avoid any social contact with friends. He frequently declined dinner invitations, passed on pickup basketball games at the campus Rec Hall, and dropped out of our ritual Friday afternoon meals at La Esperanza. But what I didn't understand, nor had I been a present enough friend to realize, was that for the past three years he had been blocking and tackling his own internal demons.

So I stood there in my kitchen staring at my answering machine feeling as if I had just been clipped.

* * *

"Gay!" he yelled, repeating what he'd said over the mild roar of the drunken crowd at the bar. We were enjoying a few beers during a Brodys intermission. "I'm gay! I couldn't sleep at night – I just kept waking up in our dorm room hearing the word G-A-Y shouted in my ears and echoing in my head." Frank paused long enough for me to wait for him to say more because I was speechless. He lowered his voice and leaned closer to me. "I was sure you heard me screaming in the middle of the night – that was why I couldn't live in the same dorms as the rest of the football team and why I can't stay here now. I thought they would all know. I thought they all knew." He lowered his head. "I've propped up a life in Davis that I can't maintain. I'm here under false pretenses. I'm indebted to whatever brought us together as roommates our first year. I was so afraid of being paired with a raging homophobe, but you were the only one – for better or worse – who didn't seem to give a shit what people were like."

I swallowed hard, replaying "innocent" homophobic remarks I was sure I had made in his presence at some point. "Yeah, not caring what anyone thinks, not giving a shit – it's a gift." I forced a laugh. I leaned in. "Frank, if it makes you feel any better, I still don't give a shit."

He smiled and then ordered two shots of Southern Comfort and a Budweiser chaser for each of us at the back server's window. That was part of our ritual at a Brodys show. By the time the band took the stage for the second half of their set, we were smiling and laughing again and singing along to "Lights Out," "Irene's Kiss," and "Weekend Alcoholic."

Frank and I splintered at the large oak tree in Central Park on our respective walks home, and things were back to normal, if only for one night. We occasionally emailed and called each other, but I wouldn't see Frank again until he agreed to be a groomsman when Annie and I got married a few years later, and after that, we were lucky if we saw each other more frequently than the earth orbits the sun.

Frank met Angelo at USF in an abnormal child psychology course. Angelo was working toward a PhD in special education part-time while working full-time as a grant writer for an at-risk adolescent advocacy group in the Mission District. Angelo, twelve years older than Frank, initially was an enigma to Annie and me. It took several years – not until Frank and Angelo moved back to Davis – for us to understand him, and Frank's attraction to him. But they seemed content with life, and that was all that mattered.

Angelo was gentle, patient, and responsible. He was credible, sincere and a loyal and sympathetic friend. But protecting his soft internal nature and the ones he loved was a tough outer crust. Part of the reason Annie and I were uncertain about Angelo was his slow release of personal information. He always knew much more about us than we did him – and most of what we knew about Angelo came from Frank.

The couple's desire to return to Davis was fueled by Angelo's love of cycling and Frank's time-sensitive opportunity to be a staff professor at Sac State while also having the opportunity to work with a special needs lobbying group in the capital city. "What I do in San Francisco can change San Francisco, but what I do in Sacramento can change San Francisco, and Madera, and everywhere in between," he told me over the phone the day that he and Angelo purchased their Trinity model on the east side of Pole Line, near Slide Hill Park.

Frank and I had both forged new lives that looked much different from the lives we had in college. It was sobering in a lot of ways.

He was still passionate about music, but equally if not more so about marginalized children – and that enthusiasm was reciprocated in his husband. Our dog park discussions were commonplace and ordinary at first, lamenting corporate rock and the boy band boom. But as the weeks and months went on, we found that we had a common thread between my work in the emergency room and his work helping children.

We lightened our discussions by comparing the dogs at the park to the social groups we saw on the playground as children, at the lunch tables in high school, or at the Coffee House on campus. We had identified at least three distinct types of dogs at the park: those that played with their owners fetching Frisbees, tennis balls, and sticks; those that engaged in play fighting, chasing each other, or stealing each other's toys; and there was always a small group of instigators – the alphas and bullies. They patrolled the yard nipping and head butting the shy and less social dogs. Their owners watched with pride, and rarely took corrective action. "Yep, my dog's an alpha," they would quip, or smile and say, "Just herding the flock."

The bullies, rarely bully breeds, didn't pick on the popular and athletic dogs; they intuitively deduced their strength, agility, and speed. They didn't pick on those dogs that were playing closely with their owners. They picked on the dogs at the periphery, those not fast enough to keep up with the others, those without owners watching closely. They picked on those without protection, and they became progressively more brazen as they picked on one of every hundred and fifty, one of every hundred and ten, one of every eighty-eight, one of every sixty-eight, then one of every fifty-nine until someone intervened. They tried to pick on Daisy, but Berdoo would have none of it. He stood and guarded her like his ancestors protected their legions from the Huns and Vandals.

It was self-evident to Frank and me that Daisy didn't, and more importantly couldn't, belong to any of the social clubs at the dog park. She lacked normal social skills. Daisy had two favorite pastimes at Toad Hollow (or dysfunctional routines – depending on your point of view). Her first was running. Rather than sniffing butts, licking faces, offering toys – making friends the old fashion canine way – Daisy ran laps back and forth along the circumferential gravel track of the park. Sometimes a few dogs joined her, but they quickly broke off when she failed to engage with them or they found her game boring. That never stopped Daisy from persisting. If she was conscious of the other dogs' presence, she never showed it.

Daisy's less benign Toad Hollow routine was to take any tennis balls she found and drop them in the border space where the hard-packed gravel met the thickets on the other side of the chain-link fence.

Frank called me as I was leading Daisy through the double-gated entrance at Toad Hollow. Angelo was out on a bike ride alone and had punctured both his front and rear tires on Cantelow Road in a sparsely populated area of Solano County between Winters and Vacaville. He only had one spare tube. So Frank and Berdoo drove off to his aid instead of coming to the park.

It happened in an instant and not more than two moments after I hung up with Frank. As Daisy was running back and forth along the far fence line, she was intercepted by a Huskie Lab mix I didn't recognize coming directly at her, while a beagle was streaking at her from behind. They were attacking her from her flanks in a pincer maneuver closing together like the mandibles of a wasp. The collision was violent and intentional. Daisy was not used to having to engage in social interactions with the other dogs in the park without Berdoo as a crutch. She tried to crouch as she was spun. With his broad barrel chest, the Husky mix stood over her, proud of his accomplishment. As she lay defenseless, the beagle rounded back on Daisy, mounting her haunches and biting her neck. Daisy yelped in pain.

I yelled, "HEY – NO – STOP!" as loud as I could and broke into a sprint. As I neared Daisy and her attackers, the unneutered dog continued to bite her head and face. Daisy had tucked her tail and was trying to bury herself into the ground. Mid-stride I unfurled Daisy's leather leash, held it at its mid-point, and lashed the offender in the rump with both ends as if I were holding a Roman flagellum. The beagle glanced at me briefly with bared teeth, and then he and his accessory to the crime fled the scene and ran off toward the center of a group playing with a ball.

I ran my hand over Daisy's head, face, and back, not finding any wounds. She dove into my chest, worming her head into my armpit.

"You don't have the right to touch my dog!" shouted a portly woman waddling toward me over the knobby turf.

I stood and faced her. "Were those your dogs?" My temples pounded with adrenalin.

"My dogs are fine. Your dog started the fight!" She shouted so loudly that the audience of dogs and their owners took notice.

"What the hell are you talking about?"

"If you think my babies started this, then you and your dog must be retarded. I'm going to report your dog as an aggressive dog to the city." She huffed and crossed her arms, satisfied that she had me right where she wanted me.

I was a growing storm. Updrafts of anger circled around me as I clasped Daisy's leash. I had fleeting thoughts of asking her how she would like it if I threw her to the ground, because she was starting this fight. With Daisy orbiting around me, I strode toward her with purpose, but as I drew within a few yards of her, I could see her hands shaking as she reached into her front pockets, then her back pockets, not finding anything, grasping for an excuse, a reason not to be at fault.

"Your dog is fucking fine," I said in as smooth a monotone as I could muster as my force dissipated. "File your report, and I'll file mine."

"This is your dog's fault! It's your dog's fault!" Her beady eyes refused to meet mine. "If I get kicked out, you should get kicked out too!" Her voice had reached a high-pitched squeal.

"Bury your head in the sand if you want. Responsible owners get their dogs fixed," I said as I passed, looking for something to verbally whip her with as Daisy yanked and pried me out of the park. Daisy darted toward my car, and when I opened the passenger door, she spilled herself into the back seat. "Report me?" I yelled as I buckled in.

Daisy's panting was frenetic. She hyperventilated as she dove down into the legroom of the back seat and hid her head under the front passenger seat. Inconsolable, she bounced back up into the back seat. She paced, spun, and flapped her ears. As we pulled out of the parking lot and crawled out of the lowest point in the city, Daisy wedged herself between my seat and my window. She violently shook her head and whined as blood spattered my face and shoulder. I didn't realize she had been injured. Blood was draining from her right ear and mixing with her saliva as she panted and drooled in a state of agitation.

Daisy's breathing had calmed by the time my Volvo's brakes squealed into the parking space in front of Pets Veterinary. The receptionist eyed my blood-soaked left shoulder as she checked us in and quickly went back to notify the staff that we needed urgent care.

Daisy wouldn't calm for Dr. Clementine. She spun more violently than she had ever done before. Ducking and dodging the diagnostician, she took shelter under a plastic chair. She whined in fear and agony as Dr. Clementine snapped her gloves on and made her way toward Daisy's hiding spot.

"I'm going to have to sedate her to get a good exam…" Her patience seemed pressed.

"That's fine. What do I do?"

"Hold her still."

I eased the chair away from Daisy as Dr. Clementine drew from a vial of midazolam. I draped myself over Daisy and held her still for the injection. Clementine then stepped out into the hidden hallway connecting the back of all of the exam rooms. I sat there, alone with Daisy, stroking her from head to haunches, waiting for her tachypnea to abate but it never did. Ten minutes later, the doctor returned with an autoclaved tray of stainless steel instruments, suture, and surgical tubing.

"Did it take effect yet?" she asked.

"I don't think so." I moved back from Daisy. She began to pace, spin, and pant again.

"Morphine's turn," she said.

I again wrapped myself around my dog as Clementine drew yet another syringe.

"Hopefully this does the trick." She plunged it into Daisy, deposited it in a sharps container, and stepped out again.

Daisy's constitution held fast, and after another ten minutes, the doctor returned to find Daisy whimpering and spinning around the room while I sat depleted against the wall.

"I'm going to have to use the gas. Why don't you go home. She will be fine. Change your shirt. Get cleaned up. I'll call you when I know more."

"Can dogs have mental problems?" I asked.

"What?" She organized her tray of tools and ties.

"You know, like being developmentally delayed or having learning disabilities?"

"No, not typically. Your dog is just scared. She was in a fight."

"I've read that some dogs can have OCD. Is that true?" I persisted.

"Where are you going with this?" She stopped what she was doing and peered at me.

"Dogs can have diabetes and cancer, right?"

"Yes…" she said slowly.

"Well, why can't they have other things we have?"

"Go home. You're a mess. I'll call you later to let you know what I find." She put her hand on my shoulder.

I reluctantly pulled out of the parking lot. My arms wouldn't steer me home. I was being driven back to Toad Hollow in my bloody t-shirt, hunting for the woman whose dogs had mauled mine. But she was gone, and so were her dogs. Finding nothing but stares and whispers, I finally called Annie, breaking down in my bucket seat. My chest collapsed into my stomach. I complied with Annie's request to come home, but before I left the Hollow, I took a picture of the sign at the entrance: "You are liable for any injury caused by a dog under your supervision."

When the whirlwind of the day faded into evening, the aftermath of the attack at the park became clear. Dr. Clementine called with her damage assessment after Charlie and Magda had been put to bed. Daisy had sustained six puncture wounds to her left upper lip, and she had a three-centimeter right auricular laceration, an injury which had created a pocket of coagulated blood between the inner and outer skin of her right ear. She would be left with a rugby player's ear, Clementine noted. Daisy had required one liter of intravenous Lactated Ringers solution as volume replacement for the blood she had lost, six staples to the wound in her ear, and two sutured bolsters to squeeze together the new dead space inside her ear. After she recovered overnight, Daisy would be coming home with a Penrose surgical drain in her ear, a debridement solution, and a one-week course of prophylactic antibiotics. By the morning, I would be out $450 and a night's sleep.

As bad as I felt for Daisy, I couldn't shake the three-in-the-morning visions of striking another dog: the dog's face turning back at me, the stinging slap of the leash, and his troll owner screaming. I was viscerally stunned by my capability of inflicting purposeful injury on a living being. I always thought of myself as incapable of doing that no matter what the provocation. I was repulsed by my actions, but I didn't know that I would do it any differently if it were to happen again.

Annie tried to offer a different perspective on the situation. "You are fixated on how you could have hurt someone else's dog, when that person's dog actually hurt yours. You were defending a family member," she said bluntly.

Three days later, when Mari tapped on the door, Daisy's cone scratched against the wall as she ran to the door to investigate. I had the fleeting thought that it was like a blind man's cane feeling for an edge. Mari was dropping off one of Tae Ng-Kabayo's pieces from the *Enterprise* denouncing how the city handles aggressive dogs and their owners.

"She is probably one of those assholes that throws their gum on the sidewalk, or dings your car and doesn't leave a note, or leaves shopping carts to roll around in the parking lot instead of putting them away – asshole!" Mari sputtered. She shook her head, turned and gestured toward our pear trees. "Next year, these might produce enough that we can start to can some pears." She brushed the leaves of our Moonglows with her hand as she stomped back home.

Frank and I stopped going to Toad Hollow. We ignored the posted signs saying that dogs weren't allowed at Putah Creek Elementary or at Thong Hy Huynh Elementary over on Birch Lane. We flagrantly flaunted the law to let our dogs run off leash at Slide Hill Park. Daisy needed to master one-on-one social interaction with Berdoo before she could manage the mainstream demands of Toad Hollow. Thankfully, Berdoo could be a friend to Daisy in the same way I had been to Frank; he didn't care what Daisy did. Play or not play, he was just as content trying to engage Daisy as he was to watch her obsess over the lingering smells of the balls that had once bounced across tennis courts, playgrounds, and backstops.

Dress-Up

"How very little can be done under the spirit of fear."

— Florence Nightingale

Months had passed since Daisy was attacked. The last of her scabs had fallen off and her sutures and drain had long since been removed. Only scattered gray patches of furless skin remained as mementos, and those were receding under the weight of her water repellent coat. Daisy had moved on, but I was still struggling.

"Ouch," Magda said as she attached one of her hair clips to a spot in Daisy's fur that was still healing.

Daisy sat patiently as Magda adorned her with a dozen of her hair clips and barrettes, which Magda refused to wear, but were "medicine" for Daisy.

Daisy sighed heavily but complied as Magda put a pair of her new leggings atop the dog's head and tried to pull her soft ears through each of the leg holes.

"Magda, do you think she likes that?" I asked.

"Daisy," was all Magda said, and she smiled with contented happiness as she trimmed the dog with more items of clothing.

Daisy then ripped through the house like a cannonball as Magda's stylings flew from her fur and landed against the floor and walls in a drum roll.

Wandering

"If a man does not keep pace with his companions, perhaps it is because he hears a different drummer. Let him step to the music which he hears, however measured or far away."

— Henry David Thoreau

The sun teased the tops of the Sierras, burning their peaks in a fiery glow as it took issue with the persistence of their snowy caps and frozen granite. In those first few seconds and minutes of the day, Daisy and I had to squint as the autumn sun shot beams of light across the flat expanse of the valley. Millions of photons caught in linear mid-flight as the dew returned itself to the atmosphere as vapor. Morning runs were always the best when we got to witness the time of day when Mother Nature turned up the house lights.

On most fall days, pallor's fog permeates and makes anemic all the valley's colors as winter snuggles between the mountain ranges. But today, the sun's unimpeded path made this morning feel deceptively like spring. A trio of blackbirds began pestering a crow that had taken refuge under a volunteer walnut tree. A pair of robins sat on a nearby fence offering no help.

Daisy had trained me for the ten kilometers of the Davis Turkey Trot and the 13.1 miles of the Davis Stampede. Now, stride for stride, breath for breath, we ran together as we trained for the California International Marathon, a flat run from Folsom to Sacramento. Daisy was unaware of my plans.

Running east, as the bottom of L Street forced us left onto Second Street. We waved at the homeless and glaucoma-riddled army veteran who had chosen the public space as his ever-changing art piece of painted rocks and plastic chairs. He never saw us as he went on creating life for all seasons in the dead space where Second Street lay broken between K and L.

Just past Toad Hollow, only a stone's throw from the modern transcontinental railroad, and a slightly stronger throw's distance from the patchwork of asphalt and concrete connecting San Francisco and Teaneck, New Jersey, sat Carmen Ventura's Caterpillar Academy. It lay nestled among many other uninteresting new buildings in a cocoon of reflective brown glass and earth-toned stucco.

Mercy Valencia had recommended we call Carmen after deciding not to pursue the public preschool. Children's Therapy Center had put us on a sliding scale payment system for Magda's therapy, which took the sting out of having the additional expense of private schooling. But after we met Carmen, we were convinced this was the right place for Magda. At Carmen's open house for new parents, she said, "You shouldn't try to teach fish to run or butterflies to swim. You have to let them work out what they are good at so they can start to feel good about it. It's much harder for someone to learn if they are being forced to do it in a way that doesn't make sense to them. It adds a layer of complexity that need not be there. It's a layer that in the least can cause a child to frustrate, in the most can cause a child to reject positive learning."

We were sold.

For the last two years, Carmen had allowed Magdalena to play with the clothes used for dress up without concern that Magda never wanted to dress in them. She also allowed Magda a safe space to play alongside the other children, even though she never played with them. And that was okay because Carmen had made clear to the other students, and to their parents, that all children were safe in her space. No one was allowed to be marginalized because of who they were or how they interacted with others or their environment.

That alone was worth the price of admission.

On this autumn morning, Carmen was outside unlocking her door, and waved as Daisy and I ran by.

* * *

I grasped my watch and hit stop on the timer as Daisy and I crossed the finish line in the concrete between the sidewalk and our driveway. Mari was standing on a stepladder with a pair of hand shears in one hand and a plastic bag and a spray bottle clutched in her left. The rusty spring in the shears cried under the pressure Mari exerted as she bounced from branch to branch pruning in what seemed a haphazard fashion, but which probably made sense to her.

"What are you doing?" I asked.

"Fire blight."

"What fire blight?"

"The tips of these branches are infected – see?" She pointed her creaky shears at a branch.

"I just thought that was fall color."

"No, they're infected, dead, like gangrene." She was stern. "You have to throw these clippings in the trash too, otherwise they will infect everything around them over and over again."

"What's in the bottle?"

"Bleach – full strength. I spray the shears between each clipping so I don't spread the infection." She scissored them in the air to emphasize her point. "You have to be vigilant. Fire blight is like cancer."

As Mari launched into her version of fire blight germ theory to me, Annie opened the front door with Magda leaning against her hip and a stack of papers in her hand. "You forgot to sign these last night."

"What are they?" I honestly did not remember her asking me to sign them.

"This is the release for the school so they can get records from the county and Children's Therapy Center. I'm taking Magda over to PCE so she can be tested for special ed. That way she can get a plan in place before she starts kindergarten."

"Right. I totally blanked on signing that last night." I paused. "I saw Carmen this morning. You told her Magda isn't coming to school today, right?"

"Yep," she replied. "Feather said this process can drag out forever," she added as her faced turned from confident to concerned. "Can you get Charlie to school? I need to get Magda into the main office early, and he isn't ready yet."

"Absolutely," I said, unsure of what the school would be doing for Magda with or without special education. My memories of students in special education were of kids with little or no verbal abilities and odd physical mannerisms, educated in a portable classroom way at the back edge of the playground, their recess and lunch breaks purposefully timed not to coincide with the rest of the school. Those kids in the trailers were the kids that you heard couldn't control their bladders or would pull their hair out in chunks and eat it. Everyone made jokes about them and mimicked exaggerated speech impediments. And there were always the ubiquitous "short bus" jokes.

I pressed the forms up against the cracked garage window, shook those memories out of my head, signed in multiple places, and handed them back to Annie.

"Have a good day." I high-fived Magda. She hated hugs in the morning; only at night were they allowed. She smiled with her face barely visible under her cap, her neck covered in a woolen scarf, and her torso covered in two jackets. She draped herself over Daisy and squeezed.

I shot Annie a look about Magda's wardrobe. Knowingly, Annie said, "Magda also brought a backpack full of lots of important things that people take to school."

"What did she stuff in there? That zipper is crying," I whispered.

"This is what you do when you go to real school like Charlie," Annie whispered back. "I tried to get her to change her mind, but it's not worth it. She has your copy of *The Art of War*, three highlighters, a fistful of cereal bars, a string of paper clips, headphones, mittens, that snow globe she got in Denver, and God knows what else."

"At least she's ready."

"That makes one of us," Annie said. She glanced across the front yard at Mari. "What is she doing?"

"I'll fill you in later," I said, and hugged her goodbye.

Annie walked Magda down the driveway and along the sidewalk. Magda twice refused to hold Annie's hand.

Daisy bucked her leash as I led her back inside. She didn't stop squirming until I put her in the garage, fed her, and opened the door to the side yard. I then came back into the house and opened a jar of canned pears as Charlie ate his bowl of cereal at the kitchen table. He didn't want to talk this morning. His face was jammed into a copy of a Bone comic book he had checked out from the school library.

"Is this what you're going to be like as a teenager?"

He was locked in another world and unresponsive to me while we ate breakfast until I told him it was time to leave for school.

He then looked up. "Okay, let's go."

"How did you get into those books?" I asked as we walked the blocks toward PCE.

"The Colusa kids were really into them, so they loaned me one, and then I found them in the library. I've pretty much read all of them about three times."

"Really? That many times? Don't you get bored?"

"Starting to. I read them once to Magda, so that kind of doesn't count."

"I didn't know that," I said. "That counts big time. Did she ask you to?"

"No, Daddy, you know she doesn't ask. She just kept standing next to me when I was reading them, so I decided to read aloud to her. I think she enjoyed it because she listened like she was totally into the story."

My eyes misted with Charlie's revelation. The morning breeze pushed against our faces and perfumed our neighborhood with the elemental smells of school. The fall bloom was in effect as school doors opened with the crisp crack of book binding glue, fragrant with the wood and graphite dust of sharpened pencils and new boxes of crayons.

By October, seasonal change is even more palpable on the playgrounds as earthworms feast on rotting leaves, and the Bermuda grass browns and recedes in the rapidly diminishing light. By winter's arrival, the bloom will have fallen off the rose, as once important petals of papers lay strewn, scattered, and crinkled, clinging to the windward side of the chain-link fences and jaywalking into the neighboring yards.

Charlie's offhand remark about reading to Magda compelled me to ask more about why he chose to do what he did, but I didn't want to put the focus on his sister, so I deflected. "How old are the Colusa kids?"

"The youngest is two grades ahead of me."

"Are those books appropriate for your age if older boys are reading them?"

"Dad, it's fine."

"Okay, but I still remember reading you books like *Pete's Pizza*, and your favorite, *Harold and the Purple Crayon*," I reminisced.

"Those are little kids' books," he said in disgust.

"Fine, just don't let me find out that whatever you're reading is warping your mind."

"Okay, I won't."

As we approached the school grounds, I could feel his interest in our conversation waning. "Do you have a lot of friends?" I asked to keep him engaged.

"Yeah, sure."

"How many?"

"I don't know, at least my whole class, my soccer team – a hundred maybe." He distanced himself from me.

"Hey," I said catching his attention. "Can I get a hug goodbye?"

He halfheartedly gave me his upper body as he one-handedly, and briefly, grabbed my waist before running off calling out to three of his classmates who were playing tetherball on the playground. I stood for a minute and watched as he seamlessly integrated himself into the game, negotiated turns, all while he maintained a running dialogue about school, comics, and what he was going to wear for Halloween. As I panned out and turned to head home, I could see more groups of boys being boys and girls already forming circles of gossip, giggles, and whispers.

As I strolled back home, I could see that Mari was still busy attending to our pear trees. The closer I got, I could hear her talking as if I hadn't left. "They have antibiotic sprays you can put on trees," she said. "But that is stupid. You don't take antibiotics all the time to keep from getting sick. You know, right? It makes them not work."

"Well, yes, that's generally how it works," I said.

"This wind is going to spread—" The shears fell from her hand and landed sharply on her left foot and stood upright holding a ballerina's pirouette. A pool of blood began to saturate her shoe as she bit her lip in pain.

"Are you okay?" I asked, reflexively pulling the blade from her shoe and putting pressure on her wounded foot with my bare hands. "We need to get you to an emergency room."

"It's fine," Mari said with her usual stoicism.

"No, it's not fine. You're going to need a tetanus shot and stitches. God knows how deep that went."

I helped Mari down from the ladder and walked her back into her open garage. I took off her shoe and saw a half-inch puncture just behind her big toe. It oozed blood when I removed my manual pressure.

"Yeah, this is going to need stitches, antibiotics, and a tetanus shot," I affirmed.

"It's fine," Mari repeated obstinately. "Let me just wash it out in the shower."

"No, it's not fine. You can barely walk. The wound needs to be formally cleaned out, and we also need to make sure you didn't break a bone."

She waved a dismissive hand at me.

"If the bone gets infected, you could lose your foot," I added.

"Fine, I'll take myself in," she huffed.

"Let me drive you."

"No, I can drive myself."

"How?" I asked incredulously.

"I only need my right foot to drive." She pulled her keys from her pocket. "Just close my garage door for me, would you?"

"Yes, but please let me drive."

"No!" she bellowed over her shoulder as she limped toward her hatchback.

I eased Mari into her car and she sped off. As I turned to close Mari's garage door, I finally noticed that my hands, arms, and clothes were covered in her blood. Halloween had come early, and I was a clumsy axe murderer. I needed to go home, wash, and change. I closed Mari's garage door and decided I would check to make sure her house was locked after I was clean.

As I washed my hands in the bathroom sink, the blood separated along the curvature of the bowl. The lighter, more serous components were easily caught in the wash of warm water and soap. The heavier bits, mixed with the weight of iron, moved more slowly. Gravity was holding strong against the current coming from the faucet. Drying my hands, I could hear the wind rattling the downspouts of our house against the stucco wall in Morse code. Normally wind confused Daisy, and she barked until she found the safety of her blanket and crate, but she had been quiet throughout all of the chaos of the morning. Something wasn't right.

"Daisy!" I shouted. I ran to the garage. Empty. "Daisy!" I called louder as I ran out the side door. Empty. I turned my head to call her name again when I saw the latch on the redwood gate hanging its head in shame. Unable to hold tight onto the latch bar against the force of the prevailing wind, the galvanized screws had given up their hold, the wood flaking and the embarrassed metal crumbling.

I bolted out the flimsy gate, destroying what was left of the metal apparatus, and sprinted into the middle of the street panicked.

"Daisy!" I bellowed. "Come!"

The neighborhood crow perched on the telephone wire thought I was crazy. And why wouldn't she? A man was running down the street covered in a bloody shirt screaming, frantically bouncing from house to house, peering over fences, and prying behind bushes like the confusing opening scene of a horror movie.

Daisy had never run off before. I didn't think she could. I didn't think she would want to. The world was too big and too loud to chance it alone. I called Annie and it went straight to voicemail; I left what I was sure was a distracted and unintelligible message.

Having no success on our block, I decided the best way to look for her would be to search on bike. I could cover more ground than I could do walking, and I would be more nimble than I would be in a car. I grabbed her leash and sped off.

Some autistics wander. It is a known fact. They don't run away from home; they just leave. They were never gifted with the horse sense to tell them it might be a bad idea, ignorant of one of Maslow's most primitive needs. When Quincy Hamlin was younger, Feather had to invest in a home alarm system, not to keep burglars out, but to keep their son in. He also had to wear a leg bracelet 24/7 like a parolee. He was a radio-collared wolf. They could track his movements and whereabouts at all times. I was now thinking maybe I should invest in one of those devices for Daisy.

As I worked larger and larger concentric circles outward from our house, I berated myself for not noticing sooner that the gate needed repair, similar to the way Annie had cursed herself the day Magda wandered out our front door. I then began to chastise myself the way Annie had herself when Magda wandered away from her in the grocery store.

Normally Magda lay in the shopping cart and covered herself with all of the cold and frozen foods Annie put in the cart. Her therapists told us she did it because she needed the body feedback. We worried she was going to get frostbite. But on one Sunday afternoon at the deli counter, Annie briefly turned her back on her cart, giving Magda enough time to climb out from under her icy blanket and wander off, ultimately hiding under a display table between the meat department and the bulk goods. No amount of overhead paging alerted Magda to the fact that Annie was looking for her, nor did it convey her hysteria. It took Annie at least six months before she would ever take Magda back to a store with her alone.

Minutes were beginning to feel like hours, and with every moment that passed, I was sure the likelihood of Daisy being hit by a car escalated exponentially. Perhaps the police would catch her before they caught the murderous lunatic on the bicycle weaving in and out of neighborhoods, shopping centers, and public school playgrounds.

Without conscious awareness of where I was headed, I crossed Covell Boulevard, rode through an open chain-link gate, and found myself atop the concrete foundation slab where the old tomato cannery once sat. Spilling out to the north was an amphitheater of broomsticks. The beheaded remains of the sunflower fields that were so beautiful in June were staring back at me on my stage. Dressed in my bloody clothes, a tragedy was playing out before them. I scanned the audience for signs Daisy had been there. Black dots peppered the landscape as crows and blackbirds laughingly flitted from seat to seat in search of any remaining seed and the best seat. As I scanned the horizon, I caught sight of one black dot stirring up the rest, moving from aisle to aisle, ushering cacophony wherever it went. "Daisy!" I yelled. With the last bits of adrenalin I had left, I dropped my bike and broke into a sprint.

As I approached, it became clearer that it was her, bounding over furrows. An invisible leash of smell was haphazardly dragging her head-first in any direction it saw fit. She was tripping the light fantastic and finding the answer to what she would do if left to her own devices. She was on a John Muir ramble, investigating the world of nature around her. As I came alongside her, she glanced at me as if nothing was out of place; she was running, and I was next to her, like we always did, every day. There was no need for the despair painted across my face in sweat and dirt. This was just an everyday occurrence, and we were just running home.

As I approached our front door, dusty and bloodied, my dog in one arm and my bike in the other, I saw that a package had been left for me on the doorstep. Annie was slumped against two planes of stucco, her arms wrapped around her legs and hugged to her chest in a seated fetal position, the cordless phone next to her. I could tell she had been sitting there for a while, caught between grief and fury. As our eyes met, her face contorted to hold back the tears until it ruptured under pressure, and a torrent burst forth.

In a gush of a run-on sentence, she told me everything. "She isn't going to qualify, she is going to have to go to kindergarten without help, she is above the eightieth percentile across the board, she has never been there. Am I crazy? Are we just making stuff up?"

"I don't understand." I sat down next to her and wrapped her in a brief hug. "Didn't Mercy say she should get special ed?"

"That's not how it works! You can't just say she needs it, and then get it." Annie tried to compose her face, but the words and tears came running out again. "He was giving her all the answers – like name something you wear, and he would grab and tug on his shirt – or how do you tell time, as he tapped on his wristwatch. There were pictures all over the wall with the answers on them!"

"So that's that. There is no other way to get her help?"

"No," she said. "We have to have a meeting next Friday so they can formally tell us she doesn't qualify."

"I'm confused. I thought they already told you she didn't qualify."

"They did." Annie stood. I stood too.

"Then why should I take a day off work to go to some damn meeting if the outcome is a foregone conclusion?"

"Those are their rules." Annie finally took notice of the state of my clothing. "Oh my god, what happened to you?"

"Mari had a small accident. Didn't you get my message? It's been one of those days…"

"You're telling me…" Annie sighed and wiped her tears.

"Well, you're not going on your own. Can I see a copy of those rules?"

"I put them on the kitchen table. Feather called and said they're supposed to give us copies of Magda's reports and the tests they used on her before the meeting." Annie's tone changed. "So is Mari going to be okay?"

"I'll fill you in on all the details after I get clean."

Parallel Universe

"We are just an advanced breed of monkeys on a minor planet of a very average star."

— Stephen Hawking

I watched the brass pendulum swing in time through its little glass door as the Regulator wall clock in Frank and Angelo's dining room ticked the seconds off, lulling me into a hypnotic state. Self-doubt was settling in as the silence progressed. I felt as if I was wasting their time, I knew something was wrong and could not let that go. Anger was welling, and winning over concession.

Frank and Angelo poured over the photocopies I had picked up from the Yolano Union School District's main administrative office downtown earlier that day. It was amazing to me how much paperwork could be generated by one day of testing. In addition to the list of wrongs I felt had happened, I added tree murderers to the list of charges.

The waning sunlight shot horizontal rays through the Bosc's sheer window fabric, illuminating the ever-present Davis dust suspended in midair. Dust is ubiquitous in Davis, a fact that even the impeccable cleanliness of my friends couldn't avoid. Frank highlighted with precision and Angelo underlined with ferocity as a scale model of the universe spun and expanded slowly, like an astronomy animation, above their oval maple table.

Dust fairies fell like snowflakes over the protocols, answer sheets, administration manuals, and diagnostic reports generated by Diego Braeburn and the YUSD in their evaluation of Magda. Among the stacks of papers we had been given by Mr. Braeburn was his report, the only document I understood, but only because I understood the meaning of its concluding statement, not its rationale: "Magdalena Mae Russell does not meet California qualification criteria for special education." The rest of the papers held no meaning for me. "Normative values." What is normal? "Standard deviations." What is standard? Percentile ranks. How does something so arbitrary and made up by someone without a disability determine the impact of a problem? I stared down at my hands, thumbing my fingernails, waiting for validation from Frank or Angelo.

Breaking the white noise of the metronome, Frank's wooden bistro chair complained as he shifted his weight to reach for a stack of individually enveloped CDs on their pinewood sideboard. "I want you to have these," he said.

"What are they?" I asked, confused.

"It's a string quartet."

"What?" I was expecting him to say something about Magda's testing.

"They are amazing. They take contemporary songs and play them classically. All sorts of bands like AC DC, Nirvana, Depeche Mode. I burned a bunch of these for you after you called about Magda's testing. People at work think I'm listening to the classical station. You're going to love 'Message to Harry Manback'."

"I'm lost," I said.

Angelo finally made a motion that he was ready to talk as he sipped from a cyclist's screw top plastic water bottle. The bottle gasped for air as it reformed its cylindrical shape. Angelo was a gangly man, as if he had never quite been able to fill the height he was given at the close of puberty. He was clothed in an odd combination of a white tank top and the blue and orange spandex shorts of the Davis Bike Club. With his torso mostly exposed, an abrupt tan line bifurcated the crease between his deltoids and his biceps, accentuating a frame somewhere between emaciated and athletic. The striations of his skeletal muscles were clearly evident.

"Well, I see several problems here." Angelo looked up at me from above the reading glasses perched at the rubbery end of his nose. "You said that Annie told you the testing room was full of posters of letters and numbers."

"Yes, Annie said there were preschool style cartoons of people's faces, foods like hot dogs and pies, stuff like that. Not only that, this guy asked how Magda would be able to tell what time it was as part of one of the tests, and when Magda couldn't answer, he pointed to his watch."

He shifted in his chair.

"It shows poor judgment to run a test in a room like that. It's distracting, and potentially nullifies test results if a child can choose answers off the wall. And certainly you cannot give children answers verbally or nonverbally, but it is not much to argue with in a meeting. It will degenerate into an us-versus-them type of argument, and you will never win that battle."

I deflated. "Annie and I are upset because the reports from Children's Therapy Center, the County, and the STAR Center show that she has significant delays, so we don't understand how on earth these tests show that she is better than eighty percent of her peers. It just makes no sense."

"All the district has to do is say that they considered your outside reports. They do not have to listen to them or follow their recommendations, or at least that is what they think. They get very defensive about parents coming in and telling them what to do."

"Then how is the district considering our testing from the STAR Center, Children's Therapy Center, or the county?" I felt heated.

Angelo smiled as he rubbed both hands over his buzz cut scalp as if he were shampooing a full head of hair. "This is what really torques me about school evaluations. They play fast and loose with testing rules and then cling religiously to state regulations. I don't know this man. I don't know if he is lazy, incompetent, malicious, under guidance, or some mixture of all of the above." His rib spaces retracted as he spoke.

"Okay," I leaned in, "so what do we do?"

Angelo's tone deepened. "Let's look at the answer sheet and scores on the language test they administered to Magda. He started the exam one and a half years ahead of Magda's chronological age. You are supposed to start the test at least a year below the child's age."

"Is that allowed?"

"Technically, yes, but only if you suspect that there is no language problem."

"Why would you be testing if you didn't suspect a problem?"

Angelo smiled. "Precisely! However, if you are testing normal subjects, or the test is part of a battery of tests for a child that clearly has no language issues, then technically, you could start testing beyond the chronological age of the child. But it is nearly impossible to say that a child is testing below age level if you don't start below their age level. Do you see what I'm saying?"

"Yes, this guy knew what answer he wanted before he started. So when Annie brings him reports that says Magda has an expressive language delay, and he decides to start the test as if he has no indication that Magda..." I threw my hands up.

"When you come to your own conclusion based not on fact but on your own opinion, especially in the world of disability, you have just opened the door to discrimination," Angelo fumed. "But it's worse. When he wasn't able to reach the foregone conclusion he had already made because of the way Magda was answering, he decided to accept a wrong answer as correct so that he could move on."

"What?" I yelled.

Angelo shuffled the papers in front of him and found the test administration manual. "In order to validate your reason for starting a test ahead of age level, in this test, the child has to get a correct score on the first three questions in a row. In technical jargon, they call it a basal score. If you cannot establish a basal score, you need to regress backward in the testing until the child can answer three questions correctly. Otherwise, the test is invalid. So when he got to the third question, and Magda got the answer wrong, he marked Magda's answer as correct on the scoring sheet."

"What the ... are you sure?"

"Yes, I've given this test a thousand times," Angelo said flatly. "The test asked Magda to list foods, but she didn't. She said mustache, clearly not a food. More to the point, he knew that the answer was wrong. He actually circled the error."

"Can you prove that this answer should have been marked incorrect?"

"Sure, I have the instruction manual right here, and I'll photocopy this page for you, but better than that, I know the author of this test. She was one of my instructors in grad school. She is now in her eighties and lives in Solvang." He smiled. "She's one of my Facebook friends."

"He's beaming that he actually has friends," Frank chimed in.

"I'm not done," Angelo said ignoring Frank. "There is other proof that corroborates your case that Magda has significant delays worthy of qualification for special ed in this testing, despite the conclusions drawn by the district."

"Like what?"

"California regulations require that you record, written or audio, fifty spoken utterances when testing these kids in the area of language. Those utterances are then analyzed by someone who knows what they're looking at, like a speech therapist. The therapist makes an assessment, which gives the tester objective information about the language skills of the child."

"Okay..."

Angelo removed his glasses and leaned in. "Diego Braeburn was only able to record thirty-four utterances during his entire evaluation. Even if what was said in those utterances was age appropriate, which it wasn't based on this sample—" Angelo held up a photocopy of thirty-four lines of text written in Braeburn's handwriting "—a child of Magda's age should have verbal diarrhea, if you find a subject that interests them. If Magda didn't have language delays, there would be no reason to be unable to record the proper number of utterances. And if you cannot get the proper number of utterances, the law says you have to explain why. I see no explanation." He dropped his pen and paper on the table. The particles of dust in the air scattered in random directions, thrust out of their natural orbit.

"The way I see it, this testing shows that she does need special education, despite what this report says, but that is an uphill battle."

Frank picked it up from there. "You are going to have to get an independent evaluation. It's the only way to nullify this pile of horseshit. You can argue that what this person did was wrong until you are blue in the face, but a district administrator is always going to back an employee. Just beware that you aren't going to make any friends in this process."

"Well, we are kind of stuck, right? We can't accept this. It's wrong. What do we do?"

"Tell them that you disagree with their assessment and you want your own independent evaluation. Then and only then will you be willing to talk about enrolling Magda in public school."

"How do I do that?"

"Let me see who you're meeting with." Frank rifled through the stacks of papers. "Where is the notice of meeting?"

"What is that?"

"It's the sheet with the time, date, and location of the meeting, and what will be discussed – never mind, here it is." He studied it. "Well, this is interesting. You're on the fast track to nowhere," he said bluntly.

"Huh?" I peered at him, dreading what came next.

"In order to determine if a child qualifies for special ed, you have to have certain people present at the Individualized Educational Plan meeting – IEPs for short. It's the law," he said flatly.

"Okay, so who are they supposed to bring?"

"You have to have a regular education teacher, a special education teacher, someone who can interpret test results such as a psychologist, and an administrator who can approve resources. There is no teacher listed as coming to your meeting, special ed or regular ed. This just cements the fact that they have no intentions of qualifying Magda or really listening to what you have to say. Otherwise, they would have a full team there."

"How do I fix that?"

"Don't. Let them fail at what they're supposed to do. It will be points in your favor later. Man, these people are bad." Frank shook his head at Angelo.

Angelo rolled his eyes. "What do you expect?" he said knowingly.

Turning to me, Angelo said, "Be firm, and don't back down. Get that independent assessment and go forward from there. And don't let them try to pawn some other district employee off as an independent. Independent means your choice, not theirs. I know people in Sacramento who are more than capable of doing this kind of testing. Just let me know when you need it."

"There is no way this won't become adversarial," I said.

"These meetings usually are. But remember, they wouldn't have to be adversarial if they just did the right thing," Angelo said. "The onus is on them, not you. Your job is to be an advocate."

"This is a lose-lose situation," I said. "If we don't do anything, she won't get help. If we do complain, they will be less likely to provide help."

"Yes and no," Frank said. "I wouldn't be passive in this process. You know what will happen if you accept this bullshit." He tapped Braeburn's report. "But what will happen if you press them, you don't know. School districts can be horribly stingy with providing services, but they don't like to lose face." He smiled. "Isn't Annie on the PTA?"

"We both are."

"That may help."

"Neither of us do politics well, if at all."

Berdoo lifted one eye as Frank got up from the table. "You want to stick around for dinner?" he asked as he walked into the kitchen.

"No, I'm good. Thank you. I need to get home to Annie and the kids. She'll be wondering what took so long."

"No she won't," he said as he popped his head around the corner and smiled. "Beer? Wine?"

"No, thanks, but I'll take a rain check," I said as I began to collect the mountain of paper that had been strewn across their table. "I need to talk to Annie."

"Personally, I would report this to the state," Angelo said, "but wait until after you find out what happens at this meeting. That's up to you, of course. Somebody like this Braeburn shouldn't be determining who does and doesn't get services. You could report this to his direct supervisor, but it's unlikely to go anywhere. Since the site administrator is supposed to be at your meeting, it's unlikely they care about these types of improprieties to begin with. More than likely, they are part of this culture too. What you permit, you promote."

"That doesn't seem right. If I falsified a medical record or tried to keep a patient from getting care and that got reported to my boss, my behind would be in a sling – at a minimum."

"Public schools are an alternate universe," said Angelo. "There is no educational malpractice. They exist on a protected plane of tenure and ego. Educational laws don't carry any criminal penalties. You could try going to the school board, a little too political for me, but technically they are there to represent you."

"That sure is not the public's perception nor my idea of what a public school is supposed to be." I shook my head.

"No, it's not, nor should it be," he said. "In all reality, it really shouldn't be the ones responsible for providing and funding services that are the same ones determining the need for services. It really is a conflict of interest. It should be an independent process."

"Thanks for all your help," I said, shaking Angelo's hand. "Thanks, Frank," I yelled in the direction of the kitchen.

A loud, "Yep," came back in reply. I heard the clicking of an igniter and the subdued roar of their gas range being lit.

"See you, Berdoo." There was no response from the mountain of fur on the floor.

Angelo walked me to the front door. "If you like running so much, you should try cycling. It's easier on your knees."

"No, thanks. I already get yelled at by farmers for running through their fields. I don't need angry motorists after me too."

"Good point." He smiled. "Oh, hey, before you run off, take the technical reports on all those tests with you." He ran back to the dining room and grabbed them from the sideboard.

"What are they?"

"It's all the internal data from the publishers of those tests, things like how accurate they are and what they actually test for. Some are more forthcoming about their limitations than others, but you might find it helpful in requesting that independent eval."

* * *

Daisy greeted me by spinning slowly in circles when I came into the house. Magda had draped Daisy in her own weighted blanket and wrapped her compression belt around her chest just for good measure, and Daisy couldn't spin with quite as much speed as she usually did. Magda had also attached Daisy's leash to her collar, and she ran with Daisy from room to room, squealing in delight.

"Run!" Magda belted. "Run, Daisy!"

"You are not going to believe this…" I dropped the stack of papers, test booklets, and manuals on the kitchen table in front of Annie. "You were right in more ways than you know. We need to figure out how we are going to approach this."

"We have to meet with ADN." Annie was flat.

"What is that, another special ed acronym?" I snorted in derision.

Daisy and Magda flew into the room, and then, as if their batteries had been removed, they both hit a wall as their rumps hit the floor. The only motion Magda could muster was a rhythmic fingering of the fur on Daisy's chest. Both of their gazes were elsewhere and unbreakable.

"Adam Del Norte, the man we're meeting with," Annie spoke softly as she stared at the two. "They call him ADN. I've been on the phone with Feather for the last hour asking her what advice she has. She said he is notorious for blocking kids from getting into special ed. This is not going to be a fun meeting."

"Not fun for whom?" I asked.

No Child Left Behind

"A penalty is a cowardly way to score."

— Pelé

We made our way down a narrow corridor of Putah Creek Elementary School, a pungent building from the Sixties. All education buildings from that era carried that scent of what I believed to be hidden asbestos, lead paint, and carcinogenic carpet glue. I was sure if I looked hard enough, I would find black spotty mildew under the windows.

Annie pointed to a door standing ajar. "That's the testing room," she whispered.

As we passed the open door on the way to the administrative offices, I caught a fleeting glimpse of the cartoons Magda had given as answers during her testing: a man with a mustache holding a wrench, pepperoni pizza, and a smiling worm coming out of an apple. My blood pressure ratcheted up several millimeters of mercury.

The smell of Diego Braeburn's drugstore aftershave lingered in the hallway as we followed him through a labyrinth of cubicles, copy rooms, staff lounges, and conference rooms. He was a gangly tall man in a way that reminded me of Abe Lincoln, and he walked with a purposeful stride. White tennis shoes, khaki pants, and a tucked-in polo shirt made him appear more ready to sell electronics or cell phones than test children for learning disabilities. His pitch-black hair was thick, without curl, and stuck out perpendicularly from his scalp about an eighth of an inch.

Diego centered the engraved plastic nameplate that read COUNSELOR in its brass mounting on the wooden door of his office, the type of sign that could have been replaced with JANITOR or STORAGE. In fact, his windowless room was the size of a broom closet. The leading edge of the door kissed the front edge of the desk, preventing it from fully completing a ninety-degree arc. I wondered how someone had managed to get a desk in the room to begin with. They probably had to take the hinges off the door. *Fire code violators*, I thought with an inward smirk, adding that to the list of reasons I found the school deficient.

Seated behind the desk was a man with small and shiny features who appeared to take no notice of us as we walked in. Diego shimmied around the desk and took a seat next to the man, who was fiddling with a bulky Panasonic portable cassette recorder. Diego sighed heavily as he sank into his padded chair.

"This is Adam Del Norte," he said in a flat tone. "He is our site administrator for special education here at the early entry program."

Adam pressed his lips together as if attempting to smile and considering a half-grimace sufficient. He extended his right arm. I was confused; was I supposed to shake it, or was he was directing us to sit?

We opted to sit.

"Thank you so much for being here with us tonight. I'm really glad you could make the time," he said in a cloyingly sweet tone, as if he had finally come alive like a Chuck E. Cheese animatronic. Despite his attempt at politeness, I felt a sense of dread.

Annie and I complied and sat down in two child-sized red plastic chairs. We looked up at the two men staring down at us as if we were about to get in trouble.

"We want you to feel comfortable," ADN said, the irony completely lost on him. Thick crescent-shaped sideburns framed his face. "That's hard to do when we are recording each other, I know." He forced a chuckle. "But it's your choice. When you agreed to this meeting, you indicated that you wanted to record, and that's your right, but that also gives us the right to record the meeting."

He smiled and pressed the Play/Record button.

Recording the meeting had been Frank and Angelo's suggestion. Initially, Annie and I were hesitant that doing so would make us appear overtly confrontational, but now we glanced at each other, knowing now that it was a smart idea.

The white eyes of the pulleys began to spin at different speeds as the mechanism on the desk whirred to life, providing the background hiss to everything that was now being recorded. I hit Record on our palm-sized digital recorder and placed it on the edge of the desk.

ADN studied it for a moment. "Just pretend the recorders aren't there. Let's close the door – for privacy reasons."

I did so then sat down again.

"You've met Mr. Braeburn – he did Magdalena's testing. I am Adam Del Norte, and I wear many hats around here," he said with an air of self-importance. "In this capacity, I'm acting as the site administrator for special education or S-A-S-E, since your daughter isn't yet enrolled in a school with a principal. Sorry we can't use my office. I had an incident in there recently – but your Magdalena would never do something like that, would she?"

He looked down at his stack of papers and exhaled through his nose, then smiled.

"Anyway, my most important job is making sure that kids who need help get it, and that's really the goal of everyone in the YUSD. I do need to put out there, however, that both Diego and I have another meeting in an hour, so if this extends beyond that time frame, we will have to reschedule the remainder of the meeting. It's a very busy time of year for us." He feigned flabbergast.

"We understand," Annie said cordially. "We have friends whose children are on IEPs. It sounds like this is the time of year to have the annual meetings."

ADN didn't look up. "Here is a copy of your parental rights." He handed Annie a pink-stapled stack of papers. "You can review these anytime you like. This tells you about all of the processes we have here for special education. I want to start the meeting formally by saying that we have reviewed the reports you gave us prior to the testing." He anointed the stack of papers on the desk.

"Let's start by talking about Magdalena's strengths." The parallel lines of his mouth drew taut into an angular circle, another attempt at a smile. "What does she do well?"

Annie took the lead. "She is smart, she is kind, she loves animals, she loves to help, and she wants to learn."

"Oh, yes, I definitely saw her intelligence," Braeburn offered. "Lots of interest in everything we were doing during the testing."

I could feel Annie's face tighten.

"That's great," ADN said as his hand furiously took notes on a yellow legal pad while his head nodded in agreement.

"And what concerns do you have?" he said as if reading from a script. "Why are you here?"

"We are worried about her ability to learn," I said.

His pen paused, and he looked at me.

I took that as an invitation to continue. "She isn't capable of doing lots of things that other kids her age can do. She really doesn't play with anyone. She really doesn't have any friends. But what we think is most important is that she doesn't ask for help. Right?" I tried to elicit a response from either ADN or Diego, but all I got were blank stares. "How critical is that for learning in school, raising your hand because you don't understand a concept?"

I paused for a response or a follow-up question – none came.

I plowed on. "A couple of weeks ago she decided to make chocolate milk without asking anyone. She didn't ask for directions, and she ended up dumping an entire box of chocolate milk powder on the floor in the kitchen. Annie was sitting in the next room. Rather than ask for help, Magda made an even bigger mess than she had to begin with. But she is smart enough to know that our dog isn't allowed to have chocolate, so she poured water on it to try to clean it, then got a broom to try to sweep it to one side, and she ended up spreading it all over the floor. Then she broke down in tears and cried all night because she was afraid she had poisoned the dog."

"Wow," ADN said. "So smart to know dogs can't have chocolate."

My face twisted. "That's not the point I was trying to make."

My words didn't make a dent. "Given what you said about how smart she is," said ADN, "and how she wants to do well, let's review that in the context of the testing Mr. Braeburn was so nice to provide for us."

Mr. Braeburn talked about the tests he used on Magda, what they tested, and how that applied to what Magda would be doing in school, as well as what the regular classroom teachers would do to support the concepts tested.

I began to lose focus. So did Annie. She placed her hand on my thigh, fingers splayed, and squeezed. She was in the silence of rage, a rage only a mother could have, the kind of rage that would allow her to lift a car off of her daughter if it ever came to that.

And here it was, the moment when we didn't get to choose our next possibility; the moment that we were forced into; the moment when disagreeing with the room meant that we would be ostracized for not falling in line. But it was also the moment we felt the car was about to crush our child.

As Diego Braeburn droned on about his testing, Annie and I knew that what our life had been like before this meeting was nothing like how it would be from now on. The blind wonder of marriage vows, the excitement and confusion of bringing new lives into the world, the pride of holding our very own first set of house keys – it all became hazy, distant, unimportant. This asshole was blatantly lying about our child. Annie and I had never felt this strong of a shift, ever, not with Magda's brain MRI, not with our first conversation with Mercy Valencia, not the first time we saw a diagnosis in writing. An uncontrollable urge led me to draw a large Greek letter delta on my notepad. "Change" I scribbled underneath it.

Diego concluded his rubber stamp impression of Magda. "It doesn't appear that she needs special education, and our classrooms are more than capable of meeting her needs with the regular education curriculum."

What little air the room held had been let out. Annie and I were suffocating.

ADN chimed in. "We have such great schools here. We have wonderful teachers who will keep an eye on her, and if she ever looks like she is struggling, she can be tested again at that time to see if she qualifies at that point. You know, I really don't like having this conversation with parents because I know you are here because you want the best for your child and you think that special education can help. I really wish some of the private therapists out there would refrain from sending nice parents like you here. And you know, pediatricians don't have a good idea of what we do in schools."

"I don't understand." Annie pushed against my thigh as if getting ready to stand.

Diego interrupted. "What Adam is saying is that it's not that we don't want to help. It's just that providing help at the level you are seeking has to meet certain legal requirements. We are bound by regulations that prevent us from enrolling everyone who meets with us. Absolutely, we want to see all these kids get help, and trust me, they will. I'm sure you are aware that people move to Davis just so they don't have to spend money to send their kids to a private school – our public schools are that good."

"Can I ask some questions about your testing, Mr. Braeburn?" I said in as calm a manner as I could muster.

"Absolutely," he said confidently.

"I take it that this isn't your first rodeo?"

"Oh no, I've been doing this for many years."

ADN shifted in his seat.

"Great, so you have a pretty solid knowledge of these tests, and you always administer them the same way?" I pointed to Magda's tests.

"One hundred percent."

"Okay, great. Can I ask you why you chose to start the first language test at one and a half years above Magdalena's age? My understanding is that you should have started at least a year below her actual age."

"The test allows for that." He beamed as if proud of himself. "You just need to achieve a basal score to—"

"I know what a basal is. But that wasn't my question. My question was why did you start the test at that point? If you start the test at a level a few years beyond her age, aren't you assuming that Magda won't be recognized as testing with delays at her age level?"

"She got the first three questions right, so the test is valid." He shifted uncomfortably in his seat.

"Again, that wasn't my question, but nonetheless, did she get those questions right?"

"Yes."

"Are you sure?"

"Yes." He didn't look at certain as he sounded.

"So if I found out that the answer Magdalena gave in that third question was wrong, what would you say?"

At that, Mr. Braeburn became mute.

"Well, I suggest we do more testing," ADN interrupted. "You guys really limited what areas we were able to evaluate, so there might be a problem with Magda, but we don't know for sure."

"Why more testing?" I snapped. "That makes no sense."

"But Mr. Russell, we are obligated to test in all areas of suspected disability," said ADN.

"Great! That's the whole point of why we're here. What disability do you suspect? Or the real question I would like answered is why you didn't suspect a disability with her language when you were given that information from us months ago."

"Diego can retest her, or at least ask the questions you think he should have."

He glanced at his colleague. Diego Braeburn nodded.

"Would you like that?" ADN asked us.

"Is that even okay?" I asked incredulously. "None of these scores are valid. We have to question everything you did with her because the tests were invalid."

The ordered fashion in which I was going to ask our questions about all of the testing fell apart. "We brought you paperwork showing you she has been diagnosed with multiple language issues including an expressive language delay. You only got thirty-four utterances, but you were supposed to get fifty. Does that sound compatible with a disability in language?" My voice reverberated off the walls.

"The language sample is valid for analysis," Diego said.

"Mr. Russell, I can see that you are very upset," said ADN.

"You haven't seen upset!"

I had lost my composure. The atmosphere had become humid and hostile. I was flushed from having been forced to breathe recycled and poorly circulated air. The hard plastic chair-back angered the middle of my spine.

With sweat beads forming at my temples, and in as calm a voice as I could summon, I said, "We want an independent evaluation. I understand we are entitled to one if we disagree with yours, which we emphatically do."

"I can't authorize that," ADN said. "You'll have to go to Tier Three to make that request."

"What is Tier Three? Is that a person? How do I contact Tier Three?" I spit rage.

"The contact information for your Tier Three administrator is on the last page of the papers we gave you at the beginning of the meeting," ADN said without eye contact. "You will have to contact them if you want your evaluation. But what we are recommending today is that Magda does not qualify for special education, and she needs more testing done in other areas of suspected disability."

"Is that what the teachers who should be at this meeting think?"

ADN's mouth fell agape, but no words fell out.

"Can you tell me what disability you suspect?"

"I hope you both have a good day." ADN stared at the desk.

Annie stood and pushed me through the door.

"That went well," I said sarcastically as I hit stop on our voice recorder.

"I think this is only the beginning of a long, uphill battle," Annie predicted as Angelo's use of the word "advocate" resonated in my head.

"How in good conscience could you act like that as an educator?" I mused.

Annie shook her head in disgust. "I have no idea."

Annie's Dream

*"Only if we understand will we care. Only if we care will we help.
Only if we help shall all be saved."*

— Jane Goodall

My subconscious is a sieve. I rarely remember my dreams. They are silent films mostly. My rapid eye movements flicker in black and white, rarely in Technicolor.

I know Daisy dreams. Her feet paddle dry land and run through mid-air. Her shoulders fasciculate as her cheeks puff and fall with each lecture she gives ephemeral squirrels.

Annie dreams in vivid high definition and Dolby surround sound. For her, dreaming is an IMAX movie-going experience.

The night before our wedding, Annie dreamt she had found some-one's wallet while we were out shopping for last-minute table favors.

When Annie tried to return it to the store manager, she was accused by the wallet's owner that she had in fact stolen it and had rung up several thousand dollars in charges on one of his credit cards. She was arrested, and we had to pay not only the man's credit card charges but also the caterer, the DJ, and the venue even though we couldn't wed since she had been booked on felony charges and was awaiting arraignment. Apparently, I was unable to bail her out.

Two days before we left Oakland for Davis, she awakened me to make sure I didn't want to move back to Davis because I had been a serial killer who preyed upon elderly patients. She was convinced I had been administering lethal doses of insulin at three in the morning in a misguided and deluded attempt at ending their suffering. I had been accused of the plot in a bad Lifetime movie.

For a long time, Annie researched dream interpretations online or asked friends what her dreams meant. Rarely was the answer positive. Typically, they meant she was stressed or B-vitamin deficient.

More often than not, they portended catastrophe.

"I had a horrible dream last night," Annie announced.

My eyes finally cracked with the morning. "I'm sorry," I said, hoping my brief reply would give the hint that I dreaded hearing more.

"It felt so real – don't you want to hear about it?"

"I suppose," I lied.

She sensed my disinterest. "I'm not going to tell you if you don't care. I can't help what I think up when I'm sleeping. Can you?"

"It's fine, but is this going to be as real as the time you changed deodorant because you woke up thinking I had threatened to leave you because I hated your Lady's Secret?"

"You had quit your job and joined the Independent Disability Evaluation Authority," she said.

"What the hell is that?"

"It was like a conglomerate of meter maids, librarians, and mall security guards."

"Okay," I said in confusion.

"On your breast pocket, you wore yellow iron-on badges in the shape of an incandescent bulb with I.D.E.A. embroidered in cursive where the filament belonged. Your outfit was like a gas station attendant from nineteen fifty-two."

"That's creative on my part," I said.

"That's not the point," she snapped.

"Did I have one of those cool hexagonal starched hats with the black brim?" I asked cautiously.

"Yes, and you had a navy blue pressed shirt with matching slacks. You carried a clipboard with a stack of triplicate forms, and you wore ridiculous mirrored sunglasses."

"Mustache?"

"No," she said plainly. "You would look gross with a mustache."

"I've always wanted one, but deep down I know you're right. What was my job?" I dared to ask.

"That was the worst part. You wouldn't let people access certain places until they could prove they needed them."

"I don't think it is fair that I get accused of things that I wasn't even awake for," I said.

"You were like a bouncer at a bar, but worse. You hired all your friends to help you too, and you were mean to me and people I know."

"Really, this isn't fair," I pled.

"You put up gates in front of wheelchair ramps and wouldn't let anyone use them, even if they were in a wheelchair; you made them try to use the stairs first. It was the same thing with those blue handicapped parking spots. No one was allowed to park there even if they had a disabled placard. You made them park in a normal spot and prove that they couldn't walk into wherever they wanted to go from where they had parked."

"I don't understand why that seems like a real thing I would do," I said.

"You wouldn't even let blind people use the braille on the keypads at the ATM machines without first proving they couldn't get their money without it."

"What? How did I do that? File off the bumps on the keys?"

"You told them that these services were being saved for people who actually needed them, and if you let everyone use these things, it wouldn't be fair to the people who really needed them."

"That sounds logical…" I sat up.

"It was awful! There were old people falling all over the place, and you would only let them use the ramp or the parking spot after they fell, but by then they didn't need the ramp. They needed to go to the hospital to have their broken bones set."

"Well, it wasn't real," I groaned as I lowered my feet to the floor to get out of bed.

"Ash Hamlin was even there, and he was in a cast with a broken leg. He wanted to use an elevator instead of the stairs, and you told him he couldn't use it until he went to the doctor to prove that he didn't have diabetes and schizophrenia first."

"What? That is patently ridiculous. Are there even any buildings in Davis that have elevators? And if so, what does schizophrenia have to do with it? I don't know how you would think that any of this was real."

She sighed. "It felt real."

"What do you want for breakfast?"

"I'm not hungry."

"Would it help if I apologized?"

"Maybe," she said in a small voice.

Sensitivity and Specificity

"Controversy equalizes fools and wise men, and the fools know it."

— Oliver Wendell Holmes, Sr.

"I don't understand why we have to shift our lives around, and I have to take yet another day off from work for something that seems so obvious," I complained. "This could have been handled with an email."

"Well, it might be good to have some face time," Annie said. "It's easier for them to be dismissive of an email or a phone call."

I had no retort for the truth.

The main office of the Yolano Union School District used to be Davis' first modern high school. It was a rigid red brick structure softened by the surrounding decades-old pines and the rest of the mint green copse. Approaching the main entrance, we were first met by a plastic horned owl that sat bolted to its perch like a gargoyle. His head had grayed and balded under the merciless glare of the sun.

His shoulders had begun to ripple and become cancerous. His single remaining eye, no longer translucent, gazed warily at Annie and me. His articulated head shook "no" under the influence of the morning breeze. He seemed genuinely upset that things no longer were the way they used to be.

As I opened the divided door for Annie, I could see that he had been failing miserably in his duty to keep the swallows from building their mud nests against the wall.

"We are here to see Tier Three – Alice Sutter, I believe," I said to the receptionist.

"Yes, she is expecting you, second door on the right, room forty-six." She was pleasant and clueless.

"Adam Del Norte has filled me in on your disagreement," were the first words out of Alice's mouth as she extended her hand to shake ours. "You'll have to forgive how cold my hands are. I think I have a vascular condition."

"Reynaud's?" I asked.

"I'm sorry?" she replied quizzically.

"Never mind. I was just guessing."

"Mr. and Mrs. Russell, how can I help you?" She fell into the cushion of her leather chair. Her lips were thin glossy streaks of Fire Engine Red held low on a canvas of meticulous foundation.

Annie and I had agreed ahead of time that she would do the majority of the talking, since according to Annie, I might come across as much more confrontational than I intended. We thought we would catch more flies with honey, so to speak.

Annie began our story, and Ms. Sutter nodded occasionally as she jotted words on her yellow legal pad. Periodically she underlined and circled words with more force than seemed necessary, and I was curious to know what those words were. When Annie got to the spot where Diego Braeburn's testing came into question, I laid out photocopies of the test protocol, the test scoring instructions, and the email Angelo had forwarded to me confirming that the test had been administered incorrectly by the test's own author and its publisher.

"The average Davis student," Alice began her reply, "achieves at a higher level than most." She smiled. "That makes it difficult in this community to assess needs, because our schema of how well our children should be doing is different. Did you know that our high school has a nearly perfect graduation rate, and ninety percent of our students pass their advanced placement tests, earning college credit before they even start? And nearly half of our high school students are taking at least one advanced placement class. Our average SAT score is 250 points above the national average." Satisfied with her sales pitch, she tapped her desk as if the statistics were all held within its confines or she was somehow responsible for these glowing reports.

Taking our silence as license to continue, she did just that. "Too often parents worry that their kid is getting behind, when in fact they would be squarely in the middle in someplace like Woodland or Dixon, or even ahead of the curve. One of the first years I worked as a school psychologist, I tested a child for autism because his mother wanted it done, and even though he had a medical diagnosis, he didn't meet the California requirements for special education. And do you know what happened?" She pinned us with a suspenseful gaze accompanied by a smug smile. "He went on to be accepted to MIT."

"I don't know that you are hearing why we are here," Annie attempted to redirect.

"We do not believe that our daughter was tested fairly," I interjected. "We know Davis is a great school district, but that is not why we are here today."

I couldn't help but be confrontational. I was playing into her hands and knew it, but these feelings were reflexive and innate. I was turning into what they thought we were. We had been shoved into a box, forced into a corner, and I could only see one way out, like a maltreated pit bull that has no recourse but to bite, labeled an animal known to be pure evil before it's even born, case closed. I had sat on Gavin Amador's couch and listened to the lie that we were the reason Daisy was how she was. We would not accept the lies this woman was beginning to spin about our daughter.

Her expression softened to one of fake patronizing empathy. "Arthur. Annie. These tests are diagnostic."

I shot a look at Annie, and she mirrored back her state of disbelief. This Tier Three administrator, whatever that meant, was actually defending what Diego Braeburn had done. In my mind, Alice Sutter's first impression of our situation should have been one of professional embarrassment, quickly followed by a strong desire to rectify a wrong.

"What does that mean?" I blurted. "Do you as a district or an evaluator diagnose conditions?"

"No, Mr. Russell, we are not doctors, we identify disabilities. I know it can be confusing."

"Then what is diagnostic about these tests? These are only screening tests, right? That's what the publishers say they are. Diagnostics versus screening might be semantics to you, but semantics have meanings, no?"

"Let me assure you, the tests we use are the national standards used by schools all over this country." She shuffled some papers on her desk to look important. "These are very good tests."

"Okay, how good?"

"I'm not sure I'm understanding your question." Her face soured.

"You said these tests are very good. I want to know how good, assuming that Mr. Braeburn did his job correctly."

She tilted her head at an exaggerated angle in an attempt to act surprised. "I see no reason to believe he did otherwise."

"Okay..." I looked at Annie in disbelief. "So I've read the statistical manuals for your tests, specifically the one we have placed in front of you, the language test that Mr. Braeburn administered to Magda. Its own authors cite that it is wrong about identifying a disabling condition one out of five times. So for every fifth kid you test, the test results are wrong." I paused to let that sink in. "Not only that, but the test manual says that the test is reliably the same when retesting the same children as low as two thirds of the time, but that's pretty shaky, don't you think – when you only get the same answer two out of three times on a test that is wrong one out of five times? So what we are asking is, isn't it possible that this test was wrong with our daughter?"

"Mr. Russell, that's why we use multiple measures to assess children. According to special education law, no one measure shall be the sole criterion for determining eligibility."

"Okay, what I'm hearing is that you are multiplying fractions, or rather probabilities, right?"

"Yes…." She sounded unsure of her answer.

"Don't fractions get smaller when you multiply them?"

There was no response.

"The product is never greater than the factors."

Again, no response.

I felt frustrated now. "I don't think you understand what you are trying to tell me. Let's say the test Mr. Braeburn gave Magda is wrong every fifth time – assuming that it is administered correctly. What you are trying to say is that if you gave Magda a different test in the same subject, and it too came back as normal, you could be more comfortable with your assessment, right?"

"Yes, exactly!" She nodded in triumph, glad that I finally 'understood'.

"I agree. But explain to me then how testing Magda for a different disability is supposed to support, or not support, the conclusions made by the poor testing choices of Diego Braeburn in this one area of disability testing?"

"Again, these tests are norm referenced."

"What does that even mean? If I test a bucket of fruit for apples, and afterward I lie and say there were no apples, why would a test for oranges show that I was right about the apples? Does that make any sense? And how am I supposed to trust that you are even adequately testing for oranges?" I fumed. "Ms. Sutter, by Diego Braeburn's definition, Magda would be considered a normal subject – part of that normative sample you referenced."

She rearranged herself in her chair.

"So from a test that its own authors say can be wrong twenty percent of the time – a test that was administered incorrectly – and despite the fact that all the prior test results that we gave to the district showed a significant problem, you believe that Mr. Braeburn is correct in his evaluation?" I peered into her face looking for ethics, morals, principles, or anything that would give me hope. "Bottom line – a test that is administered in a manner that deviates from the standard protocol is not a standardized test. It is a different test from which no statistically valid conclusion can be drawn, period!"

"Mr. Russell," her tongue became vinegar, "Diego Braeburn's language analysis supported his standardized testing."

"How so? It was equally poorly conducted. He didn't even reach California's requirement for collecting an utterance sample. It's invalid on its face."

"We believe that Mr. Braeburn's evaluation is defensible and appropriate."

"He only gave her half of the test questions he was supposed to!" Annie interjected. "How is that defensible or even remotely appropriate? What does that even mean?"

"I have an email here from Mr. Braeburn, and he says he has never doubted that his assessment was accurate, complete, or valid. In fact, he says that Magda's score may under represent her true ability." Sutter smiled.

Gravity assaulted my jaw.

"In fact, Mr. Braeburn is our expert in the area for qualification of this age group, and he states that he feels samples as low as twenty-five utterances are appropriate for analysis to determine language abilities. We really do need you to allow us to do more testing." She paused to assess us. "Mr. and Mrs. Russell, we reviewed all of your outside testing, and we are not allowed to use it for determination of special education services. This is why we need more testing here in the schools; we need to test for *all* areas of suspected disability." She pressed her hands against her desk.

I spoke first. "Ms. Sutter, we get that on some level, but what disability do you suspect? We came to you with known disabilities, and Diego Braeburn says they don't exist. More to the point, he thinks that Magda's skills are above average."

"More testing will help to validate or invalidate what you are trying to say, Mr. Russell. Like I said, no one criterion can be used to determine if a child requires special education." She clung to her perch. "There are thirteen eligibility categories to special education, thirteen doors we call them, and we want to make sure that you have access to as many as possible. That is what the law tells us we are obligated to do – it's called Child Find." Alice regained her smile.

"You don't have to find any child," I retorted. "We brought her to you."

Her left eye began to twitch.

"I might not like these tests, but what I have a bigger problem with is the fact that Diego Braeburn is either incompetent or purposefully not giving these tests correctly. I don't understand how you don't see that. Isn't it your job to supervise these people?" I was practically shaking in anger. "If you did something wrong, would you not expect your boss to hold you accountable?"

I shifted in my chair and briefly made eye contact with Annie. She was in the silence of contempt.

"Let's try to look at this one more way. What if a doctor had run a bunch of tests and told you that you had breast cancer, and you even had a biopsy to prove it." Her hands reflexively moved toward her chest. "But you had to change insurances, and you could no longer go to that doctor. You knew you needed a mastectomy. You knew you needed chemo. You knew that waiting for treatment would probably be the worst thing for you. Now, this new doctor won't provide you any treatment until he performs his own tests because he doesn't have to agree with any of the prior testing you've had done, and that's his prerogative. You know, doctors don't like to be told by other doctors what to do. So he orders you a mammogram. Do you know how accurate a mammogram is, a medical diagnostic study?" I emphasized the word diagnostic.

"No," she managed.

"Well, it's wrong one out of every five times – and guess what, your mammogram came back negative, so you don't have cancer, right?"

She sat motionless, her lips parting, attempting to formulate a response.

"But then your doctor wants to run more tests after you complain that the radiologist must be wrong, because he only read half of the images the doctor ordered. Yet when you complain, your new doctor tells you that you need to be screened for all sorts of other cancers, and he wants you to have a colonoscopy and a brain scan. Then you ask, "Will that make the results of your mammogram more or less valid?"

Ms. Sutter sat, studying me, her hands moving about her desk without the assistance of her eyes, searching blindly.

"Is that really true about mammograms?" she asked timidly.

"Do you see my point?"

Ms. Sutter finally found the pen her fingers had been casting about for. "I don't think we need to argue all day about the merits of these tests. This is just the way it is. This is state law. If you don't like it, you can talk to your congressman."

"She's a woman, and I will be reaching out to her," I said.

"If you want another test done, we can offer you an independent educational evaluation, although that test might not be up to your standards either." She scribbled something on her note pad.

"We will make sure it meets national standards and is administered according to the rules," I said flatly.

Ms. Sutter found her smile again. "I'm going to allow you to get an independent evaluation, but I will need to interview the evaluator before I allow it, and your evaluator must be able to attend a four-hour IEP in person. They may not participate by phone, and they have to do an in-class observation. We have rules and requirements for evaluators."

"May we have a copy of those rules?" I asked.

"Yes, I can't find them now, but I will email them to you. However, I do have a list of independent evaluators for you to choose from." She grinned.

"Don't these people work for the schools already?" Annie asked as she reviewed the sheet.

"Oh, I'm not sure…" Sutter sputtered.

"Well, I'm sure," said Annie. "Glenn Burgundy works at Huynh Elementary. He tested one of our friend's children, and doesn't Sonya Stonehouse work here too?"

"I'll have to look into that," Sutter hastened to reply. "Mr. Russell, do you have the day off from work today?" she asked cloyingly.

"Yes.…" I was unsure of where she was headed with this.

"And both kids are at school?" Her voice slowed to the consistency of syrup. "Why don't you enjoy the day? I know how busy life can be with children around. Relax – take your wife out for coffee." Her lips thinned and spread into a wide smile.

"Okay . . . sure." I had no other reply to her abrupt change in demeanor.

We gathered our papers and left.

As we walked past the receptionist and the owl, Annie looked at me. "Breast cancer? Really?"

"Everything we have heard from essentially birth on – Dr. Comice, the County, Children's Therapy Center, all that Yolo First Five paperwork has said how critical it is to get kids like Magda help as early as possible. So yes, I'm as serious as a heart attack, or at least breast cancer today. I don't trust Alice Sutter, but any evaluator worth their weight in salt is going to see how hard language is for Magda." I was already texting a message to Frank and Angelo by the time we were in the parking lot.

* * *

Back at our Pear Street manor, the phone was ringing and Daisy was barking as we walked through the door. The caller ID flashed "Feather Hamlin."

"I'm not answering that," I said, eying it warily. "That one is all you."

Annie rolled her eyes at me.

Just as Annie sat down to talk to Feather, my cell phone rang. It was Frank.

"Hey, I got your text. They can't do that. They can't make your evaluator jump through more hoops than they would for their own. You absolutely can phone into an IEP meeting, and I have never been to a four-hour IEP to discuss an independent eval. It all sounds like crap to me. They are playing games with you."

"Okay, where do we go from here?"

"The problem is, I'm going to have a hard time finding someone that can commit to that amount of time, and is the district going to pay for four hours of an IEP, plus at least two hours of testing, and then another hour or more of observation? You are potentially talking about eight billable hours. This won't be cheap for them."

"I will have to email Ms. Sutter and let you know. She says she has to interview the evaluator anyway," I said.

"Let me call you back. I have a couple contacts at Sac State and one at the MIND Institute that might be able to help. What names did she give you?"

"I think their names were Burgundy and Stonehouse."

"Yeah, don't take that bait – I know them both; even if they don't work directly for the district now, they do contract work for schools all the time. They aren't going to bite the hand that feeds."

Annie and I both hung up simultaneously.

"How is Feather?" I asked.

"The district called CPS on her yesterday."

"What?" My mouth was agape. "Why?"

"Quincy is having another horrible year at school: the principal pulled his aide, he is getting tormented on the playground, he is writing self-deprecating things on his homework, and he is pulling his hair out in class. So instead of helping him, the district called CPS on the Hamlins because they're convinced that he's being abused by Feather and Ash!

Can you believe it?" Annie's hands flew from her sides. "I mean, what would you do if they called CPS on us?"

"Not take it well…"

"Oh, and she hates ADN, and said he was the one who kept Quincy off of an IEP the first couple years he was in school."

"Sounds about right," I said.

"How is Frank?"

"He's working on finding us an evaluator, said it might take some time because of Sutter's constraints."

Daisy let out a series of barks from the confines of her crate when the phone rang again.

"So, can I take you out for a cup of coffee?" I asked with my best smart aleck grin.

Regulation and Adaptation

When the turbulent day is over, she is seasick and immobile. From a listed deck, people move unpredictably. She is constantly bombarded by waves of olfactory assaults and acoustical batteries. She can adapt to the daily changing angle of the sun but cannot accommodate the unpredictability of manmade light's sixty cycles. When her sleep finally comes, there is no lazy drift off. No simple secure mooring exists. For her, wake begins its end with a collision.

Her balance is loosely berthed at the end of never-ending semicircular canals. In her wheelhouse, a sticky throttle and a soft brake. Navigation is at the mercy of the current, the phases of the moon, and the multitude of the unknown. There is no ebb and flow. She is a demagnetized compass in the Bermuda Triangle.

Rudderless.

In a craft resistant to control, she gives few overt impressions of frustration. She bemuses and confuses passersby. Yet she is persistent. Is she consciously fighting sleep? Or is she finally endorsing the need for rest but incapable of reconciling the day's journey?

Perhaps it is my fault. I'm too anchored in my own needs, and constantly capable of, and culpable for, failing her routine. An enigmatic arrangement to her bed exists to which I am ignorant, and of course, she cannot tell me, readdressing that which I thought I had already addressed. It is a layered process with arbitrary rules.

Her hull groans as she's chosen the wrong tack, the wrong tactic.

Awash in insults, she knocks and kicks.

Foundering, she is discordant under the gravity and weight of a starry dark blanket.

With a heaving sigh, she sinks into sleep. Only in that moment I can see that which everybody is overly willing to see: she is normal; she is beautiful. The involuntary control of voluntary muscles has ceased, and there is peace in her paralysis. Her face has softened, the tension is gone, and only the required tidal respiratory movement remains.

Has she sunk deeper into her autism and dreams only in that language? Can she think the way that I wish for her? Or is it in a way that others think she is capable of? There are constant explanations for her nature, and backhanded questions of our nurture.

But I dare not shift my course. The jerk of her leg lets me know that this state of rest is temporary, and so is my control. No matter her dreams, she swims in shallow water, and I do not want to be yet another who rocks the boat. I know she will wake before it is necessary. It is our unified reality. She did not make today's trip alone. Aboard, she carries a manifest of depleted passengers. It is a truth only soothed by the fact that when she does stir, it will be with people who love her.

Thirteen Doors

"A door is what a dog is perpetually on the wrong side of."

– Ogden Nash

The wind whipped the trees and hurled pecans onto our roof in a steady barrage, each one landing like a gunshot above our heads. It sounded like the salvos behind Laurence Olivier's voice as he narrated *The World at War.*

"We are going to have to keep Daisy in most of the day until I can clean those up," I said to Annie, fully aware that she was already awake from the hailstorm of nuts. "Otherwise, she'll gorge herself on raw pecans and shells." I groaned in reluctance to face the day. "I don't want to have to clean that mess up again."

Magda's independent tests were done, and all scores were consistent with the state's qualifying criteria oft cited by everyone we had met at the YUSD. Magda's ability to express and understand language fell well under the seventh percentile, and well below one and a half standard deviations from the mean, the magical Mendoza Line required by the California Code of Regulations. All of this meant that she should qualify for district services. On a second confirmatory test, the percentile rank and standard deviation were unable to be computed because her raw score was a zero, meaning she got no answers correct on that exam. In addition, the language analysis took nearly two hours to obtain, and the utterances analyzed showed markedly poor linguistic skills. All of these findings were a far cry from the glowing report Diego Braeburn had submitted as factual several weeks earlier.

"Do you have that notice from the district saying where we are supposed have the IEP meeting this morning?" I asked Annie as I prepared the coffee maker.

Annie pointed to the envelope pinned to the wall next to Magda's daily calendar and picture exchange system. Today Magda would be going to preschool followed by a trip to Woodland for an occupational therapy appointment, then bath time, dinner, story time, oral hygiene, and finally bed. Inside the envelope was a single sheet entitled "Notice of Meeting" which had been sent along with another pink copy of our rights and safeguards as parents.

"The meeting starts at nine-thirty in the Blue Conference Room of the main office downtown." As I scrolled through the list of attendees, I felt better about the potential outcome of this meeting because it included all of the people required to make a formal decision. In attendance would be a regular education teacher, Barbara Smith; a special education teacher, Cruz Palmer; a specialist, Jonathan Calaveras; the PCE principal, Wayne Costa; and Adam Del Norte, who was listed as an administrator/psychologist. Alice Sutter was to be the Tier Three administrator, and Ben Seckel was listed as our independent evaluator. I was also encouraged that Sutter had left Diego Braeburn off of the list. I thought maybe she had finally realized that his input was meaningless.

Daisy spun and flapped her ears as I engaged the coffee grinder. Magda began to cry, probably because of Daisy's discord.

"It's her tag, Daddy," Charlie reported as he came in the room.

"What?" I said, turning to look.

Magda was sprawled on the living room floor, her face beet red as her arms flailed backward in an attempt to rip the tag from her shirt that was angering the back of her neck.

"Honey," I said reaching to gather her from the floor. "I'm so sorry – we must have forgotten to remove that one. Can we get this shirt off of you?"

She didn't respond, but the wailing ceased, letting me know she had assented.

"I wish you could tell me with your words when something is bothering you," I said, as I pulled the shirt over her head and set it aside

She rolled herself up like a pill bug and resumed her moaning.

I did not realize the full weight of the guilt I levied on her by saying that. It would take a few more years for me to learn that quite often she understood the subtext of what we said to her even though she couldn't express it or respond in a way that mirrored her understanding.

* * *

The north winds of the Sacramento valley painfully and angrily calve far above the rugged landscape of Siskyou County. By the time they rip through the peaks of Shasta and Tehama Counties and breach the flatlands of Yuba and Butte, they are in a full stampede. The north winds of the valley were Mother Nature's unpredictable drunken rage. We often found ourselves bound by these fits of florid mania as she impulsively ripped the calm of Davis away. Today, she was hastily throwing her lover out into the street. Suitcases of leaves and branches were strewn haphazardly across sidewalks and drives, once private delicate matters blown into another's lawn. This morning, she was on a blood lust campaign to end her current tempestuous relationship once and for all.

Ben Seckel, our independent evaluator, met us as we approached the entrance to the old red brick building, and I saw that our friend the owl had recently been decapitated. His now lifeless body held fast to the rusty spring where his head once sat.

"That Alice Sutter is pretty pushy, don't you think?" Ben probed.

"I don't really know her," I said.

"She wanted all the test protocols and reports way before they were even due to the district, and she wanted to know exactly how long I would be at the IEP meeting,"

"How long can you stay?" Annie asked.

"I have a client meeting I need to be at in Woodland by eleven-thirty, so I told Alice I would be leaving around eleven. She made it seem like the meeting wouldn't last much longer than that." He attempted to straighten what the wind had done to his hair and tie.

The wind made it difficult to break the seal on the door to the building, but once we wrangled it open, the receptionist was enthusiastic.

"Yes, Mr. and Mrs. Russell, your meeting is in the Blue room." She led us up a flight of stairs and through a groaning wooden door. When we entered, we saw that everyone listed on the meeting notice was there seated and waiting. They all stopped in mid-conversation as we entered, as if we had interrupted a meeting that we had not been part of or privy to. Their Styrofoam coffee cups were all half to two-thirds empty.

"We will formally introduce you to everyone as we start the meeting," Alice said in her most chipper voice.

Annie and I sat.

The walls were painted baby blue, and the room was spacious with large multi-paned windows, a stark contrast to Mr. Braeburn's window-less cubby. Vertical swaths of safety glass, the kind with embedded chicken wire, reached from counter height to the ceiling. We were guided to sit at a corner of the multiple portable tables that had been arranged in the shape of a square, leaving a dead space in the center of the room. I was thankful that this time the chairs in the room were all adult sized.

"Okay," Alice announced as she placed her small digital audio recorder on table. "Shall we get started?"

The room quieted enough to hear the wind tossing insults at the walls outside. I placed our recorder on the table and tapped record.

"Before I forget, I want to make sure you get a copy of your parental rights." I took the pink packet and slipped it underneath the stack of protocols and reports from Ben Seckel. Alice smiled as she sipped her cold coffee.

"The purpose of today's meeting is to hear the results of an IEE, or independent educational evaluation, regarding Magdalena Russell. But before we get to that, let's start with introductions. I'm Alice Sutter. I'm the Tier Three administrator for YUSD." She turned to ADN to her left.

As the introductions circled the room, I found myself staring at the man sitting directly across from me. He appeared to be in his late fifties. His hair was slicked back to a common point somewhere behind his head pulling his thin face taut against his cranium. I could almost make out the sutures connecting his frontal, parietal, and temporal bones. He didn't look like the typical YUSD employee. His movements were slow and purposeful.

As Barbara Smith, a white-haired woman who introduced herself as "Granny," started to speak, Annie leaned in and whispered in my ear. "She is at PCE. Thank god Charlie never got her; she is sharp with parents and kids. Thinks she is queen bee – doesn't like to be questioned."

I nodded imperceptibly as I studied the man who eventually introduced himself as Jonathan Calaveras. As he spoke, he adjusted his pinstriped tailored suit, and in doing so exposed a circumferential barbwire tattoo just above the crease of his left wrist.

"My name is Jonathan Calaveras from Hire Psych." His voice was slightly nasal. "We at Hire Psych provide a collaborative approach to defining special education needs, which includes an effective communication plan at district and school levels. Since our home base is in California, we are a local company invested in our communities. We have numerous relationships with California school districts to help them make sense of disability law and qualification criteria. We are committed to sharing our cost effective interventions and innovative approaches for servicing handicapped students with the schools we serve."

"What is he selling?" I murmured out of the corner of my mouth. Annie shrugged.

"Great, now that we all know each other," Alice said, "why don't we talk about Magdalena?" She looked at Annie and me and gave us her best camera-ready smile. "Why don't we start with you, Mr. and Mrs. Russell? Why don't you tell us about your daughter's strengths first?"

I fought the urge to roll my eyes. *This bullshit again*, I thought to myself. I deferred to Annie. Everyone in the room took notes as Annie talked. But unlike the last IEP meeting, members of the room asked Annie to provide examples of why we thought Magda was smart, what kinds of things she did to let us know that she was a caring person, and how we knew she loved animals so much. However, just like the last meeting, when it came time to discuss our general concerns for Magda, or specifically, her meltdown that morning, there didn't appear to be any eager concern to take note of what we were saying.

By the time we were done with this exercise, it was five past ten, and Ben Seckel had yet to speak. Finally, it was his turn.

As Ben explained what tests he used and the rationale behind them, he was interrupted frequently and peppered with questions from Alice about where he had obtained the materials and how he had chosen the testing environment. Some questions seemed pointed at me for asking the same questions of the district's testing choices and Braeburn's methods; other questions seemed banal and a waste of time. As Ben described the relative reliability of those tests and how he used multiple measures to ensure accurate results, Alice disrupted his flow with questions that seemed curiously obtuse for someone who not only had the report in front of her, but who'd also had the opportunity to peruse its contents for several weeks.

As the voices and questions bounced around the room, Jonathan Calaveras remained silent and motionless. Occasionally the tip of his tongue would protrude from his mouth as if he was priming his lips to speak. It looked as if it may be a tick or a reflex, but it almost appeared prepared, rehearsed, or practiced. He did it in a way that looked less like he was wetting his lips and more like he was tasting the air. However disconcerting, it was the only physical motion that let me know he was still alive.

His silence and mannerisms made me wary, and only added to the unease I had about the sincerity of the questions being asked of Mr. Seckel. I looked for answers in the faces around the room, and my mind searched for some hint as to what Annie and I were watching unfold during these proceedings. As Alice's line of questioning became more tedious and off the point, my eyes searched for something of interest and settled on the structural aspects of the room.

The room looked like it once was a science classroom, or maybe a chemistry lab. My eyes darting as if I were a laboratory mouse stuck in a maze, I followed the exposed conduit lines connecting junction boxes, duplex outlets, and single pole switches attached to the walls and the faces of the workbench. Where was the exit to this conversation? When would we start making decisions about how we were going to help our daughter in school? There had to be some small reward at the end of this exercise in tedium.

An old Simplex school clock hummed and ticked as the big hand hit twelve and the little hand landed upon eleven. Ben Seckel needed to leave for his next appointment.

"Thank you for your evaluation, Mr. Seckel," Alice said. "Before you leave, I do need to ask, why did you not include Magdalena's actual language sample in the report? You are aware that it is a requirement of the California Code of Regulations, are you not?"

"Ms. Sutter, I'm sorry, but you are incorrect." Ben stood and gathered his papers. "There is no requirement that the actual sample be written out, only that it should be transcribed, or," he emphasized the word or, "recorded, as I did, and those results reported. And that is what I have done. I recorded the language sample on my iPhone and subsequently analyzed that data and reported those results to you." He sounded clearly annoyed with how the meeting had played out.

No longer able to maintain her façade, Alice's face pickled.

Annie and I thanked Ben for coming. The door hissed as the negative pressure in the room made it difficult to open, and as it closed, the safety-glassed windows rattled as if warning that they still had the potential to injure, while the overhead tube lights flickered with the unstable current ripping through the old building.

At that moment, Jonathan Calaveras finally spoke. He had not said a word since introducing himself. "The district has asked me to review and evaluate whether or not Magdalena's testing meets the criteria for special education eligibility. I am an expert in this area. I have reviewed all of your daughter's educational records and prepared a report."

Ms. Sutter then opened her leather briefcase and took out what looked like a ream of paper. She divided the stack and passed copies of his report around the room, the last copy coming to Annie and me. I tried to read it as Mr. Calaveras droned on, but I had difficulty paying attention to two things at once. All I could focus on was the letterhead the report had been printed underneath – a serpentine string of faceless children holding hands like paper dolls, all intertwined around and through the words Hire Psych, 22 West Bonther, San Francisco, CA.

Alice Sutter confidently pushed herself back into her chair and listened to his report with overly rapt attention.

"The first test Mr. Seckel administered, the Reedley Atwater Timed Test or RATT, was published in 1989," Calaveras began. "There are many other newer tests that would be considered appropriate, and the normative sample should really be considered much too old to make this test a valid measure. In fact, there is literature to support that assertion."

I frantically skimmed through the Hire Psych report in front of me, looking for the support he was claiming. I latched on to any details that popped out amidst the sea of run-on sentences and technical jargon. I desperately was looking for something I could grasp onto – and I found dates.

"Wait a minute!" I said.

Alice cleared her throat in an attempt to remind me not to interrupt.

"Don't I get to ask questions?" I glared at her. "Isn't that what this pink packet of papers says we get to do in these meetings?" I lifted the fourth packet we had received in nearly as many weeks. "I'm just now reading your report, Mr. Calaveras. You are asserting that a test published in 1989 is invalid, but you are citing research from 1986, 1984, and even as long ago as 1971 as evidence that the test is outdated." I didn't allow him to answer. "Is it even quality research you are citing? Is it peer reviewed? Is it even relevant to the claims you are making? I see no quotations here, just names and dates." I rapidly flipped to the last page. "And I see no bibliography or reference section."

Calaveras opened his mouth to speak, but I interjected. "The test Diego Braeburn wrongfully administered was first published in 1969. How is that any better? It's twenty years older than the test Mr. Seckel used!"

"We are here to discuss your IEE, not any of the prior testing." Sutter sounded composed and rather sure of herself.

"Yes, but Mr. Calaveras said he reviewed all of Magda's educational records." I said as I searched for a better rebuttal. "What does 'all' imply?"

Jonathan Calaveras broke the silence. "The Seckel report cites very low scores in certain areas of figurative language, expressive language, and even receptive language; despite this, no further exploration was pursued, which is highly recommended. All of these scores should be interpreted with caution."

"What?" I buried my face in my hands.

Calaveras continued to ramble about coefficients of error, interrater reliability, supralinguistic testing, metacognitive competence, how certain tests are not theoretically or developmentally best representative of a disability, and how age bands should be interpreted relative to normal distribution and deviations from the mean.

I looked at Annie; she was in the silence of devastation – shell shock. We both had believed that we were well on our way to getting

Magda some measure of help as we readied her for kindergarten, and we were strongly sensing that was not to be.

"Mr. Seckel routinely references one of Magdalena's known disabling conditions as Sensory Processing Disorder, or SPD. SPD isn't recognized by the American Psychiatric Association, nor is it in the DSM-IV, and it is not clear that it will be in the fifth revision. At this time there is insufficient evidence to support that SPD affects educational competence."

Calaveras flicked his tongue and waited.

"You are not here to help the district determine eligibility," I asserted. "You're here to discredit our testing." The wind renewed its assault on the building and battery of the windows as if to emphasize my point.

Calaveras was unfazed, and continued as if I had said nothing. "In addition, given that no language or utterance transcription was provided, and we are only able to read Mr. Seckel's analysis, it is possible that the sample is invalid or inadequate. No determination of how many utterances were obtained can be made, and as such, there is no way to determine that California criteria has been met."

"But he said he recorded it on his iPhone. His report says in black and white he analyzed an utterance sample. In fact, he says in the body of his report that it took three times as long to get a sample as it did Diego Braeburn! And if this is so important, why didn't you ask him for that data weeks ago, or at the beginning of the meeting?"

I began to feel dizzy.

Again I was ignored. "It should also be noted," Calaveras continued in his monotone, "the confirmatory test that Mr. Seckel administered had a raw score of zero. It is not possible to assign a percentile rank to a zero score. Therefore, it is not possible to say that a zero raw score can be translated into a percentile rank below the seventh percentile required by law."

As Mother Nature continued her battery, the room felt as if it were moving. I was vertiginous and nauseated as she raked branches against the windowpanes.

"You are telling me that failing a test so badly that you score a zero doesn't qualify you as being below the seventh percentile?" I said.

Mr. Calaveras didn't move, nor did he appear to register anything I had just said.

"California Code of Regulations 3030 is clear," he stated, as he began to summarize how he was going to swallow whole the hope that Annie and I had brought to this meeting. "Based on these regulations and the information I have reported within the body of my report, there is insufficient evidence to determine eligibility under the aforementioned law." He reclined back into his suit, aware that he had just poisoned our cause.

The room watched us, waiting for us to die.

Annie finally found her voice. "You never met her or tested her, and you feel comfortable making these statements?" No response. She glanced around at the others. "Is that how this works?" she said softly to the room.

Our whole independent evaluation had been undone. I felt like vomiting and was having trouble seeing. My hands and feet were tingling. My heart raced. I could see that Annie too was feeling faint. We had been bit by a rattlesnake, and were systemically ill. The room was a trap, and Annie and I had stepped into its gaping jaws.

Alice sensed our weakness and attempted placation. "We really wish Mr. Seckel could have stayed longer to discuss his IEE, but since he isn't here, we cannot make any further determination than that of the information placed in front of us." She placed her frigid hands where her three-chambered heart had shrunk three sizes that day. "If you still want to pursue special education, you will have to allow us to do more testing. Mr. Calaveras's team has agreed to do the testing for us. There are thirteen doors to special education, and we need to look behind every door. You have restricted us from pursuing our legal obligation to your child. I can email you the consent for evaluation later today. I believe deep down that Magdalena will get the help that she needs."

We said nothing. We had no response. As we got up to leave, PCE principal Wayne Costa spoke for the first time since his introduction.

"There are lots of times children struggle in kindergarten and ulti-mately go on to become a success in sixth grade. Very often, learning issues are solved simply with time."

I had no energy to scream just how ridiculous that statement felt in this context and in every context I could think of. Without further com-ment, I methodically gathered our papers, the recorder, and Annie.

Annie's knees buckled as I gently poured her into the car. Her jaw was clenched and incapable of speech. Rivers spilled from her eyes onto her cheeks; waterfalls cascaded onto her blouse. She shook with the magnitude of the worst California temblor.

As I closed her door, I spotted Jonathan Calaveras leaving the main exit. He stopped and absorbed the sunlight with his face as he surveyed the surrounding devastation. The wind had died down, and only the remnants of her fury remained. He reached into his pocket and pulled out a pack of cigarettes. As he lit and puffed, he drew cancer past his lips and then blew it out into the world.

By the time we made it home, Annie had finally regained her abil-ity to speak. She reflexively reached for the phone to call her parents. I thought I should do the same. I walked out into the garage with Daisy with my cell phone in hand, but only got my parents' voicemail. I had the same luck with Frank and Angelo.

I sat down on the steps in the garage, the weight of the day prevent-ing me from staying upright. In that moment, Daisy was the calmest I had ever seen. I looked at her, and she looked back. She knew what had happened; she could feel it. My head heavy with a well of tears, I keeled forward to the floor, but before I collapsed, I landed against Daisy. She braced her chest against mine and buried her face into the space between my chin and sternum. The weight of her body pushed back against mine in support. She didn't move, she didn't lick, she didn't flap her ears. She was simply present for me.

Herpetology 101

"Snake with Human Head Found in Arkansas"
— *Weekly World News*, October 24, 2000

A nnie and I didn't eat all that day. Neither of us was hungry. We managed the daily routine for Charlie, picking him up from school, helping him with his homework, and taking him to soccer practice. Annie somehow found the strength to follow Magda's unchangeable routine: therapy in Woodland, snacks, stories, and bath time. But neither of us had the fortitude to answer the phone, do the dishes, or do anything other than takeout for dinner. By the time we both crawled into bed, I was certain I would be out like a light. But I wasn't. The darkness only made the voice in my head louder. In the void, I could hear Annie's thoughts too.

"That's our baby, that's our little girl, and she can't do things that other kids can," Annie said to the ceiling. "Are we making this up? Are we in the wrong?"

"No," I answered.

"How can Alice simultaneously say that she is sure Magda will get the help she needs, and then pull the rug out from under everything?" Annie exhaled a shaky breath.

"I have no idea," I muttered. "It's flatly unfathomable. I don't think we could have done or said anything to change their minds. Even if Ben had stuck around for the entire meeting, nothing would have changed. They had predetermined what was going to happen well before we got there."

Annie and I were up all night, tossing and turning. We went through long periods of silence in which we thought that the other was asleep, only to have the other start a sentence mid thought. We traded off our anger and grief, finishing each other's incomplete thoughts of disgust.

"This whole thing seems wrong," I said.

"That is an understatement," said Annie.

"No, I mean more than just our situation." I tried to hold on to rational thoughts as I fought the hatred brewing within. "I thought laws were supposed to help people who are disabled, right? Not be used as a means of blocking them."

Annie yawned. "I don't know anymore."

I sat up and climbed upon my high horse. "Well, if you're a child, it seems like there is a huge difference – this arbitrary roadblock, this hurdle, this additional obstruction to getting appropriate help. Why does someone have to prove to some ridiculously high standard that they are "exquisitely" disabled? Why can't you take a letter from a licensed clinician that says this person is disabled, and have that be it? The schools, the classrooms, the teachers, and the parents can sort out how to support that child separately and constructively. But to add a step that serves not only as a means to identify, but can equally be used grudgingly as a roadblock – to me that only opens thirteen doors to discrimination, not access. All it takes at the DMV to prove you are disabled is a form from a doctor. There is no bureaucratic asshole making you take a number and wait in line so they can decide if your doctor was wrong or right. There is no behind-the-wheel test you have to take. It just is what it is. You deal with it and move forward."

"Well, it is more basic than that, I think," Annie murmured, as her body finally gave in to the sleep it needed. "You either care about children or you don't. You're either ethical or you're not."

"I need a screwdriver," I said.

"That won't fix anything," Annie said as she exhaled her last conscious breath and inhaled her first of sleep.

I was more awake than I had been all day.

We had no vodka, we had no orange juice, and in fact we had nothing alcoholic in the house.

As I put on a pair of Levis and a hoodie, I could hear Daisy rattling around in her crate and licking herself repetitively. "Stimming" is what Magda's therapists called it. I gently closed our bedroom door so I wouldn't wake Annie as I called in sick to work. A migraine, nausea, and GI distress were the symptoms I gave the graveyard shift clerk. I then grabbed Daisy, her leash, and we both stepped out into the cold black sea of night.

Daisy bounced around me, shooting out in radii as she always did if we were not running, although she didn't jerk me as forcefully as she once had; she was older now, more used to routine. But tonight I didn't care. I was too wrapped in my own head to pay any attention to what was going on around me.

Daisy and I moved in spirals and haphazard diagonal lines, walking with a purpose we had forgotten about. And ultimately, like nocturnal insects, we found ourselves attracted to the unnatural fluorescent lights at the 7-Eleven.

The only person awake in Davis besides Daisy and me was a scruffy faced man in his early twenties with his thick-volumed *Defects Sorting Manual* textbook opened on the countertop at the register. He sat guarding the rolls of scratcher lottery tickets and cheap cigars with a lazy beard poorly hiding his inexperienced skin.

"You can't bring him in here." He pointed his yellow highlighter at Daisy.

"Hey, sorry, she's my guide dog." I cracked a smile and simultaneously chided him for not being aware of Daisy's gender.

"You're gonna get me fired. This whole place is under video surveillance." He kept his writing instrument trained on Daisy.

"Again, I'm sorry – all I want is a bottle of vodka and a bottle of orange juice, then I'll be out of your hair."

"No. It's after two in the morning. Even if you didn't have that dog in here, I can't sell to you." His writing instrument now pointed at the digital clock on the wall. The red colon flashed as it laughed at me. It was fourteen minutes to three.

"Ugh," I groaned. "Come on, Daisy, let's go home." I felt beaten.

I compared the measuring tape marker on the door to what I knew about my height as Daisy and I pushed our way out.

"Rules, rules, rules, laws, laws, laws," I complained as we walked empty-handed across the vacant asphalt parking lot. "There are always rules. I need to look up those rules. There has to be a way to fight this."

We strode home at a brisk clip, my brain trying to work out what to do first. I knew I needed to prove that Calaveras and Sutter had broken some rule; even if it was only ethical, it was wrong. I shook my head at every lawn sign we passed encouraging me to "Keep Davis Schools on Top – Vote YES on Bond ZZ."

"On top of what?" I said to Daisy.

I lifted the lid on the laptop and went straight to Google after opening Daisy's crate for her. The digital clock in the bottom right-hand corner of the screen said it was the hour that blood was at its thickest. I keyed in Hire Psych and hit search. The banner on the website was the same as the letterhead on the submarine that had sunk our hopes less than twenty-four hours ago. As I clicked around their website, I found a profile and a photo of Jonathan Calaveras. The photo was at least ten years old and poorly resembled the hollow man Annie and I had met the previous morning, though it felt like it had only been a few hours ago. His bio suggested that he had a wealth of knowledge about special education laws, and to prove this, it laundry-listed lectures he had given on the subject.

As I nosed around the Hire Psych website, I paused as I noticed the difference between the services directed at private payers and the services directed at school districts. The language used on the private clinical services side of the site was flowery and inclusive – a spare-no-expense view of providing services for disabled children. In stark contrast, in the sections written for potential school districts that sought Hire Psych's consulting services, the verbiage carried much more of a financially conservative tone:

"Implementing a response to intervention (RTI) program can reduce the number of special education referrals and evaluations and prevent inappropriate placement of students in special education. RTI yields large financial savings by preventing over-identification of impairments, reducing long-term costs of educating struggling learners and allowing special education resources to be allocated on the basis of highest need."

It was the same thing Feather Hamlin had warned us about. Hire Psych was profiting from teaching school districts how to shirk their responsibilities to disabled children. I began to feel sick to my stomach again. Calaveras's company was openly marketing a method to keep disabled children from getting the help they needed and to which they were entitled.

I opened a second tab in my browser and searched for free email accounts. After about five attempts, I finally found a site that didn't require a phone number or linked email address to create a new account. With my new alias I drafted an email to the intake coordinator, Luis Rome, for the private services department at Hire Psych.

"Mr. Rome," I typed. "My name is Diane Lassen. My daughter has difficulty learning. She was given a diagnosis of Sensory Processing

Disorder, or SPD. Does your company have any familiarity with treating children with SPD and the effects it has on learning? Thank you, Diane"

"I bet these assholes are willing to make a dollar any way they can," I mumbled as I hit Send.

I then flipped through the report Jonathan Calaveras presented at the meeting, highlighting all of the research citations he included as reasons that, in Magda's circumstances, it supposedly was not possible for her to have educational problems. I opened a Word document and began to cut and paste the research articles' abstracts as I found them. With each citation I could feel my adrenal glands generating vengeance, my hypothalamus brewing fury, and my heart beating a war drum.

As I read the various Google search results, I realized that everything Calaveras had cited held no relevance to Magda. I could find no association with the clinical questions being asked. How did a forty-year-old dissertation about a handful of eight- and eleven-year-olds' ability to write figurative language stories have any relevance to five-year-old Magda's understanding of oral language? How did a dozen Italian nine-year-olds' ability to take a multiple choice test support the assertion that Magda should not be expected to understand certain concepts at her age?

It was becoming clear to me that what Calaveras had done was not a fair and even-handed literature review. This was no broad literature search exploring all sides of the discussion. This was a hatchet job. He was a hired gun, and we were his quarry.

I felt clammy.

I threw the Hire Psych report on the floor and began to parse through the rest of the paperwork Annie and I had come home with. I paused as the first page of the pink Procedural Safeguards caught my eye. "As a parent you have the right to prior written notice and consent." Under that heading, a bullet point gave me a glimmer of hope: "A description of each assessment procedure, test, record, or report used as a basis for the action proposed or refused will be provided to you."

Annie and I received no notice of Calaveras's manufactured record.

The next section was titled Parent Consent. "The school district must have your informed written consent before it can evaluate your child. You will be informed about the evaluations to be used with your child. Your school district must make reasonable efforts to obtain your informed consent."

I opened another tab and searched "special education evaluations." The third link took me to the California Department of Education's special education page: "An evaluation may be defined as the act of determining a child's eligibility for special education. Assessment is a process through which one determines the child's abilities and need for services."

"He evaluated Magdalena," I muttered.

The Safeguards continued: "Consent forms must describe the activity for which consent is sought and list the records (if any) that will be released and to whom."

I looked down at Daisy licking her paws in rhythmic contentment. "No one obtained informed consent from us for any activity or to release any records," I said to her, and she briefly looked in my direction before resuming her routine.

I could smell the rain that had started outside, the sheets of it lashing the kitchen window unusually loud in the early morning silence. Heavy drops assaulted the asphalt shingles, occasionally punctuated by the thud of a falling pecan. To Daisy and me, the war that had begun outside was giving us feelings of impending doom.

I continued my scan of my parental rights, and was now reading about FERPA, the Family Educational Rights and Privacy Act: "The custodian of the records shall limit access to those persons authorized to review the pupil record, which includes the parents of the pupil and school employees who have a legitimate educational interest in the records. Unauthorized access will be denied unless the parent has provided written consent to release the records or the records are released pursuant to a subpoena or court order."

There it was, in black and pink, the biggest rule they had broken, giving Magda's protected information out without our consent. I returned to Google and searched FERPA. "Let's hope there isn't some loophole they're exploiting," I murmured. The search returned about 1,630,000 results in three tenths of a second. I clicked on a link that directed me to a copy of the law posted by a parent advocacy group. The majority of the document read as legalese to me, and it raised more questions than it answered. I was now left with questions like who is a "school official" and what is "legitimate educational interest?" As I scrolled through the document, I saw a hyperlink that redirected to a page discussing the situations when a school doesn't have to seek a parent's consent to release records.

"Here it is!" I announced to Daisy. "A school that allows school officials to obtain access to personally identifiable information contained in education records under this exception must include in its annual notification of FERPA rights a specification of its criteria for determining who constitutes a 'school official' and what constitutes 'legitimate educational interests'."

Daisy sauntered out of her open crate, looked skyward at the noise, and laid herself across my feet with a deep sigh.

I opened another tab on my browser and typed in YUSD, clicked on the link to the school district's home page, and typed in "annual notification of FERPA" into the search window. A link to a PDF file appeared entitled FERPA notice. I hesitated, almost dreading what I was about to read, then clicked.

"Student records are generally confidential. However, federal and state laws say the following people can have full access to student records:

- Parents/guardians of students age 17 or younger
- Parents/guardians of students age 18 or older, if the student is a dependent for tax purposes, and
- Students age 16 or older, or who have completed 10th grade.

For questions about the district's privacy policies and procedures, contact the principal or his/her representative."

There was no indication that Calaveras, or anyone from Hire Psych for that matter, had legal or rightful access to Magda's school records. I returned to the YUSD home page and typed in "Hiring" into the search window. I was directed to the YUSD policy on the hiring of contractors and consultants.

I fought dizziness and fatigue as I read through the YUSD's internal rulebook. It was ten after five in the morning, a time when arterial tension is the highest, and my cardiac conductivity the most vulnerable. With every school board policy and administrative regulation I clicked through, the pain in my chest blossomed.

According to YUSD's own words, only the triumvirate – the three highest district administration officials in Davis, not a lower-tier administrator like Alice Sutter – had the power to hire a consultant without getting the YUSD school board's approval. And at that, the triumvirate could only hire in the case of an emergency. Even beyond that restriction, they could only hire if the YUSD didn't have anyone already on staff who could perform the same function.

I felt light-headed and clammy.

"A consultant contractor shall submit a written conflict of interest statement disclosing financial interests," read the section on the ethical considerations of hiring consultants.

The fist in my chest clenched.

"The Board may reject a contract with any consultant based on its belief that the contract could result in a conflict of interest or in the appearance of impropriety."

My anger transferred itself to my jaw and left arm.

I clicked back to the YUSD home page and stared blankly at the search window. The cursor sat blinking at me in disbelief. I keyed in "Complaints" and was directed to a printable PDF for filing a Uniform Complaint with the school district and a link to the Procedural Safeguards Unit of the California Department of Education. I opened another Word document and began drafting our first grievance.

"Why aren't you at work?" Annie startled me from my focus. I had been typing for two and a half hours straight before I realized that the rain had stopped, the sun had come up, and routine had returned to the rest of the world.

I looked down at Daisy and repeated the question. "Why aren't you up?" She tilted her head at me.

"I called in sick," I said to Annie. "I couldn't sleep. Did you?"

"No, I thought maybe I was keeping you up, and you came out to sleep on the couch." She rubbed her face.

"I've been up reading and writing. You are not going to believe the bullshit I've found."

"We need a lawyer," Annie said.

"That's not the half of it."

Daisy finally moved as the laptop chimed indicating I had a new email from Hire Psych.

"Diane, SPD, we see it a lot. Let us know when you want to schedule an intake evaluation. Sincerely, Luis Rome"

"What is it?" Annie asked.

I looked at her and smiled for the first time in twenty-four hours.

* * *

A murmuration of blackbirds moved against a clean sky in an amoebic dance on the south side of the Yolo causeway, an ever-changing Rorschach inkblot, thousands of dark pixels in a swirling flux, held in a loose and flowing mold by some compelling outside force, like schools of sardines at the Monterey Bay Aquarium. In midflight they vacillated between fear and leadership as they schooled and swam above the shallow reflection of the grass-filled wetlands.

The closest special education attorney we could find was located in Natomas, a suburb of Sacramento, about a twenty-minute drive from Davis. As Annie and I made our way to meet the attorney, I paused my roiling feelings for Diego Braeburn, Jonathan Calaveras, Alice Sutter, and anyone else I could find complicit at YUSD as I admired the natural beauty of the Yolo Basin.

"Ruby Reyes said to look for the big Colonel Sanders on the KFC sign after we get off at the freeway," Annie offered, keeping an eye on landmarks as I drove. "It's near a business park, I think."

The pastoral fields of Yolo County abruptly ended with the industrial boundaries of the city of West Sacramento, and as we crossed the Sacramento River, the large amber waves of grassy flat floodplain transitioned to suburban sprawl.

The Colonel was there waiting with his trademark plastic grin as we pulled off the freeway. We slalomed our way through a maze of big chain restaurants into a small-rent strip mall.

"It is suite ten," Annie said as we pulled into a parking space and surveyed the flat stucco and glass façade for identifying marks.

Suite 10, denoted in small slanted bronze and black adhesive numbers, looked like an afterthought, wedged between a hair salon and On's Junior Market. The horizontal metal blinds, obscuring the floor-to-ceiling front window, blinked and fluttered as we entered the law offices of Oroblanco, Marsh, and Reyes.

"Come in, come in," boomed a short woman heading in our direction, exchanging papers with another woman, presumably her secretary, as she approached. "Follow me, follow me."

Ruby Reyes fell into her plush chair and indicated our chairs with an outstretched arm. "Mr. and Mrs. Russell, I've read your email and all the complaints you've filed, so how would you like to proceed?" Her voice displayed no apparent bitterness about her work, but her tone conveyed a length in career that had helped her build up a thick skin.

I spoke first. "I guess we aren't sure. That is why we're here. We think Magdalena should be in special education, but our school does not. We believe they have done something wrong and don't know what to do about that wrong."

"To say that what they did was wrong is an understatement," Reyes said. "This is probably the worst case of a school district trying to block a child from special education that I have ever seen, and that is saying something. The reality is, and unfortunately for parents like you and your child, it is a common practice for schools to delay and defer providing services." She exhaled heavily. "And in your case, this is particularly egregious. You have a couple or three options the way I see it. We could push forward with filing for due process and bringing this in front of a judge." She leaned forward and rearranged stacks of paper on her desk. "From what I have read, you have multiple grounds for finding the district in breach of state and federal regulations by denying a free and appropriate public education, or FAPE, based on issues ranging from prior written notice to issues of consent and predetermination, and many more, not to mention FERPA." A smile grew across her face.

"But," she paused and drew in a long breath, "there are holes in your case which could leave you open to losing, so you may want to consider whether going full throttle at this point is a wise idea."

"What holes?" Annie asked incredulously. "This is outright wrong what they did."

"No doubt it is, but your district will claim that they could not find your daughter eligible for special education because you did not allow them their federal right to evaluate her in all areas of suspected disability – as preposterous as that may sound." She cleared her throat. "That might be enough of a crack in your case to wipe out the credibility of your claim."

Annie and I sat motionless, stunned to think that they could get away with something so malicious on a technicality. I looked around the room for an answer. All I could find were stacks and stacks of manila file folders and bankers' boxes placed in haphazard organization, the mess of other people's lives. I studied Annie's face for our answer but found her mouth partially open in speechless shock.

"What was the third option?" I asked.

"Oh yes, well, what Hire Psych did was clearly an evaluation." I nodded in agreement. "That report was the sole basis for determining eligibility, so you're damn right that in the eyes of the law, it was an evaluation to determine or deny special education placement. Whether they actually saw Magdalena or even tested her is a moot point." She clapped her hands together with a pop. "That will be a fun question to ask Mr. Calaveras on the stand: 'Just how do you evaluate a child you have never seen?'" Her grin grew.

Ruby continued. "I agree with the assertion you put forward in your complaint to YUSD and the State. For every evaluation they do, you are entitled to an independent evaluation."

I was confused. "So in this one particular area, Magda will potentially be evaluated four times before she is finally found eligible or ineligible?" Annie and I shared a quizzical glance.

"Potentially more if we go to due process and we have to get experts involved," Ruby said calmly. "Consent to whatever evaluations they want to do is my recommendation at this point," she said, stifling a cough. Her hands blindly searched her desk for a cough drop. "Regardless if you think they are worthwhile or not, you don't want to give a judge rationale to think that you are obstructing school district personnel from doing their job." Her fingertips finally found the cough drop on top of a paperback copy of *The Mussel Slough Tragedy*.

"Even with all the facts in your case, you don't want to lend credence to anything the school's attorney is going to say about you. You want all of the judge's sympathy to fall in your favor. And they will throw everything they can at you. I've watched them use how many times a child is tardy, absent, or misses a field trip as rationale for proving that the parents are difficult people to work with. And God forbid you raise your voice in an IEP meeting." She waved her arms in flabbergast. "Listening to those school district attorneys, you would think you were making bomb threats."

"But we have done so much with and for the school since Charlie started kindergarten – he's our firstborn," Annie said. "We've been involved in the PTA, assisted teachers on field trips, organized and run donation drives, and God knows what else."

"I hear you," said Ruby. "Truly, I do. I would continue to pursue your complaints, as those are completely valid, and doing so will possibly force them into doing something without having to go to a due process hearing." She fell back into her chair. "If it is a good something, great. If it is a bad something, then they will have to explain their motives and rationale to your school board trustees, who in most cases don't like hearing that money has been wasted and that school administrators are hiring contractors without school board approval." Her smile returned.

"But I wouldn't put much faith in getting a written positive result to your complaints." She began to crunch the remnants of her lozenge. "It is unlikely the district will admit to any wrongdoing that would make them vulnerable to further action. And the State is useless. They don't have the manpower or the willpower to fully investigate your complaint. More often than not they believe what school districts tell them or just simply agree with the school district's investigation."

I sat with Annie in her silence of disbelief.

"Some people call it a racket, some call it bureaucratic incompetence, and some realize it's a mixture of both," Reyes said, sensing our mounting shock. "In Davis you have the triumvirate, correct?"

"Yes," I managed.

"Reach out to them. Send them an email with a request to meet in person to discuss your complaint." She paused. "And let them know you come in peace. Tell them you are not looking for a long drawn-out process, but rather you want a meaningful and appropriate response to what appear to be significant violations of policy. And let them know you are willing to allow the schools to do whatever testing they deem necessary. Does this sound fair to you?"

"Hardly, but it is what we have to do I suppose," Annie said.

"Good, because unfortunately, when you bring an attorney into things, you will have to continue bringing an attorney into things," her voice graveled. "You can be absolutely positive that they have an attorney working on their behalf, reviewing all of this, strategizing their best defense, and you might be able to avoid having them involved in your case for the remainder of Magdalena's tenure in Davis if you can resolve this amicably."

"I hadn't thought of that," I said, turning to Annie. "I think we were just so upset that we felt we had to do something."

"Yes, of course you did," Reyes said. "That's completely understandable. You did nothing wrong, but what I'm saying is that their level of resistance to you will escalate with how difficult they perceive you to be. So if you have no attorney, they see a small threat. Conversely, if you have an attorney, you will always be a large threat."

"I don't understand," I said. "If we're a threat, why not just do the right thing?"

"That's the million-dollar question." Reyes laughed. "In the cases I have seen, with the clients I have, there is no doubt that it would have been ultimately cheaper for the school district to just do the right thing rather than put up a fight." She shrugged. "Ten years ago I would have said I think it is pride that gets these folks. But in an increasing number of cases now, it is the school district's attorneys who have no interest in seeing things end fairly or justly. The more of a wall they can build between schools and parents, the fatter their wallets become. Even if I win your case, their attorney still wins. Schools have become a market ripe for the picking, and the biggest losers, other than the children who are being discriminated against, obviously, are the taxpayers. The schools are so scared shitless of being sued and of bad press that they end up deferring common sense to their legal consultants."

"I don't know what to say to that," Annie said.

"Look..." Reyes leaned forward and took a more serious tone. "Your complaint is very good, don't get me wrong, but you're missing some elements. It is true that the school has to notify you if they are going to release records, but in order to make a complete claim, you need to see a contract between Hire Psych and YUSD. If there is a contract, it needs to be valid and enforceable, meaning that just because some jackass wrote up a contract with an outside agency doesn't give YUSD carte blanche to do whatever they want with said consultant." Her voice began to rise. "And, to top it off, I find it highly unlikely that Alice Sutter was ever given such high administrative powers by the board that she is allowed to enter into contracts and sign off on them. This means one of two things: either Alice Sutter spent taxpayer money without the consent of the school board, or the triumvirate was aware and agreed to sign off on something they knew was unlawful. If that's the case, you are dealing with the political will of your town's highest administrators, or those administrators don't care what their subordinates do with taxpayer dollars."

Ruby Reyes drew a few deep breaths to calm herself.

"Now, when they fail to do the right thing after Magdalena has undergone whatever tests they think they need to do, give me a call and we will file a formal complaint with the Office of Administrative Hearings." She had returned to a more calm and collected demeanor. "At that point, we will have a strong enough case that the likelihood of recovering your legal fees from the district will be good."

"How does that work?" Annie asked.

"Today's initial consultation is free. If you want me as your attorney, I will need a two thousand dollar retainer, and our office charges two hundred dollars per billable hour, which includes phone calls, emails, and texts. So, if we push forward with the case against the district, we will ask for your attorney's fees as part of the settlement, so ultimately you may not lose much in terms of out-of-pocket costs to you. Just so you are not blindsided, I am very upfront about my costs." Reyes handed me a sample bill for the work that was done in preparation for the meeting with her that day. "Legal representation can be a major expense, and my partners and I are willing to set up payment plans for folks who might not be able to pay straight away."

I was unable to hear the rest of what she said as I reviewed the sample bill. Reyes had spent four hours reviewing the complaints we had filed, reviewing our email correspondences with YUSD, and drafting a complaint to file with the Office of Administrative Hearings in Sacramento. She had also included the one-hour meeting she had anticipated we'd have today. The total: one thousand dollars. Thankfully, below the amount due, the word WAIVED was stamped in large red ink.

"How many mortgage payments do you want to skip?" I said to Annie as we stepped out into the daylight and surveyed the lot for our car.

"Seriously," Annie said as she fumbled for her sunglasses deep in her handbag. "Am I just missing something here? Why does something so obviously wrong require attorneys to fix?"

"Probably because it is so obviously wrong." Taking a lighter tone, I said, "I can't pay for your attorney, but I'll buy you a cup of coffee." I looked for the smile I was beginning to see less frequently.

Annie shook her head and mimicked a grin.

"Look," I said, "why don't we do what Reyes said and write YUSD letting them know we are consenting to whatever the hell they want to do, but at the same time let them know that we would like to meet to figure out some constructive way to move forward. Magda has at least a dozen years of school ahead of her. We can't live through twelve years of animosity and fighting. Maybe the triumvirate, or trinity, or whatever the hell they're called will be sympathetic and not want this kind of BS going on in their schools. Who knows, maybe they're figuring out how to fire Alice Sutter after reading our complaint." I unlocked our car. "And if they blow it again, maybe we'll just find another attorney willing to give us a first-time free consultation."

I smiled.

Annie laughed. "Right."

Consecration of the House

"Once you agree upon the price you and your family must pay for success, it enables you to ignore the minor hurts, the opponent's pressure, and the temporary failures."

— Vince Lombardi

Through the closed door, I could hear the sound of high heels and wingtip shoes tapping in determined lockstep as the trinity made their way to where Annie and I sat waiting. The processional march was brought to full volume as they closed in on us. A woman and a man played off of each other in an indistinguishable conversation like background music.

"What do you think is going to happen?" Annie asked.

I ran the pads of my fingers over the faux wood laminate surface of the conference table at which we had been placed in the Green Conference Room of the YUSD main office.

"I don't know. I don't think we are going to have some kind of knockdown drag-out type of fight. My guess is that they will try to size us up." I shrugged. "See how threatening we are."

Annie nodded. "Probably. Do you think they will take any action against any of the clowns we have been dealing with?"

"Hopefully something, but I guess we'll find out soon enough." I removed one hand from the tabletop and squeezed hers.

The back door to the conference room swung open with the draw of a cello.

The three filed in walking in a straight line. Sierra Gravenstein entered first followed by Jonah Kern then Stan Foxwhelp. All avoided eye contact until they abruptly turned ninety degrees to the table, leaving Kern bookended by his two taller colleagues as they faced us. Uniformly they all stretched out their arms to shake our hands. I'm sure mine felt clammy and nervous. Theirs were all business. As we sat, Mr. Kern pulled out his iPad, made a few swipes and taps, then set it down in front of him with its cover folded like an easel. There was a collective exhale in the room as we completed our pleasantries. The lyrics to a Pink Floyd song ran through my head – "Mother, should I trust the government?"

"Shall we start?" Kern smiled.

The other two remained quiet and motionless, staring at us, studying us, perhaps. I couldn't tell. Their faces were expressionless, dense, unyielding granite. Did we or did we not match the mental image they had created of us by reading our complaint or by listening to Alice Sutter? Or, as Ruby Reyes surmised, were they listening to the advice of their attorneys and approaching us with caution? Were all three here as part of the unnatural dance between good faith and due diligence?

As Annie spoke about why we chose to move to Davis, she pulled together themes of how well Charlie liked school, and elements of our work on the PTA, all while describing where Magda had missed critical milestones along the way. I looked for something in their faces that resembled an empathetic response. I looked for blood flow.

Did this trinity view us simply as whiners? Had we now been lumped into the same category as Feather Hamlin? Were they concerned about the seriousness of our complaint, or just the lengths to which we would go to stand up for our rights?

Jonah Kern was the only member of the triumvirate who engaged Annie in conversation. His rosaceal complexion seemed to migrate as he spoke, and every sentence he uttered in response to Annie's sentiments seemed a simple rephrasing of YUSD's website, the *Enterprise*'s puff pieces about Davis schools, or the political rhetoric used in every campaign to raise school parcel taxes during the last twenty years. All he seemed adept at was recapitulating the theme we had been hearing about the benefit and beneficence of Davis Schools, over and over again, as if they felt compelled to give us a sales pitch instead of a workable solution.

Sierra Gravenstein seemed unmoved by our personal history in Davis. Her face was fixed and her hands were anchored against her lap. She wouldn't look at me, but instead only looked at Annie, who was nervously trying to get as much of our personal story into their minds as she possibly could. She provided the humanistic counterpoint to the dry, rule-oriented, rigid complaints I had written.

Stan Foxwhelp cleared his throat and spoke. "Mrs. Russell, we would really like to hear more about why you have asked to meet us." A small butterfly bandage sat where his jaw met his ear.

Annie was silenced by Mr. Foxwhelp's interruptions. I stared at the white apple with the bite taken out on the back of Kern's iPad and wondered what was displayed on the other side "Sure, I suppose it's best to start at the beginning."

I rephrased and retold the story that Annie and I had been struggling with for the last few months, a story we hoped would conclude with this meeting, or at least produce some sort of resolution. I began with a brief history of Magda, her struggles as a child, the private testing, assessments, and therapy she had been through, and the litany of diagnostic labels she had been given.

Annie followed with a review of the testing done by Diego Brae-burn. We both traded back and forth, in counterpoint, as we delivered the details of how he had misadministered and incorrectly scored the testing, how Alice Sutter had supported these findings, and how she never let us know about Jonathan Calaveras's evaluation.

As we talked, I caught them all at one point or another wince and shift uncomfortably in their chairs, as if their voodoo dolls had just been stabbed. It was impossible to tell if it was fear of reprisal or anger at an employee's incompetence.

"I can assure you both that the reputation of our special education department is sterling," Mr. Kern said after I finished our opening argument.

"Well, we hate to be the ones to point out the tarnish," Annie said.

"What I'm hearing reminds me of, you know," he fumbled to find his words, "those stories about parents who find the physical strength to lift a car off of a child. You know, how do they do that? Such focused strength. They lose track of whatever else is going on around them just to take care of their babies." He laughed. "Inhuman strength."

The others nodded. I could feel my face contort and recoil as I struggled not to retort, *You're damn right we are going to lift that car.*

"I hear many issues," Kern added, his tone deepening. "Ethical issues, moral issues, legal issues. I assure you we will fully investigate this." He counted out the issues on fingers from his left hand with the index finger from his right. "I would like to have you both talk to a special investigator we have hired so we can fully detail your complaint. We have rules and policies which undergird the protection of children with physical or mental disabilities. Our staff is here for the children, period. Everyone here has dedicated themselves to protecting and including kids like your daughter." He paused to draw a deep breath. "And we are utterly committed to the protection of our students' information and privacy."

Stan Foxwhelp interjected. "I understand you do a great deal for the PTA at PCE, and we greatly appreciate your hard work and efforts to support our schools." He smiled and pushed himself back into his seat.

Kern nodded at Stan and took the baton. "We are pleased to hear that you are willing to allow the district to complete its federal obligation to fully explore every aspect of Magdalena's educational needs."

I was caught off balance by the sincerity of Kern's brief declaration because the sentiment was contradictory to everything we had been told about him. I ran my hands over the tabletop once more and said, "We hope you understand our trepidation about allowing greater access to Magda for more testing given what has happened to her educational records thus far. Can you arrange it so that Mr. Calaveras and his Hire Psych team are not doing the evaluations? We don't trust them."

"Yes, I think that can be arranged," he said, "and thank you for letting us investigate these matters. Can you spend about another hour here to talk to our investigator?"

"Sure." I nodded.

Kern tapped and swiped his iPad screen a few times, and then the triumvirate stood and marched out of the room in the same festal procession they arrived.

"Do you think he was recording us with that iPad?" I murmured to Annie.

She stared at me in the silence of missing the point.

"He wasn't taking notes or reading anything."

"Why would he do that?" Annie asked. "What does it matter?

"I'm pretty sure it is illegal to record someone without their consent. That is why we have to declare before those stupid IEP meetings that we intend to record, and they are supposed to do the same."

"Well, if he did, it's not that big of a deal. Let them have a recording of this mess." Annie exhaled. "I actually think they are going to do something about this. They hired a special investigator. They are going to fire Alice Sutter, I would bet anything." She spoke barely loud enough to imagine the thought without jinxing it, and I heard hope and positivity in her voice for the first time in months. "They just can't tell us. They have to go through the proper steps first."

"Well, I didn't hear much from them, at least not anything definitive. Gravenstein didn't say a word. Don't you think that's weird? Foxwhelp seemed annoyed that we complained. Kern didn't outwardly say what Diego or Alice did was wrong."

"It's progress," Annie said, "and I find it hopeful."

"Did you see that the owl was missing from the front of the building?" I smirked.

"What owl?" Annie replied with one eyebrow arched.

* * *

"Mary Ellen Lake!" exclaimed the hurried woman who burst into the conference room, announcing her arrival. Mary Ellen didn't make eye contact; her brain was too busy trying to manage the oversized bag in her left arm and the laptop tucked under her right to operate the portion of her cerebrum reserved for normal social graces. She spilled herself onto the table in front of us, and a yellow pencil rolled across and onto my lap.

I reached across the table to return the instrument, and she quickly shoved her hand forward in an effort to shake mine. "Mary Ellen Lake," she said again, "associate at Meyer, Key, and Lisbon." Her handshake was soft and awkward, the kind where you only grab fingers, not palm. I watched as she similarly grasped Annie's hand before sitting down and opening her computer.

Ms. Lake's fingers attacked her laptop keyboard, her pencil now having come to rest behind her ear. "Okay, so you filed a complaint with the district." Her eyebrows lifted as if she were looking at us inquiringly, yet her gaze remained fixed upon her screen.

"Yes, we did," Annie replied.

"You know, the only way to get a child qualified for special education is through the IEP process," she said. "I cannot get her qualified for you – not even the triumvirate can do that."

"Yes, but we went through the 'IEP process'," my hands made air quotes. "That's why we are here."

"But Mr. Russell, surely you know that federal law requires that process. A district investigation will not change whether Magda is placed on an IEP." Her face rose above her computer.

"Here's what we need to know: was what they did legal? We feel strongly that it was not."

I glanced at Annie for support, and she nodded. I continued. "Who gave Alice Sutter the right to give Magda's records to a private company, and how on earth is it acceptable to use that company as your hatchet man?"

Mary Ellen's head snapped up at the last two words. "All depends on how they define their contract," she said bluntly, her eyes finally meeting mine.

"I haven't seen a contract. Does one exist?"

"You can be assured that I will review that relationship as part of this investigation."

"When will we hear from you about your findings?" Annie asked.

"I am investigating this for the district, not you. I will be sending them my report, and yes, they have authorized me to share my findings with you after they review them, of course." Her eyes scanned the table for her belongings.

"Okay, well you can call us anytime if you have questions," Annie said.

Mary Ellen slammed her laptop shut with more force than was necessary. She plopped her bag on the desk. She jammed some papers and her computer into the bag. She looked at some point tangential to our faces as she shoved forward her soft hand. She collected the remainder of her things, slung her bag on her shoulder, and left.

"Are we done?" I asked Annie.

"I guess so. She seemed to type a lot." Annie's statement sounded more like a question.

"Let's find our way out of here."

Annie smirked. "How about that coffee now?"

Held in Trust

"If you have the feeling that something is wrong,
don't be afraid to speak up."

— Fred Korematsu

The additional tests Alice Sutter and the rest of the administration at YUSD thought Magda needed came fast and furious after our meeting with the triumvirate, and they took nearly a week to complete. None of the evaluators were from Davis. Alice Sutter or Jonah Kern (it wasn't clear who was in charge) had brought in private contractors from well outside of Yolo County to do the majority of the evaluations. Annie and I found this infinitely more infuriating given our recent ordeal and ongoing complaints against Hire Psych.

Annie and Magda spent an afternoon of testing at our kitchen table with a special education teacher from Sacramento Unified. After that,

Magda went through back-to-back days of tests, home assessments, and observations at Carmen Ventura's preschool by a psychologist from Elk Grove and a speech therapist from Fairfield.

Daisy hid from everyone who came into the house. I think Magda wished she could do the same.

Halfway through the testing, I turned to Annie. "Guess we weren't specific enough about not wanting Calaveras. We didn't want anyone private. Why couldn't YUSD do their own testing? How many tax dollars is this costing? Do they not have anyone inside the district that can do any of this testing?"

"It's this or we get Diego Braeburn and ADN," Annie quipped.

"Just shoot me," I cocked my thumb and drew two fingers to my temple.

But arguably the most frustrating part of the entire process was the lack of any feedback. Throughout all of Magda's developmental testing, whether with Yolo County, Children's Therapy Center, or the STAR Center, Annie and I were always kept in the loop. We knew where Magda faltered on tests, where her motor planning evaluations showed where she had room for growth, and with what tasks in her daily life she needed an incredible amount of support. Those people in Magda's life were tangible and familiar. They had become her therapists and in turn friends, then part of our family. In Daisy and Magda's opinion, the people traipsing through our home had no business there, and I couldn't agree more. With people we didn't know, and who likely would never be responsible for treating or educating Magda, we discussed everything from her difficulty with toilet training to how she chews and swallows food. Yet, despite how much we opened ourselves to them, there was no indication from anyone as to what they would say in an IEP meeting or write in their reports. For the evaluators, this was a forensic autopsy. There was no need to report the findings to the patient. That die had been cast.

Annie and I completed mountains of paperwork for YUSD. I rearranged my work schedule so we could both sit through hours of interviews with the evaluators, and unfortunately for Charlie, we displaced or cancelled many of his afternoon play dates with friends.

* * *

My brakes squealed as I pulled in front of our East Davis home. With a ratchet and a groan, I engaged the parking brake and removed the keys from the ignition. I paused and stared at the ring of keys. My right thumb had already begun its subconscious search for the key to the front door. I had no memory of leaving work. I had no memory of the drive home. I had no idea if I used my turn signals. Had I sped home, or was I the slow idiot everyone was trying to get around? My mind was somewhere that my brain wasn't. What would be found, or actually reported, by YUSD during Magda's latest round of testing had pulled me away from living in the moment.

The red door gave way as I went to insert the key into the deadbolt. Annie's face was three shades brighter.

"You're not going to believe this!" she sputtered.

I only had enough strength to sit down and take my shoes off.

"The IEP meeting notice arrived in the mail today, and not just the regular mail – it was registered, and I had to sign for it, but I couldn't answer the door in time because I was dealing with Magda having a meltdown, and your dog was going crazy! So I had to drive all the way down to the post office, wait in some ridiculous line, just so I could find out this."

Annie shoved a folded wad of papers into my chest. I stared blankly at the forms and then at her. She charged down the hallway to our bedroom.

"Look at them – just look! Guess who is coming to our meeting?" She groaned.

"Who?" I said, finally speaking my first word since arriving home.

"Not only is Jonathan goddamn Calaveras coming, but they are also bringing the school district's attorney!"

"Wait, what?" I stumbled for words. "That Lake woman is coming?"

"No, she is the investigator. It's someone named Rangpur." She paused to put on the silver necklace I had given her in grad school. "It says why he is coming to the meeting, and next to his name it has 'Attorney for the District'."

I fumbled through the papers in my hand.

"They have five business days before our IEP meeting to get us the reports from all those evaluations they just did!" Annie shouted from the bedroom. "They have two days left, or they will have broken yet another rule!"

Annie's footfalls were angry and heavy.

"Can you get Magda ready for bed for me please?" I could hear the drawers of Annie's dresser flying open and closed.

"Sure," I said half paying attention.

Magda, in her fleece pajamas, was lying against Daisy in the middle of the living room floor, spooning her. Magda's matching white top and pants were now darkened and mottled with the soot of Daisy's shed fur.

"I'm supposed to be meeting Feather and Mercy for a drink downtown tonight," Annie said walking into the living room. "I just don't remember where they wanted to meet," she said trying to find the hole in her earlobe. "I need to check my email. Where did you leave the laptop?"

"I don't know, kitchen maybe. I haven't been home," I muttered.

"Quack quack, bing! Good dog!" Magda softly patted Daisy's head as if ringing for a bellhop. Daisy lay motionless, her eyes closed, her lips drawn up slightly as if smiling and enjoying Magda's attention. "Quack quack, bing! Good dog!" This time Magda tapped the side of Daisy's rib cage with a dull thud. Daisy extended all four limbs in a stretch with a long slow exhale, and then she went limp again. "Quack quack, bing! Good dog!" Magda squealed as she rang the side of Daisy's pelvis.

"Arthur, you're not going to believe this," Annie said as I gazed at the two on the floor.

Magda slid back and away from Daisy in an effort to get up off of the floor. As she did, Daisy rolled over and stared directly into Magda's face. She pushed her paws toward Magda's chest. Magda took both paws in her hands and smiled. Neither one moved. In each other, they had found their inner calm and the emotional peace that was so elusive on their own.

"You are not going to believe this," Annie repeated, knowing that she had lost my attention. "Do you read all of those school board meeting agendas through the PTA listserve?" She stepped between Magda and me.

"I just delete them."

"Well, guess who is on the agenda for tomorrow's school board meeting?" Annie's mouth drew taut.

"Who?"

"Goddamn Hire Psych!"

"What? How?"

"I don't know. I don't get it – here, look at this." She pressed the laptop into my hands. "I have to go. I'm late as it is. Feather is going to explode when she hears this." With that, Annie was out the front door.

I stared at the screen in the silence of feeling duped.

Charlie tugged on my sleeve. "Daddy, it's time for a story."

"I'm sorry, bud, I didn't realize..." I searched for a smile to give to him. "Go pick one out and I'll be there in a second. I have to read to your sister too."

Charlie complied. I scanned the sea of black type with an occasional blue hyperlink on the otherwise all-white webpage. The school board agenda looked formal and logical, yet at the same time it was all without reason.

I read to both Charlie and Magda before putting them down for bed. I had no clue what stories I actually read, or if what I was saying out loud even made sense. It must have, as both kids would have complained if I had even paused in the wrong place or exchanged a single word. As my attention was increasingly consumed by YUSD, the activity that I typically enjoyed as a nighttime ritual with my children was becoming just an automatic task, like getting dressed in the morning or shaving. I felt disgusted with myself for giving Charlie and Magda less of myself than they deserved. I poked my head into each of their rooms to apologize, but they were both fast asleep.

All I could think as I flipped through the registered mail in front of me was why. If the issues at hand were ethical, moral, and legal, as Jonah Kern stated, why would Hire Psych be on the YUSD school board's list of contractors to approve? Why was Jonathan Calaveras listed as coming to Magda's IEP again when he had never met her or tested her? And why would YUSD find it necessary to bring an attorney to our meeting? Were they trying to intimidate us? Was this a show of force? Was this the person that Ruby Reyes said they had been using all along?

I opened another tab on the browser and searched the phrase "attorneys at IEP meetings." The first search result with a PDF file attached was a link to a letter from the Director of the Office of Special Education Programs to Senator Hillary Clinton. It was a response to a constituent's complaint filed in New York about the school district inappropriately bringing attorneys to IEP meetings. The response was clear:

"The presence of an attorney could contribute to a potentially adversarial atmosphere at the meeting. The same is true with regard to the presence of an attorney accompanying the parents at the IEP meeting. Even if the attorney possessed knowledge or special expertise regarding the child (§ 300.344(a)(6)), an attorney's presence would have the potential for creating an adversarial atmosphere that would not necessarily be in the best interests of the child. Therefore, the attendance of attorneys at IEP meetings should be strongly discouraged."

I opened yet another browser tab and began to draft a terse letter to Jonah Kern, cutting and pasting portions of the linked letter to Clinton into my email.

I saved the email as a draft and returned to the YUSD webpage labeled Board of Trustees. I scrolled through the board's proposed agenda for the meeting tomorrow night. The Call to Order was to be held at seven followed by the trustee roll call, a patriotic observance, the approval of the agenda, a special recognition of an art teacher from the

Seven Mills Charter Academy, and then finally the approval of contracts and personnel. The first contract to be approved was Hire Psych. Hire Psych was hyperlinked in blue, so I clicked on the name that for Annie and me had become synonymous with evil.

A separate page appeared and another link entitled Rationale was underlined and hyperlinked. I clicked.

"The Ratification of the Limited Contract Between Hire Psych and the Yolano Union School District. Reviewed and uploaded by S. Gravenstein." Daisy rattled in her crate as I subconsciously held my breath. "The Requested Action is Contract Ratification." I kept reading. "Rationale: The YUSD currently does not employ enough therapists to meet the needs mandated in IEPs. YUSD currently contracts with the non-public agency Hire Psych to provide therapy services."

I gasped. "Bullshit!"

I scrolled down. "Financial Impact to the YUSD: $3000."

"What therapy? What IEP? She isn't even on an IEP! How can you provide therapy to a child you have never seen?" Daisy shook violently.

Charlie's door opened. "Daddy, are you okay?"

"Yes, sorry, buddy, I just read something on the computer and it got me very excited." I tried to compose myself. "Everything is fine. I'll put you back to bed. I'm sorry I woke you."

The concern was written across his face as I tucked him in and apologized for how distracted Annie and I been lately.

On my way back to the laptop, I stopped in the kitchen, poured a cold cup of coffee, and put it in the microwave.

Below the financial impact section was another link titled Contract. I clicked.

"This document serves as the Master Contract between the YUSD and the non-public agency known as Hire Psych."

My head pounded and my heart raced as I read through four pages of what sounded like legal mumbo jumbo to me: terms and limits of the contract, the defining of Hire Psych as a contractor, not a YUSD employee; the non-assignability to a subcontractor; and payments pursuant to an audit (if warranted). I searched for something I could understand, something that would promise some relief from the quicksand that Annie and I were sinking into.

And, as with Calaveras's report, the only things I could tangibly understand were numbers. The rate that Jonathan Calaveras and his company would charge was $85 per billable hour, which was especially troubling considering that Alice Sutter had wanted him to start on the day we originally met in her office to discuss our concerns about Diego Braeburn and to request our own independent evaluation. Sutter's obnoxious signature sat there staring at me, laughing the last laugh. This was all the proof I needed that Alice didn't want to hear about problem employees or test accuracy. She wanted her way, not ours. This was her program, not Magda's.

The owner of Hire Psych, Scarlet Snow, signed the contract the same day our independent evaluator, Ben Seckel, submitted his report to Alice Sutter, the same report that said Magda had met the qualifications for special education.

"Sutter had this all set up the first day Annie and I met with her, the same day she told us to relax and go get a cup of coffee." I seethed under my breath. "No wonder she wanted Ben's reports early. She wanted Hire Psych to have ample time to destroy them – and as soon as Ben's report came back favorably for us, Hire Psych agreed to be Sutter's hatchet man. Disgusting!"

My heart sank and my ribs felt as if they were collapsing inward. I had no words. I could only tremble. I scrolled all the way to the bottom of the scanned contract, looking for a real answer. All I found was Sierra Gravenstein's signature under the word "Approved" signed a few days after our meeting with the triumvirate to discuss our complaint.

My coffee had again turned cold and was burning a hole in my stomach, but that was nothing compared to the acid of this bureaucratic vicious cycle consuming me from the inside.

* * *

The YUSD school board's monthly public meetings were held in the chemistry lecture hall at UC Davis. Every undergraduate at Davis was familiar with Chem 194, as it was called. From any one of its four hundred and sixteen seats, new adults attended lectures on more than just chemistry. Economics, nutrition, physiology, and human sexuality were all taught from the movie-theater style classroom.

The room had weeded out generations of would be chemists, geneticists, doctors, and accountants by lopping them off of the back half of the bell curve. Before I met Annie, I had seen her between classes on the concrete steps leading up to the main entrance of Chem 194. We passed each other three times a week between Organic Chemistry and Human Development. Our glances became smiles. Our smiles eventually became hellos. Our hellos became brief conversations and questions about mutual friends and activities. It was a series of encounters that ultimately led to the events unfolding in front of me tonight. I smiled in reflex as I stepped on the crack in the concrete stair that I had repeatedly stared at in nervous distraction during my first conversations with Annie.

In that space, in the jagged gap of the monolith, I knew I was walking into this room with a purpose shaped by the desire to right a wrong, the desire to protect, and the anger of being taken advantage of. I walked in with the confidence that this was the room where the rules mattered and accountability meant something. In this room, deviation from the standard meant you were out on your ass. This, I was sure, was the room where the progressive pressure of the public influenced the building of strong schools for the children of Davis.

I passed under the globular lights of the foyer and in through the doors that opened to the top of the hall. As a student, I always sat in the cheap seats, far in the back. It was less crowded in the back. I learned my chemistry next to the people who were more interested in completing the crossword in the campus paper or shading in Willow Cook's simply drawn comic strips about undergraduate life. They didn't judge me.

But tonight, I got as close as I could to the front of the lecture hall. The seats were familiar but the view was vastly different. The front two rows had been reserved for district administrators and officials. I sat down directly behind the seats reserved for Jonah Kern, Sierra Gravenstein, and Stan Foxwhelp. As I waited for the meeting to start, I read and reread a statement I had prepared on 3 x 5 cards to deliver during the public statement portion of the meeting. "Waste of public funds, unlawful release of records, unapproved use of contractors, disabled child," I muttered, shuffling through my cards, occasionally glancing up at the oversized periodic table of elements on the wall. My brain searched for ways to change sentences and phrases into convincing rhetoric rather than complaints and ramblings.

At seven on the dot, the triumvirate walked in the side entrance to the hall followed by the YUSD board of trustees. Jonah Kern whispered to Sierra Gravenstein as he made eye contact with me. Looking all too obvious, she glanced in my direction. I stared back.

The president of the school board pounded her gavel on the long portable table that had been brought to the front of the room.

"Call to order," Mrs. Bixby proclaimed.

I had seen the names of the board members on street signs and voting ballots – Ryerson, Malcom, Regan, Freeborn, and Wellman – but had never imagined that one day I would be calling upon their stewardship.

The YUSD trustees stood abruptly and turned to face the flag standing by the side entrance. I too stood for the Pledge of Allegiance and recited the lines by rote except for the last line, to which I proudly belted "with liberty and justice for all" in the general direction of the triumvirate. We all took our seats.

The meeting was monotonous and procedural. Robert's parliamentary Rules of Order prevailed.

After the agenda had been approved, the previous meeting minutes briefly discussed and approved, and ultimately the consent calendar approved, Bixby again spoke. "We now will have a recognition of long-time art teacher Mrs. Rosemarie Monache by Mr. Jonah Kern." She gestured to Mr. Kern. He stood, gave me a very pointed side-glance, and strode to the podium with the confidence of a man who thinks he's won the battle before it has begun.

"Thank you, President Bixby, as well as the other distinguished members of the Board. It is truly a pleasure to be able to bestow upon Mrs. Monache this high praise." He motioned her to the dais.

The petite woman's reading glasses chained around her neck bounced against her sweater as she walked with a deliberate and careful step, as if tiptoeing along a fault in the floor.

"Mrs. Monache exudes and embodies that which we hold dear in this community, our dedication and commitment to children." His voice echoed around the room. Kern put his left arm around Mrs. Monache's shoulders and displayed her to the audience. "In her nearly forty years of service, she has fought tirelessly to get school bond measures passed. She has labored over the kilns at just about every elementary school in town, and she has reached out to every student she possibly could, no matter their station in life, and has said, 'Come on, you can do this. I believe in you.'"

I began to thumb feverishly through my notecards as Kern continued his praise. I was rewriting in my mind what I should say in light of the mood and recognition happening before me. I considered leaving. Should I have just emailed the board members? Was this going to blow up in my face? I, the asshole who pooped in the punch bowl, was going to forever ruin the close to Mrs. Monache's vaunted career.

Kern turned back to the Board. "How much more beautified are our campuses now because of her work? How many children have been enriched by the exposure to the arts she has provided? And how saddened are we that such a jewel has considered retirement? She should be a model for us all." He turned and stared directly at me. "With an entire platoon of your former and current students present, we here at Yolano Union School District would like to say thank you for everything you do and have always done."

The room erupted in applause and stayed in such a state for what felt like ten minutes as Mrs. Monache was handed a plaque embellished with a chrome apple, after which she embraced every trustee and was mobbed by many in the crowd.

"Okay, okay," said Mrs. Bixby, smiling and waiting as everyone settled into their seats and the room was quiet again. "That was wonderful and truly representative of what we strive for here in Davis. It reminds us that even we here on the Board should be as thoughtful and deliberate as Rosemarie." Bixby's hands opened to those around her. "We are all here because of our dedication to children, and I think that is something to be applauded."

A mild aftershock of applause rippled through the room.

"Now, back to business. First item is Public Comment. Do we have any public comment tonight?" Bixby looked to the crowd. "For those of you who wish to speak, I will remind you that you are limited to two minutes each." She clicked her pen twice. "Thank you."

I stood and walked to the podium hoping my stride looked deliberate and purposeful. The PA system groaned as I adjusted the height of the microphone.

"Name, please," Bixby politely requested.

"Hello, Mrs. President, members of the Board. My name is Arthur Russell." I shuffled my cards. "I'm sorry to have to change the mood in the room. My son Charlie goes to PCE. Before she transferred to Seven Mills, Mrs. Monache taught him how to make his own rubber stamps." I hoped that was enough to establish a connection with the six faces staring intently at me.

"Yes, she's a wonderful teacher . . . and what brings you here tonight?"

As Bixby stared at me and waited, I realized I had already burned through 45 seconds of my two-minute time allotment.

I could feel the tension and burden of proof in the room. All eyes focused on me. Someone dropped a pen somewhere in the auditorium. It clattered to its resting place.

"Board Policy 19-84 states clearly that an employee or administrator cannot hire anyone without the Board's approval unless an emergency condition warrants. I have been trying for months to get my disabled daughter special education services." My voice began to shake. "These administrators are asking you to validate an unlawful contract with an agency under investigation by the California Department of Education."

Six sets of eyes were burning a hole into my head.

I continued my poorly prepared statement. With every word, every sentence, I was Charlie Brown's teacher. I was yet another Davis parent trumpeting crazy. Unintelligible noise, the rotor wash of yet another helicopter parent incapable of seeing the big picture, only concerned about their own child. I searched the dais for a sympathetic ear, but I found none. There were no faces of concern, only mounting disgust that I had brought such a thorny issue to them in public. The podium rang and flashed at me. My two minutes had expired.

"As you know," Bixby began, "during public comment we are under no obligation to engage or answer the public."

I scowled, folded my notecards, and strode back to my seat. The whole the auditorium watched as I edged my way down the aisle to my seat. The triumvirate stared intently at the dais for a response.

Kern rose from his seat. "Mrs. President, this contract is valid, and we have an obligation to pay our invoices."

"Yes," Gravenstein added, "our contractors will be expecting payment."

"Is there a motion to approve?" Bixby asked.

"Can I talk to you?" Kern murmured, turning to me.

"Why not?" I muttered.

He gestured toward the side exit of the room. I stood and followed.

"So moved," said Ryerson.

"Second," mumbled Wellman.

"All in favor," I could hear from the front of the room just as the closing metal door echoed across every angle of the concrete stairwell.

Kern paced ahead of me then turned on his heel and launched in, his face beet red. "This is not the appropriate place to discuss this matter."

"How's that? This is my public forum, not yours." My voice no longer conveyed uncertainty as to whether I belonged at this meeting. "Why are you doing this? How is this appropriate? Why not wait until we have the results of the investigation before taking this before the board?" I gave him no chance to answer between questions. "Unless you already know the outcome of the investigation."

Kern stood still and speechless.

"And you are bringing an attorney to my daughter's meeting? I want to know why!"

"District staff does not believe that bringing an attorney to an IEP meeting is inappropriate, given the pending current complaints," he said, punctuating his proclamation with an annoying sniff of superiority. "Our staff and I remain hopeful the IEP team will come to agreement regarding your daughter's needs at her upcoming meeting and be able to move forward together in her best interests."

"Is everything okay in here?" Stan Foxwhelp said as he opened the side door, the din of the adjacent room spilling into the stairwell.

"Oh, yes, we're fine, Stan," said Kern.

"I'm not," I said at full volume.

I looked up the empty set of concrete stairs and fought the compulsion to run away from this madness, but something visceral made me stand my ground, something reflexive that said this was wrong. I knew it – and so did they.

"Suppose you asked the School Board to approve another janitor position for PCE," I challenged, locking eyes with Kern, "and they said sure, but instead of having that person clean PCE, you had them personally clean your office, maybe even your home – that would be fraud. Do you agree?"

I got no response, so I pressed on.

"This," I gestured toward Kern and the dais on the other side of the door, "is fraud."

Kern stood blankly unmoving. I had no idea if it was fraud or not, but I knew a fraud was standing in front of me.

"I need to get home to my family." I turned, clambered up the side stairwell, burst out the door, and stormed into the night.

I threw my notecards onto the passenger seat and turned over the ignition as my head fell into the steering wheel, through the steering column, and into the center of the earth.

The Foo Fighters screamed at me all the way home, repeatedly asking if someone was getting the best of me. I was sure their song was about a girl, but mine was too.

* * *

The next day, the postman knocked at the door with two pieces of registered mail. The first package, thin and flimsy, was from the Law Offices of Meyer, Key, and Lisbon. The second, fat with excessive postage, was from the YUSD main office.

Annie and I sat down at the kitchen table, she opened the package from the school district with a steak knife. I opened the finding of the district's investigation with my index finger. I flipped to the last page.

"With respect to the ten allegations set forth by the parents, this investigation found no evidence of fault on the part of YUSD. In summary, the broad allegations of FERPA violations and failure to consider an IEE are without basis. More to the point, Alice Sutter did seek to consider the IEE fully through the evaluation of the IEE by the independent contractor Jonathan Calaveras. This investigator resolved the issues by analyzing 34 CFR 99.31, which under this interpretation allows Alice Sutter to release the record of Magdalena Russell, which was authored by Ben Seckel, to Jonathan Calaveras. Further, the allegations of denial of FAPE fall under the purview of the Office of Administrative Hearings (OAH), and as such, if the parents wish to pursue this allegation, should be adjudicated in that venue. Of note, this complaint was also filed with the California Department of Education (CDE), and they will investigate further. This concludes this uniform complaint investigation. The following actions will be taken by the YUSD as a result of this investigation:

Action #1: The district will amend its annual notification to parents to comply with the provisions of FERPA.

Action #3: Once Jonathan Calaveras's involvement with Magdalena Russell has completed at the conclusion of the next scheduled IEP meeting, the YUSD will request that Mr. Calaveras return the educational records to the YUSD Special Education Department."

"What happened to action number two," I moaned. "This is horseshit." I flopped the investigation in front of Annie. "Of course, the attorney that they hired didn't find any fault in their course of action, or should I say inaction." I cupped the back of my head with my palms.

"You mean the attorney the taxpayers paid for," Annie said as she moved stacks of papers around the table.

"And how the hell are they in compliance with giving away private records if their FERPA notice, by their own admission, isn't in compliance?" I palpated my scalp for the source of my new headache. "And what do they mean they will ask for the records back? Why do they have to ask? Aren't the records under their control? Isn't that what FERPA says? Records are supposed to be under their control!"

Annie sat silently, not responding, flipping through pages.

"What have you got over there?" I asked.

She didn't respond.

"Can I look at those too?" I probed again.

Annie paused, then pushed the base of her palm into the depression between the bridge of her nose and her forehead. "There are no conclusions or recommendations in any of these reports. And guess who else just wrote a second report on a child they have never met?"

"You have got to be kidding me," I said.

"Yep, everyone's favorite hired gun, Jonathan Calaveras," she added with an eye roll.

"I have no words. This meeting is going to be ridiculous. What do we do? We can't afford a lawyer."

"Clearly they can," Annie said flatly.

"Fine, let's go through with the meeting first, and then when she doesn't qualify, we go back to Reyes. That's what she said, right, come back after they fail to qualify her." I seethed.

"Fine," Annie said throwing her stack of papers in front of me, her hands trembling, her voice failing. "I need to get to the grocery store. Do you want anything?"

"Yes, but you aren't going to find it there," I muttered. I got another eye roll, but this time it was followed by a grin.

Compromising Positions

"You come here to tell us lies, but we don't want to hear them."

— Sitting Bull

As we made our way into the district offices, I pointed out to Annie that the brick edifice was stained with bird droppings in the absence of the old owl.

"We are in the Red room today," I announced to the receptionist.

She gave me a tight, nervous smile.

The attendants were packed tightly in a room that looked as if it had been renovated in the early nineties with its padded teal chairs and molded gray armrests. The cloth-paneled walls that covered the original concrete and brick structure deadened the conversations that appeared as if they had been going on for hours before our arrival. Consistent with everything I was learning about YUSD, the "Red room" was a misnomer. Annie and I sat and took out our note pads as well as the stack of assessments we had been mailed. I locked fingers with Annie under the table and we waited.

No one talked to us. No one looked at us. We sat there quietly surveying the scene, waiting but knowing better than to expect a pleasantry, a knowing nod, or a half smile. We were the troublemakers with whom no one wanted to associate. We were the ones trying to destroy what they had worked so hard to build.

"Hi, you two," Carmen Ventura said, pulling out the seat next to Annie.

"You came!" Annie cheered. "Thank you so much." Annie stood and they hugged.

"I'm not leaving here until they get your daughter what she needs." Carmen smiled. "I have taught a lot of these people's kids." She glanced around the room. "They should know better."

At exactly nine, Alice Sutter strutted into the room shoulder to shoulder with Mr. Rangpur, the school district's attorney. They smiled and whispered with one another as they pointed out various aspects of the stacks of papers in their hands. They were followed soon thereafter by Jonathan Calaveras.

"Okay, let's start, shall we?" Alice sharply cut through the room.

Jonathan Calaveras sat down on at the far edge of the hypotenuse from Alice. It was the longest distance from any one person to another in the room, an attempt at the illusion of separation and unfamiliarity.

As everyone introduced themselves, I sketched a map of the room and where everyone was sitting. I noted the exits first, just in case the building caught on fire. Six portable tables linked end to end or side to end created an abyss in the center of the room. The area was perfect for a media pit as if this were some form of government hearing or confirmation. Yet there were no photographers, and no video cameras. There was nothing to record this scene aside from the audio recorders now sitting in front of Mr. Rangpur and me.

The attorney for the YUSD, in his oversized tie and navy pinstriped suit, initiated the reading of reports. Everyone in the room took turns monotonously regurgitating the tests they had used, the reasons the tests were valid measurements, and how Magda fell within the normal ranges for all the areas in which we the parents had concerns.

As the readings went on, I could feel Annie becoming angrier as I became more disconnected. I was only pulled back into the reality of the moment when Annie squeezed my hand every time someone assigned an emotional state to how Magda had performed.

"Magda happily participated in my administration of the Weinberg 7th Edition." Annie crushed my palm. "Magda was eagerly engaged in the 3MTA3 exam." Annie ripped my thumb forward. "Magdalena loved playing the logic games on the PAC-2." Annie attempted to flatten my wedding band.

"They don't know how she was feeling," Annie scrawled across the top of my note pad.

"Annie happily participated in this meeting!" I scribbled below it, and I could hear her suppress a snort of derisive laughter, the kind that escapes you when you're supposed to be silent and you don't want to be.

With every report that was read, my gaze was another mile away. I wanted to be free of this circus. I just wanted to be a parent, a husband, and a friend again.

I imagined my life as I wanted it. I was running with Daisy in the farmers' fields. I was catching crawdads with Annie, Charlie, and Magda in the frigid waters of Lake Tahoe under a blistering summer sun.

Life in motion was comforting. But this moment was an exemplar of a life frozen in an abstract world of make believe, a world I wanted nothing to do with. Everything that was put forth as true here was actually false, paid for by COD.

I expected this outcome. My game plan didn't include any tactics for today's meeting. I was weeks and months ahead of where we were in this moment. I had already made copies of all of the reports for Mrs. Reyes. I knew that the next time I would be opening my mouth in front of Alice Sutter, Jonathan Calaveras, or any other member of the charade with which we now shared a table, it would be in front of a judge.

Jonathan Calaveras broke my meditation when he cleared his throat to read the results of his second report on the child named Magda that he had never met. "According to Schaff, et al., current scientific literature in the area of language and neurodevelopmental disorders shows a definite causal relationship between deranged sensory processing skills and the ability to effectively communicate." He read without looking up from his paper.

Annie let go of my hand and opened her mouth. She was unable to speak.

I snapped back into where I was. I leaned into Annie's ear. "I bet that must have tasted like vinegar. Why the change of heart?"

Calaveras had reached his summary. "If it is the recommendation of this meeting that Magdalena Russell be placed on an IEP, I believe that she should receive speech therapy once a week to address this issue." He slid back into his seat.

The room sat still in its own silence. I could hear the traffic outside. I could hear Daisy at home flapping in her crate. I could hear liability being mitigated, and I could hear fiction becoming fact.

"Well, I think it's a good segue into the district's readiness to make an offer of FAPE," Alice said. "Based on all of our testing and parent input, we have determined that Magdalena should be qualified under the heading of Speech Language Impairment, or SLI."

Alice then dropped her papers onto the table and tilted her head downward so her eyes could peer at us above her reading glasses. "We know how concerned you are about her scores in the area of speech. We have determined that Magdalena should receive twenty minutes of speech therapy once a week, and we know she gets occupational therapy at home, so until we can transition her into school, she will get some occupational therapy consultation time each week.

"What does that mean?" Annie said. "Consultation?"

"Consultation is time during which the therapist works with the teacher to best support the learner."

"So they won't be working directly with Magda?" I pressed.

"What about an aide? It's clear she cannot ask for help or initiate any sort of normal conversation. All we've heard from you is your opinions about how adept she is at creating workarounds for what she struggles with, yet none of you have given us any concrete examples of how that is true. No one here has addressed how you are going to support the concerns we have raised individually with each and every one of you. How is she supposed to even access what is being taught in the class-room?" Annie was so upset that she was shaking at this point.

"Mrs. Russell, what you need to understand here is that Davis is a different animal altogether. You know, you can't compare Magdalena to all the other kids in Davis, because Davis is so far ahead of the curve. If you lived in Woodland or even Dixon, Magdalena would be solidly in the middle of the pack. Davis kids are just different."

"I'm sorry, what?" I said.

"Nowhere else in California are parents so very involved in their children's schooling. It has such a drastic effect on their perception of what is just and right or what the child actually needs," she said.

"Imagine if there was something wrong with your child and no one believed you," I countered.

There was no response from the room.

"What are parents supposed to do when someone else has already made their minds up about what is best for a child they have never met? Seems to me it's part of any parent's DNA to speak up for their kid whether they live in Woodland or Chowchilla." I placed my hand over Annie's.

"You must do the right thing here." Carmen spoke slowly and delib-erately. "I have taught this child for two years now, and without a doubt she will not be able to survive in a general education classroom without significant assistance. It would just plainly be unsafe. I've listened to all your reports, and your scores, and your percentiles, but that tells you little or nothing about what a child actually needs. Look into your hearts and do what is right. Is this how you would want me to treat your child? Is this how I treated many of your children when I taught them? Imagine this is your daughter. Imagine I'm your daughter's teacher again, and imagine you are coming to me for help. Because I will not leave here until you make the right choice." She took a deep breath and folded her arms.

Principal Costa finally spoke. "We can give her an aide for a month as a means to help her transition."

"I don't think it's needed," Sutter rebuffed.

"Possibly," Costa said, and after that, he was silent again.

"Well, it's your school, your justification, your site funds," Sutter retorted. "Go ahead, do what you want."

Mr. Rangpur whispered in Alice's ear as Costa mulled his decision. Sutter stared in Costa's direction as the attorney spoke at a level I could not hear.

"I wonder what he is saying," I whispered to Annie.

"We will give Magdalena an aide for a one month," Sutter proclaimed. "Her case manager will be Joaquin Crispin from Hire Psych. He will be placed at PCE to oversee service delivery."

"That sounds reasonable," Costa said.

Alice pronounced her closing remarks. "Magdalena's next IEP meeting will take place no later than four weeks after the first day of school in order to withdraw the aide. Until then, we are adjourned."

I turned to Annie with a stunned expression after the officials departed the meeting. "This is how they're confirming the lie they told the Board," I said. "They're employing somebody from Hire Psych to oversee Magda's special ed. That means Hire Psych is providing special education services instead of the school district. How much does all this cost, between Calaveras, their stupid attorney, and a year's salary to another Hire Psych employee? I wonder what the citizens of Yolo County would think if they knew what their tax dollars were actually paying for."

The Butterfly Effect

*"Kindness is the language which the deaf can hear
and the blind can see."*

– Mark Twain

I stared out our back window and watched Daisy and Magda play together. The backyard was in full bloom with indigo explosions of starflowers, flickering flames of salvia, and long shooting stalks of penstemon.

Over the clanging of plates and silverware coming from the kitchen, I could hear my father, my father-in-law, and Frank talking about Magda's graduation from the Caterpillar Academy. Mari and Angelo were complaining about the enumerable inane things that required a building permit from the city, including mundane maintenance tasks like replacing a dishwasher and swapping out ceiling fans. I could also hear my mother and my mother-in-law teaching Charlie how to play gin rummy on the coffee table while offering their own commentary of the morning's event.

"That was a very nice speech. She really gets kids," my mother said fanning out her cards. "You've got to build runs and sets, Charlie, like this."

My gaze was broken when I felt a hand rest on my shoulder. "We're going to head out, buddy. We have a long drive ahead of us. Thank you for the lunch and cake," my father said.

"Let me get Magdalena for you," I said. "She needs to say goodbye and thank you."

"No thanks needed. It's our pleasure." My father smiled as he watched her play with Daisy in the yard.

"That's not true, Dad. We want to teach her gratitude, and it's not okay for her to avoid social situations, especially when it comes to family."

"That ceremony, as Annie's father and I were just saying, was very nice," he returned. "I loved when Carmen said about the curiosity of the mind, the instinct to belong, and society's obligation to educate everyone to be a conscious person. So eloquent. I think it is so true how education serves not only to transfer information but to cultivate connections with and empathy for our fellow human beings. Great school." He smiled and clapped an arm around my shoulder.

"Agreed. I guess we will find out how many other people share that ethic soon."

"How on earth did she manage to get those wings on that dog?" he asked.

"I have no idea," I replied.

As part of Carmen Ventura's graduation ceremony, each graduate had to don a pair of butterfly wings that they had made over the course of the last few months. It was a preschool moving of the tassel and a symbolic metamorphosis into the next stage of childhood.

The wings were tissue paper celled and framed in wire hanger forms. Magda had made hers in the image of a Pieris rapae with light yellow tinges to the leading edges of the wings with an occasional smattering of gray dots and a gradual transition to a black wing base. Each side had a singular black dot on the forewing, and when both wings were splayed open, they gave the appearance of the wide-eyed, forward-facing countenance of a bird of prey.

Magda had refused to wear her wings for the graduation ceremony. Instead, she stood holding them out away from her body like a bag of kitchen trash because, as she so eloquently put it, "I'm not a butterfly. I'm a girl." Annie and I had no argument against concrete facts. Despite her own personal feelings of identity, Magda somehow managed to calm Daisy enough to bungee cord the wings onto the dog's back.

They were kindred spirits, dancing amongst the dandelions pushing through the high grass and flitting from blooming bush to flowering tree. Magda would throw a tennis ball and yell, "Fetch!" Daisy would sometimes recover the ball, but sometimes she would appear to take pleasure in watching Magda fish it out of the bushes for her. Whatever it was they were doing, it was their game with their rules, and both were winning.

* * *

"Today was nice," Annie said from the kitchen table as I closed and locked our heavy front door.

"Yes, it was."

"Do you think your parents had a good time this afternoon?" Annie asked.

"Of course, they love you and the kids."

"If Magda can barely tolerate the calm environment Carmen created or a get-together with her grandparents, I just don't see how she is not going to crumble under the weight of a full-blown kindergarten class."

"I don't know either, but we will get there when we get there, and we will deal with whatever happens when it happens," I offered.

"I suppose." Annie studied the label on a bottle of wine. "I left you a present in the fridge."

"Oh yeah, what is it?"

"You'll have to look," she teased.

Before I could make it to the fridge, there was a knock at the door.

"Registered mail," said the postman. "I'll need your signature here."

I complied and she handed me an oversized mailer.

"What is it?" Annie asked.

"I think it is our complaint to the California Department of Education." I ripped open the envelope, scanned the contents, then read aloud. "Dear Mr. and Mrs. Russell, herein is contained the Department of Education's findings and conclusions. This concludes the State's investigation into these matters."

"Well?" Annie prodded.

"The complainants allege that the District failed to use trained and knowledgeable personnel, Diego Braeburn. Findings of fact: Mr. Braeburn is licensed in the State of California. The District requires that its personnel be licensed. Conclusion: The District is in compliance."

"Bullshit!" Annie erupted. "We weren't debating whether he was licensed. We were saying he is incompetent."

"Precisely!" I said. I skim-read a few empty blather sentences and got to the meat. "The complainants allege that the District failed to obtain consent before disclosing private information to Hire Psych, an outside provider. Finding of fact: The District states it contracted with Scarlet Snow of Hire Psych to review an IEE for an IEP meeting. Conclusion: The District is in compliance."

"Bullshit again," Annie said.

"The complainants allege that the District failed to obtain consent before an evaluation for eligibility by Jonathan Calaveras of Hire Psych. Findings of fact: Jonathan Calaveras wrote an evaluation of Ben Seckel's IEE regarding the student's potential eligibility. Jonathan Calaveras presented his report regarding eligibility at the IEP meeting. Conclusion: The District is in compliance."

"If what that snake wrote was an evaluation, how the hell are they in compliance?" Annie belted. "Their finding of fact even says it was an evaluation! The CDE agrees with us!" She uncorked her bottle of Napa Cabernet and poured a glass.

"The complainants allege that the District failed to consider the results of an IEE. Findings of fact: The IEP meeting notes indicate that the IEE was discussed at the IEP meeting. Conclusion: The District is in compliance."

"Horseshit," Annie said between sips of wine. "Does consider mean the same thing as prepare to destroy?"

"A request for reconsideration must be postmarked thirty-five days from the receipt of this investigatory report."

"If all they had to say is that we were wrong and YUSD is right, why is that packet so thick?" Annie asked as she recorked her bottle.

"I don't know. I think there are exhibits like affidavits, contracts, and invoices in here." I thumbed the stack of papers. "The usual."

"I'm sure from a bird's-eye view Magda looked perfectly normal today," Annie mused, as she watched our little girl playing in the backyard.

"I don't know about that."

"Sure they would. Look at her now: from a distance, she's playing fetch with her dog. How much more Norman Rockwell could her childhood look?" She sipped again. "But if all those school officials could be with Magda for days, weeks, and years, as we have, they would see that she spends countless hours interacting with a dog and not with the people who love her, and why? Because she's incapable of that level of social interaction, something that is natural and easy for neurotypical kids." Annie paused. "No one wants to look at the details, and I don't think anyone cares." Her eyes misted.

I cradled her hand in mine. "I think it's because if they find something, they have to own it, and ownership means responsibility, and responsibility means caring, and they really don't care."

A tear fell from her chin onto the table.

Annie stood slowly. "I need a shower, and I need to go to bed. How are you not as worried about kindergarten as I am?" She fell into my hug.

"I am. We just worry in different ways," I whispered.

* * *

After Annie's shower and the kids' baths, I tucked them all in and headed to the sofa by way of the kitchen with Daisy, our laptop, and the stack of papers from the state. Opening the fridge, I found Annie's gift to me: two bottles of Pliny the Elder from Russian River Brewing Company. Even though the brewery was only two counties away, Pliny was an exceptionally difficult find in Davis. Annie must have had to proactively request the beer since it never made it onto the shelves in any local grocery store. It was only sold in low whispers and secret handshakes from refrigerated back rooms marked for employees only.

The Pliny poured a summer sunset into my glass and its head gently laced the sides as I sipped.

Amongst the packet of exhibits from the state's so called "investigation" were affidavits from Alice Sutter and Diego Braeburn. Alice said absolutely nothing about her involvement in hiring Hire Psych, but rather only that "the parents" were repeatedly resistant to testing their daughter despite her pleas. Diego, for his part, was relatively mum, offering only a few terse sentences stating that he was in fact licensed in California, the testing he performed on Magda was valid and accurate, and no one at YUSD ever questioned such.

The carbonation and lupulin danced along my tongue as I took another sip.

The next collated set of exhibits had to do with Hire Psych. The "evidence" tried to suggest that Calaveras had lawful means to access Magda's records, and the contract between Calaveras and the district had now been fully approved by the YUSD board of trustees. With every pretentious condition of the contract, I drank. With every page of the contract, I drank, and by the time I had reached the end of the contract, I had nearly finished my beer. I poured the remainder of the bottle into my glass and returned to the stack.

The last set of exhibits contained the invoices held as "proof" of an existing agreement between Hire Psych and the YUSD. The owner, Scarlet Snow, had submitted bills to the YUSD business office with an itemized list of billable procedures and hours. The first entry was for a total of 38.5 hours for report writing and IEP meeting attendance. Jonathan Calaveras had charged YUSD nearly $3300 for reviewing Ben Seckel's report and writing his own.

"That's an awful lot of money to charge someone for IEP services to a child you've never seen," I quipped to Daisy.

Calaveras then spent 13.5 hours writing his second report in which he willingly or reluctantly shifted his conclusions. That rang up another $1100 in charges invoiced to the taxpayers.

"Holy crap," I whispered. Daisy had draped herself across my feet. "Altogether, that's about three mortgage payments."

I typed the word "budget" into the YUSD website search bar. The first link returned a PDF document titled "Independent Review of Fiscal Compliance and Health Risk Analysis." I clicked the link then keyed Ctrl-F and searched "special education."

"The YUSD is concerned that general fund contributions to special education continue to rise annually. In addition, many parents have moved to Davis to get the services they feel are necessary for their children. In cost containment, the most efficient method of controlling special education costs is to limit the number of children placed in the program. Student study teams can keep many disabled children in regular classrooms. Providing aides is very expensive and should only be done after all other alternatives have been exhausted."

"How is this acceptable?" I asked Daisy.

Daisy's ear flicked as Mari's garage door opened. Mari started her car, pulled out of her driveway, and sped off to her graveyard shift.

"They put in print that YUSD should keep disabled kids out of special education to save money. How are people not outraged?" I asked at full volume.

I opened another tab on my browser and searched "California online impersonation law." The first link took me to an LA defamation attorney's website. "You can face up to one year in jail and/or pay a $1000 fine if you are found guilty of impersonating another person for the purposes of harming, intimidating, threatening, or defrauding."

"I can live with that." I opened another tab and searched for a free email server.

"Johnny dot Calaveras underscore Hire Psych," I said as I typed in the name of my new alias.

I typed with the fury of revenge served cold:

Alice, I was hoping you could remind me who referred you
to our services on the Davis case. Thanks, Jon

I hit send and smiled.

"We'll see if she bites." I pulled my feet out from under Daisy. "I have to pee," I apologized.

As soon as I returned to my laptop, it dinged with a new message.

Hi, Jon.

It was our attorney, Rangpur. Hope all is well.

Alice.

Sent from my iPhone.

"Of course it was," I murmured.

Daisy stood, turned, and thrust her nose between my chest and my arm. My forehead collapsed upon the nape of her neck.

"It's all a conspiracy."

Daisy agreed.

KINGS PLAY CHESS ON FUNNY GREEN SQUARES

ACT II (SIMPLE TRUTHS)

SETTING: We are in the kitchen and dining area of Arthur and Annie's home in Davis. It's late in the evening, and Arthur has just returned home from work. His green scrub bottoms are spattered in blood, and he is tired from a long and stressful day at work. Annie has had an equally difficult day.

AT RISE: Annie is moving rapidly across the room sweeping the kitchen floor as Arthur enters the front door.

ANNIE

Do Labs ever stop shedding?

ARTHUR

(removes shoes; places by door)

It doesn't appear to be the case. Are you okay?

ANNIE

Why does Mari keep pruning our trees?

ARTHUR

She is trying to help, I suppose. She thinks they are going to die without her attention,

and she knows we are busy. I don't think she
knows any other way.

                    ANNIE

Well, it's weird.

                    ARTHUR

          (walks toward Annie)

True, but it's nice to have someone in the
neighborhood that cares. I can tell that Mari
isn't what's bothering you.

                    ANNIE

We got a letter from the insurance company
today denying our appeal for Magda's last six
months of therapy. They say there is no medical
justification.

                    ARTHUR

Did they give any explanation?

                    ANNIE

No. I told you, they say the therapy isn't
justified.

                    ARTHUR

Then why are we paying for the most expensive
health plan? They are supposed to cover
therapy, right? Did you call?

                    ANNIE

I didn't have time.

ARTHUR

(flips through a stack of mail)

I'm sorry. I'm off tomorrow. I'll call. You
know how much they take out of my paycheck? A
lot, and for what? If Magda had cancer, they
would pay for treatment.

ANNIE

Our property tax bill is due again soon too. Do
you know how much they take for those school
parcel taxes?

ARTHUR

I don't remember, but I know it's high.

ANNIE

(walks to the sink and moves
plates from the drying rack to
the cupboard)

It's over a third of the bill. I want to move.

ARTHUR

I don't know if I'm ready for that. That would
be a pretty big upheaval for Charlie. Besides,
we might owe more than this house is worth
right now. And where would we move to?

ANNIE

I hear there is a school in Marin, maybe
even one back in Oakland that might work for
Magda.

ARTHUR

(moves closer to Annie)

How are we going to afford to live in Marin
County, for one? And two, aren't those schools
private and expensive? I guess I can find another
job, probably not one that pays any better. I'd
lose the hospital's retirement program.

(pauses)

I suppose I could commute.

ANNIE

This shouldn't have to be about money.

ARTHUR

Unfortunately, that's the reality of just about
any choice we make.

ANNIE

(turns away from Arthur and
stares off stage left)

Maybe other hospitals have better health
insurance, or at least a plan where we don't
have to pay out of pocket for most of her
services. People move here specifically for the
schools, right?

ARTHUR

That and the university.

ANNIE

(speaks softly)

I was sitting in the waiting room during
Magda's OT appointment today, and one of the

other moms told me that Woodland buses some
kids to Davis for special ed services.

                    ARTHUR
I've seen them.

                    ANNIE
She said she heard that an autistic girl was
being molested by a bus driver, and the special
ed people at YUSD found out about it.

          (pauses)

It took them seven months to tell the Davis
police, and they never told the parents.

          (pauses)

Can you imagine?

               (a plate slips from Annie's hand
               and shatters on the floor)

                    ARTHUR
Don't move! You aren't wearing shoes. You'll
cut your feet.

               (grabs the broom behind the
               pantry door and sweeps around
               Annie)

                    ANNIE
          (standing still)

Magda is struggling, Arthur. She's really
struggling in school.

                    ARTHUR

I know.

                     ANNIE

The PTA approved a chocolate fountain rental
last night for the school's monthly teacher
appreciation party.

        (pauses)

Not just the fountain, but all of the fruit and
bullshit that goes with it. And on top of that,
they wanted me to solicit parent donations for
cheese platters and coffee. How am I supposed
to appreciate what is happening to our daughter
when I see this kind of waste?

                    ARTHUR

Setting aside our situation, did no one say
anything about this being pretentious? I would
find that offensive if I were a teacher. I find
it offensive as someone who has donated time
and money to that school.

                     ANNIE

        (begins to cry)

I miss teaching.

                    ARTHUR

I know.

                     ANNIE

I feel like the entire financial burden is on
you, and that isn't fair.

ARTHUR

They don't pay high enough salaries for what
you do at home and what it means for Charlie
and Magda.

ANNIE

I wanted a career too.

ARTHUR

I know. It will just be delayed. For better or
worse, this is what we both have to do right
now.

ANNIE

The Hamlins are getting a divorce.

ARTHUR

That's too bad.

(pauses)

Predictable, but still, she would be a tough
nut to live with.

(pauses)

For that matter, so would he.

ANNIE

They say divorce is more frequent among couples
with special needs kids.

ARTHUR

I heard that wasn't true. Faulty reporting – a
blogger's myth.

                         ANNIE

Well, it feels real. All the special needs
parents I know are on Prozac or in counseling
or something.

                        ARTHUR

          (collects the glass shards in a
          dustpan and empties them in the
          trash)
Well, we aren't. I'm not saying this isn't
stressful. Disabilities or not, parenting or
not, or just plain life for that matter - all
of it is hard.

                         ANNIE

          (walks to refrigerator, opens it,
          and stares into it)
I can't sleep at night. My mind is always
racing, wondering what they are going to do
next. How are we supposed to get her the help
she needs, especially now that we have been
made out to be awful parents to all of her
teachers in this town. I see it in the way the
principal looks at me in meetings. I see it
in the way the teachers are standoffish toward
me. Kindergarten is not working out for her.
The aide is gone, not that she did anything
anyway.

                        ARTHUR

When I picked up Magda from school the other
day, one of her classmates told me that all the

aide did was sit in the corner and sip from
a Coke that she kept hidden on the top of a
bookshelf.

ANNIE

But of course she showed up with a stack full
of papers at that IEP meeting showing how
well Magda was doing at school and why an aide
wasn't needed.

(speaks in a mocking,
condescending voice)

Everything is totally normal. She is totally
fine.

(pauses)

Her teacher let it slip the other day that the
aide was told just to watch Magda and not help
unless Magda went to her and specifically asked
for help.

ARTHUR

(gesticulates wildly)

I don't know what to tell you, Annie. Can you
imagine if I did this at work? What if I took
Diego Braeburn's blood pressure and lied about
what it actually was in his medical record, or
took Alice's chart and gave it to a private
company without her consent so I could prevent
her from getting her appendix removed or her
soul transplanted? Or worse yet, what if I
knew that there were people taking care of
Jonah Kern who were conspiring to keep him

from getting cancer treatment, and I covered
it up?

>   (speaks in a mocking,
>   condescending voice)

Jonah is perfectly fine. I see no evidence of
cancer here. There is absolutely nothing to
worry about.

>   (pauses)

My ass would be fired, my license yanked. A
malpractice lawsuit would be the least of my
worries.

ANNIE

Well, you are not going to win that argument in
this town, not with these schools. What Magda
has isn't life threatening.

ARTHUR

The hell it isn't!

ANNIE

The kids will hear us.

ARTHUR

>   (speaks to Annie in a loud
>   whisper)

You can't tell me that these kids aren't at
higher risk for self-injury, accidental or
purposeful. All sorts of research shows that
kids like Magda are at higher risk for suicide.

So like hell this isn't life threatening. These
idiots want to make her condition worse, not
only by not helping, but by actively making her
environment worse.

> (sits on the kitchen floor
> and places his head against a
> cabinet)

You don't think that has permanent effects?
What happens to us when we are stressed? I know
that I decompensate, but at least I have some
sort of coping skills.

> (points off stage right)

What happens in her head when she is
stressed?

> (slowly and methodically bangs
> his head against the cabinet)

If everything from a doorbell to an oven timer
is that much louder in her brain, what else
does she hear amplified?

ANNIE

She is starting to kick herself at school. She
is coming home with bruises on her legs.

ARTHUR

What? How long has that been going on?

ANNIE

I started noticing marks on her around the time
they were getting ready to pull the aide.

                        ARTHUR

You mean about the time that jackass aide was
saying that everything was perfectly fine? We
have to tell the school. This is on them.

                        ANNIE

              (moves to the kitchen table and
              collapses into a chair)

Oh my god, I forgot to tell you. In the middle
of Feather's rant about Ash and the divorce,
she started telling me how bad things are for
Quincy at school. She has had to file another
suit against the district.

                        ARTHUR

Not surprising.

                        ANNIE

No, but do you know who is representing the
district?

                        ARTHUR

Rangpur or whatever the hell his name was.

                        ANNIE

No. It's the same firm they used when they bent
over backward to help us investigate Hire
Psych. It's Mary Ellen Lake's firm.

                        ARTHUR

That's sickening. Maybe the district was so
impressed with how they helped completely screw
us over that they wanted to share that with a
broader audience.

ANNIE

It's disgusting. They took my blood pressure
at the doctor last week, and they said it was
really high.

ARTHUR

You didn't tell me that. How high? It's never
been high. Why?

ANNIE

Have you seen the news at all?

ARTHUR

No, it's been a busy day.

ANNIE

There was another school shooting today.

        (pauses and rubs face)

They say he was on an IEP. And of course it's
the parents' fault for not getting him enough
help and not noticing all the telltale signs
that something was wrong.

ARTHUR

The media just says crap to fill space. They
don't know. Where was this?

ANNIE

Not California. I feel like we can't celebrate
any of her successes because they will be used
against her, or against us.

ARTHUR

It certainly feels that way.

ANNIE

(grabs the tax envelope from the
table and waves it in the air)

This is public money. This is goddamn public
education! This is our neighborhood! Those are
our goddamn taxes!

(long pause - speaks slowly)

I just feel like this is some ridiculous
nightmare, and we are going to wake up and
say, "Wow, that was weird. No one would ever
act like that. No one should ever act like
that, especially someone in charge of helping a
disabled little girl."

ARTHUR

(stands and approaches Annie)

I know. Trust me. I know.

ANNIE

They should all have been fired.

ARTHUR

(sits next to Annie at the table)

Yes. The people we're dealing with now at PCE
may not be as malicious, but they certainly are
just as negligent.

ANNIE

What happened to your scrubs?

ARTHUR

(waves his hand)

There was a riot at Folsom Prison.

ANNIE

Are you okay?

ARTHUR

Me? Fine. Are we?

ANNIE

I need a hug.

ARTHUR

(lounges back in seat - pushes
one hand through hair)

Can I change and shower first? I don't need
to give you whatever I'm wearing right now.
I found another gray hair this morning.
Curiously, it looked like the hair started out
normally, but halfway through its growth, it
turned gray. It just gave up mid-grow. Said to
hell with it, why try anymore.

ANNIE

We need to go back to Ruby Reyes.

                              ARTHUR

We've been down that road. We can't afford an
attorney. Even if we won, what are we going
to win? Have we met a family yet whose kid is
getting what they need from YUSD? I don't think
they are even capable of doing what is right,
even if it was spelled out for them.

                              ANNIE

What can we do?

                              ARTHUR

Honestly, I really don't know.

(BLACKOUT)

Apathy is an IEP Team Meeting

I'm here on holiday, vacation, with compensatory time accrued,
We've come at a time that's strictly convenient for you,
Accommodations and transportations we have made, not to be rude,
We are here to collaborate and participate; what else can we do?

When we gush and blush about her strengths,
Your pens fly with fury,
When we prioritize and itemize our concerns,
Flat in your hands, they see no hurry.

When we say she has no friends and she doesn't get along,
You tell us that lots of kids are shy, and we couldn't be more wrong.

When we say she frustrates easily and can't get her words out, You say
you've never seen her angry; happiness is all she is about.

When we say she cries at home because she felt picked on in school, You tell us teasing is just the childhood way of telling her she is cool.

When we say she can't control her hands to make scissors and crayons go the right way, You tell us lots of students make messy art every single day.

When we say that without a lot of assistance she's never learned very much, You say kids learn how to be helpless if we're always giving them a crutch.

When we say about her writing and reading, she really has no clue, You tell us lots of students moan and groan about doing their work too.

When we say she needs lots of breaks because she rapidly loses focus, You tell us thank god for coffee; otherwise, you'd be the worst among us.

When every time we pick her up we have to put her back together,
You say lots of kids fall apart after school; it's just something with the weather.

I'm here on holiday, vacation, and compensatory time accrued,
We feel like we are supposed to sit here quietly and only agree with you,
To hear our concerns be ignored or deliberately misconstrued,
Or to hear that what we worry about simply isn't true.

When we gush and blush about her strengths,
We've only minimized her pain,
When you trivialize and criticize our concerns,
It makes us go insane!

Theory of Mind

*"The reason I talk to myself is that I'm the only
one whose answers I accept."*

— George Carlin

Usually, Annie and I can hold off using the whole-house fan until the twilight of the spring. Simply opening the windows at night is sufficient to ventilate and cleanse the house with cool air for most of the rest of the year. While the whole-house fan is a marvelous invention, it does have drawbacks. Annie and I could lie to ourselves all we wanted about the noise it created, but we reflexively began to cringe with the annual birth of life that heralds springtime.

There was a time when spring weather lulled us into dreaming that Davis was truly as temperate as advertised. After the burden of months of disorienting Tule fog or frost warnings that send citrus farmers scrambling, everyone in town embraced the sun's higher zenith in the sky. Families frolicked in the mild warmth and the accompanying explosions of California poppies. The return home from work meant that I was first greeted by the perfume of the peppermint in Magda's sensory garden.

But I'm jaded now. All of it is fleeting.

The cool rain of winter that keeps the town clean is given up for Lent. And, a more insidious problem appears, one that is much worse than the incessant rattle and hum of a whole-house fan. The spring renewal is when we in Davis begin to hum "Goodbye, Blue Sky" and we get a taste of what life must be like on Mars.

The dust, pollen, dander, and mold kicked up by the Sacramento Valley's northern winds pass over the town in broad red strokes, deepening the sun and changing the hue of the stucco above every threshold, carpeting doorsteps and putting a dusty layer on the windows and everything in the house if the windows are left open.

After it gets too warm to sleep comfortably at night, the whole-house fan turns our whole house into the inside of a vacuum cleaner. The yellow anther's dust from the Roma tomatoes frantically mating in the fields lines our windowsills, settles on our kitchen table, and stains Annie's table linens. Silica and silt form layers of sediment on countertops, light fixtures, and picture frames. Daisy's fur coagulates into tumbleweeds that waltz in clumps of dust that form along the edges of the hallway. From May until September, our home becomes a filter that needs to be shaken out weekly.

Nighttime in the spring, before the whole-house fan is turned on, is the closest I can get to understanding what Magdalena and Daisy live with every day. Davis is quiet at night, certainly much quieter than Oakland. With our bedroom window open and my eyes shut, I am more conscious of my other senses. At times, this can generate bouts of insomnia. As I lay with eyes forced closed, head slightly propped on a pillow, hands gently folded, and doing my best impression of the guest of honor at my wake, my brain buzzes as I process, sort, and sometimes discard my daily events. My day at work is projected against the back of my eyelids. I'm like a coach reviewing video of the game, pausing, rewinding, watching plays in slow motion, and starting the whole process again.

But now, in the dark, as is true with autism, everything shares equal volume, and not one nerve impulse is less important than another. I can smell Mari's tulips closing for the night, the detergent used to launder our sheets a week ago, and the crumbs that are continuing to caramelize in the oven that has been off for several hours. I can feel the thread count of our cotton sheets, the elastic of my pajamas, and the backside of my haircut. I can hear that Annie breathes at fourteen breaths per minute with an occasional and unpredictable physiologic sigh. I can hear the refrigerator as it compresses and circulates coolant. I can hear the Doppler effect as motorcycles chopper arcs along the Mace Boulevard curve. I can hear the Jake brakes rhythmically popping diminuendo as eighteen-wheeled chariots contend with a reduction in freeway lanes just south of the university. I can hear the locomotives shove and knock their loads along the California Northern Railway between Davis and Tehama.

But it is the static stimuli that become clearer.

In the spring, with the windows open, that which surrounds Davis is magnified. The distant portable diesel motors are governed at 2300 RPMs as they draw water from the ground and slosh it into the sluices. The constant movement of non-potable water reminds me of the hiss on my grandfather's reel-to-reel tapes. Because the wavelength of the sound doesn't expand or compress like that of the traffic on the freeway, my ability to echolocate is compromised. Everything just stands still, pointed at me, in the dark.

From its home in the ground, water is drawn by the pumps into the V-notched irrigation ditches that encircle the fields. Makeshift dams of tarpaulin slap as they contain and control the flows. Davis is surrounded by a moat, and I feel trapped. As the siphon tubes slurp from the ditches, irrigating the furrows, the ground crackles as it slakes its parched thirst. The soil fissures and quakes as germinated and genetically modified seeds punch through the crust like mindless zombies. They moan as they unfurl their first set of leaves and prepare to photosynthesize their first breath.

I can hear Daisy knocking around her cage, recovering after being bombarded by a ringing telephone, the wet hum of the dishwasher, the four cycles of the lawnmower, the two cycles of the leaf blower down the street, and the squealing brakes of the mailman. She is struggling to engage and integrate the violations of the concrete rules we have created for her. She simply cannot access the preoperational skills required to manipulate my symbols and information. She is again locked in an ego-centric pattern of repetitive behaviors and self-stimulation.

I can hear Magdalena thrashing about her bed wrestling with auton-omy and shame, broadcasting the contest between initiative and guilt, and falling deep between the walls of industry and inferiority. She is grasping for coping skills, and is only minutes away from sharing her maladaptation with Annie and me in our bed. Finally, Annie can hear it too, as she is staring silently at the side of my head. She has heard what we share together. We listen in concert as Magda sounds the alarm of a fire drill that she wasn't given advanced notice of, announces the sched-uled assembly about "stomping out bullying" that never made it into her daily picture schedule, and gives notice to the planned substitute teacher that came without warning.

Above the din, I can hear the big nothing outside – the monster made of no substance, the absolute and all-powerful expanse sleeping soundly in its bed without concern, complacent and comfortable in its own thoughts and cares.

But loudest yet, I can hear Annie's thoughts reverberating inside my head: *How can they sleep at night?*

No Effects

"The real war will never get in the books."

– Walt Whitman

"I ran into Mari outside," I said. "She just bought an excessive amount of Mason jars for canning our pears this fall."

"Maybe first grade will be better. The academics will get harder. The expectations will be higher. Grades will matter more," Annie said, skipping right over the Mari news as unimportant.

"You think they will notice that she is struggling because there is actually something more tangible to struggle with?" I asked.

"I hope so," said Annie

"You're more optimistic than I am. I looked into that school in Sacramento – it's absolutely not a fit for her. It is designed mostly for kids with serious behavioral issues."

"No one sees this is just as big an issue for girls as it is for boys," Annie whispered.

"Where are we going to find someone who does?" I asked.

"Private school, maybe. I don't know. Why can't we find Carmen Ventura's Academy for Autistics?" Annie tempted the fates. "Even if we did, I'm sure it would cost an arm and a leg."

"I think we need to redefine what we think costs too much," I said.

It's Called

The kids called it a game

The teacher called it a misunderstanding

The yard duty aide called it her choice to play with those kids

The psychologist called it something we didn't want to blow out of proportion

The principal called it something that she was part of too

The kids called it something that she instigated

The principal called it just things kids do

The other parents called it things kids work out on their own

The principal called us too sensitive

The teacher called banning the game a way to fix the problem

We called it unbelievable

Without Principle

"[C]hildren with autism spectrum disorders are bullied far more often than their typically developing peers — nearly five times as often..."

— Time.com (Sept. 05, 2012)

Annie was in a full-blown argument with someone from the school when I returned from the grocery store. I knew it was the psychologist because I heard her say, "Look, Mr. Melrose," in a tone I knew I never wanted to hear. The remainder of the conversation was muffled by our closed bedroom door.

As I placed grocery bags on the kitchen counter, I heard an equally frantic racket coming from the living room; it sounded like someone was clanging cymbals. As I peered around the corner, I saw Magda lying in Daisy's crate kicking the metal frame repeatedly and rhythmically with both feet.

"Honey, what are you doing?" I kneeled at her side.

Her face was flushed and sweaty.

I got no answer. She struck her head three times against the back of the crate, reached in her pocket, and threw a thin circular piece of string at my chest.

"Magda, honey, what is this?"

Still no verbal response; only a face fit to explode.

I could hear Annie striking the bed with an open palm, beating whatever point she was making into the other end of the receiver.

I thumbed the string in my hand. "Magda, this looks like a bracelet maybe."

Magda howled then grabbed both sides of the crate and shook it as violently as she could.

"I'm sorry, honey, but I need to know. Is this from school?"

Magda began violently throwing Daisy's belongings from her crate, first her tennis balls, then her blankets. She rattled with such force that if she could, she would have thrown the crate inside out.

Daisy bounded in front of us panting feverishly. She flapped her ears and spun. A look of concern and confusion was welded into her brow.

"Daisy, do you know what happened?" I asked softly.

"I said nothing!" Magda sputtered.

"Okay," I responded.

"No answer!" Magda began to rock again.

"Who gave no answer?" I tiptoed into the first crack in the conversation.

"He ate his apple!" Her rage resumed. The crate was striking the wall so hard that depressions were forming in the drywall and flakes of paint were falling to the floor. "Loud crunching! Hurting my head!"

"Who, Magda? Who are you talking about? Who had an apple?"

"The scissors were broken! I hate friendship bracelets!"

"Is that what this is?"

"They are not friends! They were laughing! I wasn't laughing!" Magda erupted in tears. Snot was pouring from her nose. "My brain was crying! I just wanted to leave! They were laughing at me! He didn't help. He ate his apple – crunching, loud!" She screamed into the knees she had tucked into her chest.

"Honey, I'm so sorry." My eyes were beginning to well.

"And they were laughing! He was crunching, crunching, crunching! I was dying!" She curled into herself, whimpering.

I pushed the friendship bracelet into the palm of my hand, stood, and headed to our bedroom.

When I opened the door, Annie shot me a look and angrily raised one finger as she continued her heated discussion with the school psychologist. "That is absolutely not what we discussed! What makes you think that any of that was okay! She is a wreck right now, and that is a direct result of the choices the school made without our consent!"

I looked at the bracelet in disgust, turned silently, and walked out of the room.

* * *

"I could just scream, just scream!" Annie yelled as I hammered the laptop keys. "How can they be so stupid?" Her face twisted. "Do they just not care?"

Magda had finally calmed. Daisy had finally stopped her frenetic pacing and had crawled into her crate and laid her body across Magda's. I finished typing and turned to Annie. "I've already written the principal an email," I said. "Tell me what you think."

Dear Mr. Costa,

At our last meeting where we discussed how Magda had been bullied, we had agreed that as part of the constructive process we would be using to move forward, Magda would not immediately be placed in a situation where she would have to confront the children with whom she does not feel emotionally or physically safe. It was our understanding that we would be implementing a scaffolded plan for Magda, first by building social and play skills during recess in small groups with similarly situated children, then measuring her responses to that intervention (RTI as you called it), before ever escalating the social demands placed on her.

Yet, we found out tonight that Magda was asked to participate in a group with the kids, who by their own admission, were pushing and knocking Magda to the ground last week.

As you know from the reports in Magda's IEP, she has difficulty with expressive speech and had no practical way to answer any questions about participating in the group. You should have asked us – that is in fact what you told us you would do. In addition to her complex social problems, Magda has motor planning difficulties and has a hard time manipulating pencils, scissors, etc. She cannot perform fine motor tasks, such as bracelet making, at the same level as her peers. Placing her back with the group of children who bullied her and who are all capable of engaging in physical tasks that Magda cannot do makes her feel worse about herself. It also makes her easy fodder for those who wish to marginalize her.

She has been inconsolable since this most recent intervention. For that, and for allowing an environment of bullying to persist at your school, we hold you accountable.

If, as you have said in repeated IEP meetings, the faculty and staff at Putah Creek are here to support all children and create a safe space for learners, can you please explain your decision to disregard our agreement?

Thank you,
Arthur and Annie Russell

"Think we'll get a response?" Annie asked.
"Doubt it," I spat.
"Asshole!" Annie exclaimed.
"Which one?"
"All of them."

Magdalena's Sixth

"Nothing is more intolerable than to have to admit to yourself your own errors."

— Ludwig van Beethoven

"Daisy is happy I am her friend," Magdalena said. "She doesn't have friends, maybe Berdoo, but I'm her only friend, and she is my only friend."

My eyes started to well as I sat listening to my daughter tell me that she didn't have any friends. Daisy flapped her ears and spun wildly in circles as Magda helped me with the fall chore of clearing out all of the summer's overgrowth from the yard.

"Look how big our pumpkins and butternut squash have grown," I said trying to change the subject.

"It's hard to have friends," Magda said. "It's a bowl of rocks. It's hard."

"You are absolutely right," I said. "Just look at Daisy. She has a really hard time having friends. We all love her very much, but it doesn't mean things are easy for her."

"We have Mommy," Magda said.

"Yes we do."

I could see that her face had become locked, her brain wracked in thought, her mouth unable to translate.

"Honey, Daisy has Mommy too." I could see her frustration brewing below the surface. "We don't know where Daisy came from or who her parents were." I tried to guess what she was thinking. "We adopted her from the shelter. And it kind of doesn't matter because she has been ours for a long time now."

"I know," she agreed. "I want to go see where she used to live. I want that for my birthday. I don't want a party. I hate parties."

"If that's what you want to do, I'm happy to take you, but just know that we cannot get another dog, so don't ask."

"I know, Daddy. You've already told me that before. Mommy would kill you, but not really kill you, only you said kill... But it's not really kill – right?"

"Of course not. Mommy would never kill me."

Her face wrinkled.

"Okay, I'm done out here. Do you want to go right now?" I asked.

She didn't respond.

"Do you want to invite anyone else to go with us?" I couldn't tell if she had heard my first question.

"No, just us. Daisy can't come either," Magda insisted.

"Okay, but first we need to put a plan in place, right?"

"Yes," she said.

"Do I need to put it on the picture board, or can we talk about it?"

"Talk," she said.

"Okay, let's talk about smell. It's not going to smell good. Probably like a lot of dogs all went to the bathroom at one time."

She nodded. I was preparing her brain for the sensory assaults she was about to encounter.

"It's going to be loud too, with lots of dogs barking."

I could see the beginnings of the meltdown I was hoping to prevent creep into her shoulders.

"Is that going to be okay?" I asked.

She nodded, her expression stern and intent.

"There will probably be a lot of people there too. And they might not see you because they are looking at all the dogs, and they may accidently bump into you, okay?"

She stood still for a moment then nodded.

"And we have to do a good job washing our hands before and after. And we have to listen to all the shelter's rules."

"Fine," she said, indicating she was ready to leave.

On the horizon, tractors were ruminating over the remnants of tomato vines and sunflower stalks as we drove toward Woodland. An overnight rain had cleared the air, and we could see all the way from the purple crests of the Berryessa Gap to the tops of the Sierras. The glass skyscrapers of Sacramento gleamed in the midmorning light after their bath. Above the landscape, squadrons of migratory birds flying south in V formations honked noisily at the transient great egrets and blue herons flying below.

Magda sat with her shoulders shrugged and her face contorted into itself, refusing to absorb the scenery. The STAR Center had taught us not to ask Magda direct questions when it looked like she was beginning to slip down the slope toward a shutdown. Asking her questions only made her feel worse about what she was thinking and suggested that what we thought she was thinking was wrong. Instead, we were supposed to talk about things in the environment. It was an attempt to reboot the circuitry and interrupt the negative feedback loop she was spiraling into.

"I see where the sunflowers used to be. I'm guessing they are getting ready to plant winter wheat," I said.

There was no response from the back seat.

"When the ground isn't wet and sticky, Daisy and I go running out here. I don't think the birds like it very much."

"Mommy's car goes to Woodland," Magda growled.

"Honey, I'm sorry, I didn't want to take her car because I was kind of dirty from working outside."

Magda only glared into her knees.

"I'll bet my car knows how to get to Woodland. This is the car that took me to Daisy the first time I met her," I said.

Her face softened.

I smiled as we breached the Davis city limits and gathered speed.

"Daddy! Wind!" Magda wailed.

"I'm sorry, I'll roll up the window."

As we approached the Willow Slough, I saw the slender woman I had met at the animal shelter six years ago. It was Anjou, and she was standing next to her car and its spare tire on the soft shoulder of the road, the same sticker-plastered car I'd seen in the parking lot the day I adopted Daisy.

I slowed and pulled over, rolling the front passenger window down to Magda's disgust.

"Magda, that is the woman that helped me bring Daisy home from the shelter. She looks like she needs help. I'm sorry to change the plan, but we have to stop."

Magda's protest was silent.

"Do you need any help?" I asked.

"Yes, I could use some. I have a flat. I got the spare out. I'm just having a difficult time loosening the lugs." She hoisted the tire iron up for my inspection.

"You probably won't remember me. I'm Arthur," I said as I got out of the car and went to shake her hand.

Behind and below me, I could hear the reeds hum and vibrate with the breeze, like woodwinds playing. The birds were calling from their hidden places as the water trickled through the slough.

"You look familiar . . . maybe." She eyed me carefully. "You work for the county?"

She had lost the pepper in her hair. It was now nearly translucent. I knelt and began to loosen the lugs.

"No, we adopted a Lab from the shelter several years ago, and it was you who helped me." I replaced the flattened tire with the spare.

"Oh, that's wonderful. I hope it all worked out. I can generally get a sense of people as they come in, and I try to match them with just the right dog."

"Well, she hasn't been without her issues." I grinned. "But we love her a lot."

"Daisy!" Magda sang from the backseat of our car, her mood lifted at the mention of our dog.

"My daughter Magda," I said pointing. "She wanted me to take her to the animal shelter to see where our dog came from. I'm sure that sounds a little strange." I tightened the final lug, lowered and removed the jack, and put it in the trunk. "She has some special needs, and this is what she wanted to do," I said.

"That's great! There are rules about who can have access to certain areas at the shelter, but I can certainly give you both a tour if you're interested," Anjou offered.

"Yes," I said, feeling surprised at the serendipity of this encounter.

"Magda, this is Anjou. She helped me choose Daisy. She still works at the shelter and can show us around. We get our own special tour."

Magda studied Anjou's face, not yet capable of responding.

"I think I may have known Daisy," Anjou said with a smile.

"I'll follow you," I said to Anjou.

"Okay. See you in a bit."

* * *

As Anjou pushed the metal door into the shelter, we were met by a riotous gathering of people; everyone was in some form of distress, including the deputies behind the counter. The man at the front of the line was attempting to describe his Doberman, sobbing that the dog had found a weak spot in his redwood fence. A portly woman, obstructing the sign-in sheet at the main desk, was dropping off an unwanted screaming litter of kittens in a cardboard box. Anjou instructed us to head into the main kennel room, and she would take care of signing us in. She turned and then politely made her way through the remainder of the room, which was left grumbling to itself about fees and nuisance barking.

Magda and I walked the loop of kennels, stopping to look at dogs that we found interesting. The room was as crowded with odor as it had been the day I spotted Daisy. As we squeezed through the narrow lanes between the chain-linked stalls, I pointed out to Magda where Daisy had been when I found her and what she had been doing. Magda studied the narrow space and the brindle pit bull that now rented that stall. She froze and didn't speak.

"I see a pretty dog," I said.

"She's alone," Magda finally pushed out.

"Well, I think they're trying to make sure that all the dogs are safe and don't get into fights, or smaller dogs don't get run over by larger dogs. But yes, I'm sure they are lonely, and could use a friend to play with."

"Do you want to take her outside?" Anjou said from behind us.

Magda nodded yes, and her demeanor could only be described as gleeful.

"What is her name?" I asked.

"You know what, no one has given her a name yet. She just has a county ID number." Anjou took a knee and came to eye level with Magda.

"Would you like to name her" she asked with a warm smile.

"No," Magda barked. She had cycled back to being unhappy.

"I'm sorry," I said to Anjou. "Magda..." I said sternly.

"Don't worry about it," Anjou said, still focused on Magda. "If you change your mind, just let me know."

"No!" Magda repeated.

"I'll get her leash and walk her out to the yard for you," Anjou said.

"Daisy, our dog, is pretty forgiving," I said to Anjou as we watched Magda play fetch with the nameless dog in the pea gravel yard. "Daisy knows she has to be different for her – at least I think she does."

Anjou smiled and nodded her head knowingly. "Dogs are pretty intuitive."

"Daisy might be," I said. "More like very kind-souled."

Magda was in heaven as the pit lay on its back, full sprawl, while Magda rubbed her belly.

"They are the only two that can interrupt each other's personal space and rules and not have it dysregulate one or the other," I explained. "If her older brother, a teacher, or her mom and I, for that matter, interrupt her routine or whatever she may be doing, there is usually hell to pay. But that's not the case with the dog for whatever reason."

"A lot of sensory issues I imagine, too," Anjou said.

"Yes," I nodded.

* * *

The sun slowly disappeared as a waving curtain of dark clouds marched briskly across the valley floor. Scattered misty drops quickly gave way to sheets of hard rain. Magda and her new friend were oblivious to the world around them.

I called Magda several times with increasing volume. I got no response. I found it equally as difficult to call a dog with no name.

I ventured out into the deluge from under our shelter and touched Magda on the arm. Touch was the only way for her to hear me in that moment. "Magda, honey, come on in. We have to get out of the rain. We don't want you or the dog to get sick."

"You can come back to the office with the dog if you like, Magda," Anjou offered.

"Can she have hot chocolate?" Anjou asked me.

I nodded.

"Magda, I have a hot water dispenser in my office with packets of hot chocolate. Would you like one?"

Magda clapped then squeezed her hands together tightly as she followed Anjou.

"I appreciate this," I said, sitting down on a metal folding chair.

The dog with no name seemed perfectly content lying next to Magda while she gazed mesmerized by the movement of the foam and the dissolving powder as she stirred her chocolate with a plastic straw.

"When my son turned six, my wife and I were at our wits' end," I said, sharing more than I thought I should be with someone I hardly knew. "We had twenty-five kids at the bowling alley on campus. You know, from start to finish, it was only about a three-hour affair, but there was the shoe rental, getting the inflatable bumpers set up in the gutters, some God awful cake from Safeway, and about twenty-five sets of parents who felt completely absolved of parenting for that afternoon. On the drive home, I think we said to each other 'never again.' Yet the following year it felt like we were doing the same thing, but at the city pool. But that's my son – he wants to invite everyone from his class, all of his friends, anyone he's ever played soccer with. The list seems never-ending."

Loud claps of thunder reverberated throughout the cinderblock building, sending the kenneled animals into a frenzy. Magda and her new friend seemed unfazed and content with their companionship.

"I'm sorry, I'm over sharing," I said.

"No, no, please don't worry about that. My son has what they're trying to no longer call Asperger's." She forced a smile as the windows behind her flashed with lightning then rattled with the force of the accompanying thunder.

"Only about a second's difference," she said. "It's close."

"You know she has never wanted to invite anyone to a birthday party with the exception of her family and maybe a couple of her therapists. I love my dog, I do, and I know she loves her too. But it breaks my heart to see that at this point in her life, she is only capable of calling a dog her friend." I realized my voice was trembling. "She has never even been invited to a classmate's birthday party or a play date for that matter."

"Where does she go to school?" Anjou asked.

"Putah Creek Elementary."

"Who is principal there now?"

"Costa is his last name."

Magda had finished her hot chocolate and curled up next to the dog on the floor. She stroked the dog's head in slow, even movements.

"I remember him as a teacher," Anjou said as hail began hammering the building. "He wasn't very well liked."

"I'm struggling to find many teachers that I do like," I added.

"Costa plays staff against each other rather than build community." Anjou looked to the ceiling for her next thoughts. "Teachers are underappreciated and underpaid, and those with less of a constitution will cave to the party line. Some are beaten into submission, and some assume it with ferocity. But believe it or not, there is a silent majority who hold fast to their integrity. The bigger problem is that there is no mechanism to reward or recruit good teachers, and it is exceptionally hard to get rid of the bad ones." Anjou nodded toward Magda. "She will eventually walk across a high school graduation stage, and it won't be because of anything the administrators have done for her. It will be because of everything you have done."

I didn't know what to say, so I simply nodded.

"They will happily sell you the line about how ninety-eight percent of their students graduate, or how they're so progressive that they even teach classes in feminism at the high school," she said as ten thousand photographers snapped their pictures in the darkness that had consumed the valley. "What they won't tell you is that they like to suspend kids with disabilities. It keeps them out of the classroom so they can't disrupt the 'good kids'." She did air quotes. "The ostracism wreaks havoc on those kids too, because Davis's dirty little secret is that one in three kids – kids like your daughter, like my son – won't finish school. But it's not these kids that fail; the whole community fails them. It's a systemic problem, especially when you have broad financial backing from the parents of the gifted children."

"Are you in education?" I asked.

"Was. Then I became an attorney, and this," she gestured around her, "this is what I have always done."

She paused as an especially loud rumble of thunder rattled the windows.

"I taught seventh grade English for many years at Andrew Michael Jones. It killed me." She paused and looked at Magda. "All these kids came to me so injured after being kicked down the line. There were no IEPs, no 504s, nothing in their files to suggest they needed academic help or social support. Parents would come to me in tears after the first report cards went out. Their kids had all been floated along on the elementary school promise that things eventually will be fine." Anjou rubbed her face. "I can't tell you how many kids opened up to me about thoughts of suicide. I would go to the counselors and psychologists asking for help, and nothing happened, no help." She stopped to wipe a tear from her eyes. "Of course all the counselors were paid with soft money – PTAs and the like, never with any consistent district funding. And who wants a job where there is no security?"

My own eyes welled up in sympathy.

"At first I was skeptical about the stories I heard, but ultimately knew them to be true. I don't know why people do that," she whispered. "Why so quick to deny? Like Saint Peter, I suppose."

The wind huffed and puffed at the block building.

"Parents and kids came to me and opened up about everything, perhaps because I was the first one who had ever listened to them. And in a roundabout way, that is how I became interested in law, and what I found myself fighting for." Anjou placed her hands flat on the table in front of us and chose her words with care. "Sometimes it's overt, and sometimes it's subtle. I have seen teachers stand up and complain about 'white flight' and the 'brain drain' from their classrooms, even going as far as to say they got stuck with all the leftovers because they ended up with a kid on an IEP in their classroom. It's disgusting." By this point, she was whispering so Magda wouldn't hear. "And then, those same teachers were the ones who posted signs outside their classrooms proclaiming things like Diversity Matters, or, Everyone is Welcome. Horseshit."

The sky rumbled.

"Oddly enough, I used to get so mad at some of the teachers, but then I realized they were doing it because they could."

Her choice of words piqued my curiosity. "Could how?"

"Leadership," she said, "or lack thereof. I once toured an elementary school just to get a sense of what was happening in those classrooms as part of a transition to middle school project, and I could not believe what I saw. It was barbaric." She wiped her face again. "I saw children sitting behind cardboard barriers in the back of the room with oversized industrial earmuffs over their ears – you know the kind people use at a gun range – because they simply couldn't handle the sensory overload of the classroom. And these weren't kids on IEPs or 504s. These were children wetting their pants in the classroom and being teased for it, and kids hurting themselves in a vain effort to make the pain go away. These kids were getting nothing in the way of help, and I mean nothing. And God help the families who did try to get their kids help – they were ostracized too." Anjou was weeping now. "I should know. I was one of them."

"I'm sorry, I didn't mean to upset you," I said. "Would you like us to leave?"

"No." She shook her head. "I don't know where you are in her process or what you expect, but I think it is important that people in our community support each other and share information. We don't need to hide in shame, and we don't need to feel alone."

"I completely agree."

"You know most parents aren't litigious. It takes repeated insults before parents really feel the need to get a lawyer," she said. "Districts know it is easy to break the backs of special needs families because attorneys are expensive, and families like ours are under so much pressure as it is. And those school district attorneys," she said in disgust. "They certainly found a cash cow in Davis. No one in the administration, or the school board for that matter, is going to question their attorney's advice – and the attorney groups know this. It is in the lawyer's best interest never to resolve things amicably. The more long and drawn-out the process is, the more billable hours they submit."

Anjou fumbled for a box of tissues she had hidden in a bottom drawer.

"I've been reading the paper and watching how many board meetings and special hearings they've had for their gifted program," she added after blowing her nose.

I nodded.

"But how many have they had for special ed? None, right? Get a bunch of special interest parents together in Davis and they call it a gifted program or a language immersion program. You get a smaller group together and they call it a PTA. Get one special needs parent in Davis asking for help, and they put you on a list and label you as more than just a minor threat. There's no Autism program in Davis. There's no ADD program in Davis. There's no fill-in-the-blank disability program in Davis. But we have a gifted program, because God forbid those exceptional children be left to the mediocrity of the regular classroom." She thumped the table. "How is it that a city so enlightened as Davis finds it acceptable to focus all of its energy on the group of children who arguably need the least amount of help, and at the same time marginalize and antagonize the children who need it the most? It's simply and purely publicly funded discrimination. The irony of it all is that they think they are protecting those kids, but they are actually hurting them." Anjou waved her hand.

The lighting began to outpace the thunder outside as the storm distanced itself from the Yolo County Animal Shelter.

"So," she said straightening her shirt, "I couldn't work for a system that did that. I needed to be able to do something. So I went back to night school to become a lawyer, and I eventually got a job with a disabled rights advocacy group."

"That's amazing," I said.

"No, it wasn't," she said. "As passionate as I was about helping children, I just wasn't cut out for the work. It was stressful and more time consuming than teaching. I could never separate myself from the emotional aspect of what was happening. I couldn't handle watching school administrators congratulate themselves with high fives and fist bumps as they simultaneously pulled or blocked services from disabled kids. Just not in my DNA."

"We haven't had an easy go of it, with the schools, I mean," I said.

"They will label you," she said.

"They already have," I responded.

"They will scare you into believing that you can't win or it's just not worth it," she said.

"That seems to be our reality," I replied.

"Remember, when there is no consequence for breaking the law, the law won't mean much," she said. "But you also have to remember, it isn't their money that they care about; it's their reputation. That's what hurts them."

"I know, but how do you damage the reputation of someone who has preemptively branded you the lunatic?"

"I always thought the best way to go after them was to keep our kids out of school. Coordinate sick-outs so they don't get their ADA dollars. Jam school board meetings and invite TV news crews. Run for school board, march around the district office with bullhorns and picket signs, scare the shit out of them!" She laughed.

"My friend sent me an internet meme that said they only give special kids to special people," she said. "The same is probably true with dogs too. I always thought sentiments like that were pretty cheesy." She scratched at the nape of her neck. "I don't think that way anymore, but I also don't think you are born special. You have to earn it, and not because of how these kids are, but how special you have to become to deal with the way everyone else is."

Anjou stood as the sun shone through the rain-washed window behind her.

"And when you are in the middle of it, clinging to life, asking for help, and the people who are supposed to extend you a hand slap yours away, all you want to do is stand up in front of a room filled with all of those assholes and play a major F chord on each hand while you scream, 'Fuck you! Fuck you!'"

She jabbed her middle fingers skyward, and I felt her pain.

Color of Depression

"What's right is what's left if you do everything else wrong."

— Robin Williams

All I could see out the window was gray – the top of the gray fence separating our house from Mari's and a pair of gray doves huddled together on it as if waiting to be struck.

The absence of color had invaded the inside of our home too. The ceiling and the walls echoed the gray that had taken hold of my thoughts. I could not see past the pervasive colorless mist. It felt like it had always been there, and had no plans to leave. December had ushered in her gloom. January refused to see the sun. February wholly consumed me.

"I don't want to go running," I said to Annie as she sorted through her emails. "I'm tired. I just want to go back to bed."

Annie did not respond.

"Have you been outside?" I asked. "The air is so thick with moisture that you almost can't breathe. And there is this annoying white noise that sounds almost like it is raining, but it's the condensation dripping off of everything."

Annie continued to scroll and click.

I slumped next to Annie on the couch. "We need a break from this. All she does is come home from school and cry or spend hours in her room screaming."

"It has to be hurting her," Annie said. "I'm really worried we are doing permanent damage."

"What do we do, pull her out?" I sighed.

"I just don't know. I feel like we have put her in some ridiculous shit sandwich," Annie said. "If she doesn't go to school, how is that fair to her? She will continue to fall behind. Her reading and writing is already below grade level, and if we home-school her, how will she ever make friends? But if we keep her in school, it's like we are torturing her. And all that rage, all that negative self-talk, all that self-loathing behavior, every time she bites herself or hits herself in the head –all of that is on us. We have the power to protect her from that, and right now we're not."

"Well, they have that power too," I said.

"Doesn't make it any better." Annie looked at me. "She is our daughter, not theirs."

The dull nothing stood motionless outside, offering no help or hope.

"She is having headaches every day, to the point where she is getting nauseous," Annie whispered.

"We should call Dr. Comice," I said.

"I have two ways to make her headaches go away," Annie said. "They are called Saturday and Sunday."

I hadn't the strength to laugh. On a different tack, I muttered, "Magda told me her teacher doesn't like any noise in the classroom."

"Yes, I know," Annie said.

"Magda has to spend so much energy just focusing on being quiet. How she learns anything, I don't know," I said.

"Her brain is working to the point where she melts down every day at home, and then she won't eat dinner, and then she zonks out rather than falls asleep at a normal time," Annie said.

I felt totally bereft of hope. "I don't know what to do."

"Spring break is around the corner," said Annie. "Let's just get her there. Maybe that will be enough of a break to get us through to the end of the school year."

"Don't you find it pathetic that we are hoping on a fart and a prayer that we can somehow duct tape together a way to get her to the end of a school year?" I shook my head. "That's not right. It's not normal."

"You think?" Annie retorted.

I kicked off my running shoes, pulled a gray blanket over me, and curled into the corner of the couch.

Least Restrictive Environment

"To sit back hoping that someday, some way, someone will make things right is to go on feeding the crocodile, hoping he will eat you last — but eat you he will."

— Ronald Reagan

"I need to talk to Mari about those pear trees," I said to Annie, as I came into the house. "I can't tell if something is wrong or if they aren't getting enough water. Maybe it's this drought."

Pears were the least of Annie's concerns.

"Magda has been a wreck ever since she got home from school today. She's not talking. She alternates between lockjaw and wailing. We are only weeks into second grade, and it is hitting her like a ton of bricks. It's worse than it was last year." Annie sighed. "I just don't see how she is going to survive a year of this. She needs an aide, or at least a teacher that understands. Sorry . . . what did you say about pears?"

295

"Doesn't matter," I mumbled.

The sky blushed as the sun settled into a cleavage in the coastal range. Obtuse angles and long shadows stretched across the floors and walls of our home, and Daisy was beginning to frenzy.

"I take it Charlie hasn't fed the dog yet," I said, throwing my voice down the hall. I got no response.

"Arthur!" Annie screamed. "Arthur, come here now!"

I bolted toward the bathroom.

"Oh my god, look at this!" Annie trembled and pointed at Magda, who stood naked in the bathtub in a few inches of water. She was shaking violently.

"What?" I asked.

"Look!" she pointed. "Her shirt was ripped in the back."

Magda's torn Winnie the Pooh t-shirt sat wadded on the floor in front of the tub. Magda stood staring at me, her eyes wide and bloodshot. She handed me a wad of hair.

"What the..." My voice and thoughts trailed off.

"I couldn't see anything when I picked her up from school," Annie said. "She wears so many layers of goddamn clothing."

Magda's face was mottled, her left cheek freshly bruised, claw marks down the front of her neck. I spun her round. Hair was missing from where her scalp met the nape of her neck, and long thin scratches overlapped petal-shaped bruises. She had been tattooed in roses and fallen into their thorns.

My heart sank. I felt faint. I closed my eyes, pursed my lips, and fought every urge to vomit.

Magda began to wail uncontrollably. "I hate this. I hate this. I hate all of this. I am bad. I am bad. I am bad!"

"No, honey, you are not bad," said Annie, fighting the urge to cry, pleading with Magda.

"We are taking pictures and sending them to every asshole in that district," I said, regaining my strength. "She is not going back to that school until they can keep her safe. I don't want to hear a bunch of lip service and bullshit this time."

"They called CPS on Feather when Quincy showed up with bruises at school," Annie said quietly. "They tried to blame it on her and Ash."

"Try to blame us," I said through clenched teeth.

"We need to take her to the doctor to make sure she is okay," Annie said.

"Yes, we do, and when we get home, we need to start looking for an attorney."

* * *

The paper swung back and forth from the psychologist Matt Melrose's hand as if suspended from the invisible arm of a pendulum. Then, like the leaves outside, it wavered slightly then tumbled end over end and landed below the point from which it was released adjacent to the metal waste bin.

Annie and I were in his office across from Principal Costa and Magda's second grade teacher, Ms. Opal. They watched wordlessly as Annie fought back tears describing the physical and emotional pain Magda was enduring at school. They had no pens. They had no papers. They appeared to have no concern.

Ms. Opal stood. "Ms. Russell, I have been teaching for a very long time, and you do not know what goes on in my classroom. Kids teasing each other is a normal part of child development," she sneered. "Bullying is a term that has just become overblown, used way too much. You came to me last year so concerned about her first grade classroom, and wanting to have Magda sit in my classroom for a little while just so she could see what second grade was like, and I agreed. She worked on second grade projects and fit right in with the class and the curriculum. And you were so happy about it." She practically looked beatific with her angelic smile and dewy skin. "So what happened? Why are you now upset? I just don't think you know exactly what you want." She stood and made her way to the door. "Sorry, I have yard duty, and I'm going to be late."

The metal blinds reverberated as she slammed the door behind her.

"Let's address her in a minute," I said pointing toward where Ms. Opal had just departed. "I want to talk about Magda. What you are telling me is that you cannot do anything for her safety because it is not included on her IEP? And in order to get any of that help on her IEP she has to be tested again? And that is only if the testing shows that she needs any such help. Is that correct?"

"Yes," Mr. Melrose said. "Unfortunately, Maggie is only qualified under speech."

"Magda," I said.

"Yes, we really are limited in what services we can provide under that heading," Melrose pontificated.

"So, I just want to clarify, you cannot protect a child who is being assaulted at school, IEP or not?"

"Of course we protect children," Mr. Costa blurted. "But I would like to ask Magdalena what she did to provoke this."

I was speechless at his victim blaming.

"And the fact of the matter is that Ms. Opal doesn't believe that what is going on is truly bullying. She says all she sees is typical childhood behavior, and thinks that you are blowing things out of proportion."

"Out of proportion," I said. "Is that what you believe?"

"Well, I'm afraid this is a bit of a he said she said situation." He shrugged his shoulders.

"What you just carelessly, or purposefully, threw to the ground is a letter from our pediatrician, Dr. Comice," I said, pointing to the floor next to the waste bin. "It confirms that Magda has autism. Why can't she just be qualified under that, and then get the protection at school that she needs? What more do you need?"

"Mr. Russell, there is a higher standard for autism in schools than there is in the medical world. There has to be an educational impact," Melrose said without affect.

"Can you explain to me how there isn't an educational impact with her medical diagnosis, or the marks on her skin?"

"I know the system can seem frustrating at times," he said, giving me a morsel of his attention while most of it was focused on his phone.

"I apologize. I do have an observation in a classroom in about ten minutes. I've known lots of children who've struggled with lots of different things, and it never meant they needed something written into their IEPs. If we put too many rules in an IEP, it can become too restrictive and doesn't allow for the natural learning process to occur." He never lifted his eyes from his phone.

"And when would this testing take place?" I asked his forehead.

"Well, let me see…" He sighed as he laid his phone down and flipped through the calendar on his desk. "We have sixty days from the time you offer consent, less Thanksgiving week, which might push us into Christmas break … gosh, we are really backlogged this year." He shook his head.

"So in the meantime, how are we supposed to guarantee Magda's safety?"

"We are not sure that she needs more than what we are already providing," Costa said.

"I just don't get it. Did you not see the photos?" I could feel Annie's silent rage next to me.

"It's not clear to the district what has happened," Mr. Costa said.

My mouth stood ajar. Annie grabbed my thigh.

"What happens if we put Magda through this testing and she doesn't qualify for help, or some different moniker?" I asked. "Is it possible that she will lose her IEP?"

"It's possible," Melrose said. "She has been making nice progress from what I've reviewed."

"You've got to be kidding me," I said. "How many people do you have assigned to yard duty for each recess period?"

"Two," Costa replied.

"And how many students are out on the playground at recess? It's staggered, right? So two hundred fifty, three hundred maybe?"

"About."

"Do you see my point?" I asked. "I'm failing to see what you are already providing."

The room was motionless – expressionless – blank.

"Did you know that the district office is sending us truancy notices," I said, looking for any sympathetic bone in the pudgy man's body. "They say if we keep her out of school anymore, we risk fines or a year's worth of jail time, fines which start at $500 all the way up to $2500. You tell me what you would do, if your child came home covered in bruises and you weren't going to be able to get her any help for another sixty days…"

"I will draft the proposal for testing today, and you can sign it before you leave the office," Melrose offered.

"Magda cannot go back into a classroom with that woman. It's not safe. She's not safe," Annie said.

"No, she can't go back." Costa shook his head.

"Then where the hell does she go?" Annie asked.

"I don't have classroom for her right now," Costa said.

"I don't understand that," Annie said. "Even Charlie's teacher offered to have Magda sit in his classroom so she could at least get credit for being at school," Annie said. "And he was even willing to give her assignments, unlike Ms. Opal, who seems hell bent on making this all so much worse."

"Yes I know, but there are classroom size limits," Mr. Costa said. "Have you considered the independent study option?"

"Are you serious?" escaped my mouth.

"Did you know that Magda doesn't play with any girls, only boys?" Annie said ignoring Mr. Costa's question. "That alone isn't typical. She is ripe for being picked on."

"Are you concerned about her sexuality?" Melrose was flip.

"I can't help you," Annie blurted.

"Can you just email us the consent for testing?" I demanded. "We need to leave." I grabbed Annie's hand and headed toward the door. "I think we are done here."

"If Ms. Opal won't send assignments home, I can leave some in the office for you tomorrow," Costa said.

"Fine," Annie said.

Charlie Is

*"If we lose love and self-respect for each other,
this is how we finally die."*

— Maya Angelou

The answering machine flashed three messages as we walked into the kitchen from the garage.

"This is bullshit," I said.

Annie slumped into a chair at the kitchen table, holding her head. She hadn't spoken since we had left Melrose's office.

"Remember those conversations you weren't privy to because of your age? You know, because the adults knew what was best?"

"What?" Annie finally spoke.

"I don't know, don't listen to me. I don't know if I'm livid or delirious."

I pushed the button on the answering machine. It announced, "You have three messages." *Beep.*

"Maybe someone called to let us know this is all some big joke and they want to apologize for leading us on for so long," I said.

"Maybe it's the attorney we called," Annie said.

"First message: Annie, call me, it's Feather. You're never going to believe what they did this time." *Beep.*

"Next message: Hey, it's Frank. Arthur, call me, we need to catch up. My number is 555-5555 – just kidding. I tried texting you earlier, but hadn't heard from you. Hope all is well. You know how to reach me. I'm headed downtown tonight if you're free. Angelo's not interested." *Beep.*

"Next message: Hi, Annie and Arthur, this is Bart Alameda, Charlie's teacher. Would you call me please? I would like to find out how you two are doing. Maybe we can meet for coffee. I would like to talk with you guys." *Beep.*

* * *

"What did Mari say?" Annie asked.

"She said she would be happy to watch the kids tonight for an hour or so."

"Great. Charlie's teacher wants to meet at the coffee bar at Nugget at six."

"Perfect," I said.

* * *

Bart Alameda's glasses steamed as he sipped his coffee. Annie spoke with a thousand-yard stare as she filled him in on what had transpired earlier in the afternoon. The combination of Magda's physical and emotional reality and the culmination of years of resistance, intimidation, and insults from the district had her shell-shocked.

It wasn't just Annie who struggled to find the positive and the light side of life anymore. I too had curated and preserved everything unhappy, as if I kept it stored behind glass for ready viewing. Recounting the story to anyone who would listen may not have been therapeutic, but it helped to remind me of how unreal our reality had become. Bart's request to talk was the first time anyone affiliated with YUSD truly sought to understand our situation.

As Annie spoke, I could see Bart trying to process all of what he was hearing. As he sipped his coffee with one cream and two sugars, I occasionally caught him swallowing hard. His cheeks blushed as the steam kissed his face. He listened to Annie in a way that no teacher had ever listened to us about Magda. He didn't minimize, he didn't interrupt, and he wasn't dismissive. He was supportive.

As I watched Bart listen, I realized that I had become almost incapable of that kind of fully present listening. I had been trained by every IEP meeting, every parent teacher conference, every meeting with the principal, and every discussion with the school psychologist to tune out the static noise that constituted the majority of what they said. Without fail, every meeting we had with anyone who was legally obligated to care progressed in the same manner. Annie always tried desperately to make tangible for them what Magda's life was like, and I punctuated the conversations with illustrative anecdotes or copies of her schoolwork. But no matter how enthusiastically we tried to make the case for Magda, Annie and I were ultimately forced to watch their faces lose expression as their minds wandered off to someplace else they would rather be.

I found myself doing it too. I blamed it on chronic stress. My mind drifted to where I thought I should be. And in the contest between desire and reality, I was always the loser.

Over Annie's shoulder, I could see a small boy clinging to his father's pant leg as if the polished concrete floor was falling out from underneath him. His father stood clinging to the simple interaction between himself and the checker. The only thing the man seemed sure of in life was that he wanted his groceries in a plastic bag. I wanted to talk to him, but I didn't know what I would say.

"We cannot thank you enough for being willing to let Magda in your classroom," Annie said to Bart. It brought me back to the conversation.

"She really feels like she has done something wrong. This whole experience has been horrible for her."

"I think it has really angered Ms. Opal too," I said to Bart, glancing at Annie in support. "I can't imagine she is happy with you accepting Magda in to your classroom."

"Well, it doesn't help to have a principal who feels comfortable pitting staff against each other so he doesn't have to lead," Bart said. "Oops, did I say that out loud?" He smiled. "It would be nice to have a more supportive administration. Perhaps that is a more PC way to say it." He smiled again and centered the cup in front of him. "I actually have ulterior motives for asking you here tonight."

"Okay…!" said Annie in surprise.

"I'm worried about one of my students." He blew across the top of his coffee then sipped. "I would like to talk about Charlie. I'm a little worried that in all this–" he waved his arms like he was making a snow angel in the air "–his needs might slip through the cracks. I love having him in class. He is so eager. He loves learning and having friends. And he is so inclusive of everyone else, but there are times when he is quiet and seems to be consumed by something other than where he is."

Probably genetic, I thought, as I watched the man carry his petrified son in one arm and his groceries in the other toward the exit.

"He is a very smart and resilient kid, but every stage of development demands something new of a child. I just want to make sure we don't lose sight of helping him navigate his world."

I was flooded with waves of guilt. For the first time in a long time, I realized that I needed to be here in the present moment – not thinking about anything else and not feeling sorry for myself.

Annie reached across the table for my hand.

"Charlie was the first reason we did anything," I said to his teacher. My coffee had soured my stomach. "He was the first thing we had before we had things; he was the first child we imagined before we had children. He was the first real thing we anticipated or planned for. He was the first thing to scare the crap out of us." I forced a laugh.

"I think Charlie needs to know that," he said.

"Oh my god, you're right," Annie said. "He does so many things so well that we take it all for granted."

"I'm not trying to put you down as parents. I know this is an incredibly difficult time for you both, but time is a precious resource, and we all learn what we are taught," he said. "Don't let things like this prevent you from being the family that each one of you needs."

* * *

"Your trees are very sick," Mari said. "Those leaves aren't turning with the fall. They're dying. I'll work on them tomorrow, but I can't promise we aren't going to lose them."

I tossed the car keys on the kitchen counter. Mari and Charlie were finishing a game of Sorry at the kitchen table.

"How is Magda?" Annie asked Mari.

"Well, I don't think she liked our game, so she took Daisy into her room and has refused to come out since. Charlie said she does this a lot, and we should just leave her alone. Every once in a while we hear Daisy banging around."

"Arthur," Annie threw her glance down the hall.

"Yes," I said walking toward Magda's room.

"How was your meeting?" Mari asked Annie.

"Good," Annie answered. Turning to Charlie, she said, "We're going to check on your sister, but after that can we talk to you? You're not in trouble at all, in fact it's the opposite, but we want to ask you some questions."

Charlie nodded and smiled.

I opened Magda's bedroom door. The room was a void. The light was out and the window shade was pulled down. I heard Daisy flap her ears and lick her paws as Annie walked up behind me.

"Magda?" I said quietly.

Magda spoke into the abyss. "Charlie kept saying sorry, but he wasn't sorry. He was smiling. That's a lie. It's not a real sorry, it's just the game Sorry, not real sorry," Magda wailed. "It's mean! Mean!"

"Magda, honey, I'm going to turn on the lights so we can see you, okay?" Annie said.

The illumination showed what she had done to her room. Hurricane Magda had made landfall. All of her books had been thrown on the floor. She had strewn her blankets into every corner and stacked her dresser drawers like a failed game of Jenga in the center of her room. Magda was barely visible from her favorite hiding spot under her desk, riding out the remainder of the tropical depression. Daisy sat in front of her panting and smiling, proud she had remained faithful to her friend throughout the storm.

"Magda, what happened?" I asked.

"I had this in speech," she said.

"Had what?" Annie asked.

"Lying," Magda said.

"Lying about what?" I asked.

"Eating crow. Getting cat tongues." Magda whimpered as she spoke.

Magda metronomically struck the back of her head against the wooden desk. It resonated with a hollow thud.

"I don't want to break my leg! I know Charlie wasn't sorry!" Magda shook and folded into herself. "It's hard!" she wailed. "It's hard!"

Annie looked at me. "Will you see Mari out and talk to Charlie? I'll stay here."

"You sure?"

"Yes."

I closed the door behind me, thanked Mari, and saw her to the front door.

"I don't think these are going to make it," Mari said as she fingered the blackened branches. The leaves and branches had stiffened and lost their pliability. "Burned from the inside," she added with a shake of her head, and walked home.

"Is Magda okay?" Charlie asked as I closed the heavy front door.

"I don't know, buddy. She has a lot of stress in her life right now, and your mother and I are trying to figure out how to get rid of that for her."

"I'm sorry," he said as he made his way to the bathroom to start his pre-bedtime rituals.

"It's not your fault. Sometimes things that are easy or fun for us aren't for her." I stood in the hallway and watched Charlie diligently brush his teeth then wash his face. His Star Wars pajama pants ended a few inches above his ankle. "You've gotten taller," I said.

"I guess," he said crawling into bed.

"Story?" I asked.

"No. What do you want to come back as after you die?" he asked plainly.

"Are you talking about reincarnation?"

"Yeah, you know, what would you want to be? I would want to be a dolphin or a killer whale."

I turned off Charlie's overhead light, closed the door, and sat down on the floor with my back against his bed looking up at the glow-in-the-dark stars on his ceiling.

"Do you hope there is reincarnation?" I asked. "What about the cool things about being a human?"

"I hope for some people there is reincarnation," he said. "Like for Magda."

"Why?"

"I want her to come back as something that is happy," he said turning on his purple lightsaber and waving it back and forth above my head.

"Is this whole situation hard for you?" I asked.

"Some kids are mean to her at school, and I don't know what to do."

"Mean how?"

"Teasing her, saying stuff about how weird she is, but I don't know if she knows they are teasing."

"I think she knows. That must be very hard for you to watch."

"No one else is watching," he said. "Except for Mr. Alameda maybe. He won't let you say anything bad about anyone in class. Ms. Opal wasn't like that."

"You know we love you, right? We would do anything for you."

"Yeah." Charlie yawned.

"It's not just that I love you, but there are also many things I love about you."

Charlie rolled onto his side, his lightsaber aiming a point of light at the wall.

"We love your super-fast lightning speed and scrappiness on the soccer field. I love that *Empire* is your favorite Star Wars movie. I love that you and I go to the movies on my birthday and see movies that Mommy won't. I love that you used your own money to buy Mommy that Adele CD for her birthday. I love that you have consumed all of the Calvin & Hobbes books that I collected as a kid – and love reading them too. I love you for your fear of bees and your mastery of Legos. I love that I got to be the one who saw you draw your first breath. I love that when you were four, your favorite story was *Harold and the Purple Crayon*. I love that I knew you would look just like your mother from your twenty-week ultrasound. I love the big brother you have become."

"Daddy, can we watch Star Wars tomorrow?" Charlie murmured as his arm dropped his purple weapon and he dropped off to sleep.

I sat there staring at the galaxy above my head, looking for patterns and constellations, trying to make order out of chaos.

"Sure, buddy," I whispered. I stood up and kissed his forehead.

Annie came out of Magda's room at the same time I emerged from Charlie's.

"He's asleep," I said.

"So is she," Annie said.

"Do you want help with her room?" I asked.

"No, we can deal with that tomorrow. How is he? Did you talk to him?"

"Yes." I shrugged. "He is Charlie. I feel like we've let him down. His brain doesn't have to worry about making up monsters that live under his bed or in his closet. We've drawn them throughout this house for him."

"No, we haven't." Annie motioned for me to walk away from their bedroom doors.

"Do you care if I go running?" I asked. "I just don't feel settled right now."

"Do what you need to do. I'm exhausted."

Almost a Fantasy

"There is no what should be; there is only what is."

— Lenny Bruce

I slipped on my running shoes, put on my running jacket, snapped Daisy onto the leash, and stepped outside. The fall air smelled of softening pumpkins and distant fireplaces. The oversized blood moon cast its hue over everything around us.

As I walked the concrete path out the front of our house, I reached up and snapped a twig from the pear tree closest to the street. The darkened leaves and branches had been scorched, burned by a fever, dehydrated at the hour of their deaths. A formation of Canadian Geese honked a sorrowful eulogy as they flew over our house.

"Let's follow them," I said to Daisy as we broke into a trot.

We ran through our neighborhood at a pace much faster than normal. We ran the route we could have run in our sleep behind Brown

Elementary, through the original Mace Ranch grove of trees, and up to the top of the I-80 pedestrian overcrossing.

The moon's influence began to wane under the newly forming fog, and the tubular lights along the parenthetically shaped chain link sides of the path glowed in the mist. The freeway below was static noise. Coming down off of the overcrossing into South Davis, the lights of the overpass had been broken, and we descended into the darkness of the night. We headed for the warm glow of the sodium streetlamp at the base of the ramp and turned east toward Willowcreek Park along the bike path. I could hear music playing through an open window in duplexes ahead of us. Happy voices were singing along.

We turned south into the park and traveled a path rippled by tree roots. Path lights punctuated the darkness. Somewhere, high above us in their evergreen perch, a dense murder of crows mocked us under their breath. We ignored their insults and pushed through the mist into the greenbelt path between streets named after the first peoples of California.

Through the tunnel of trees, the air became acrid and thick with sulphur. We came to the clearing between Miwok and Pomo Places and rounded on a dark figure standing on a granite stone at the edge of a flooded field. A broken sprinkler head forced a stream of water up behind its silhouette until the power of gravity ripped it back down to the ground where it spattered like strips of firecrackers. The figure seemed unaware of us as it cast arcs of orange and white fire from its hands into the soggy marsh.

I was unsure that what I was seeing was real, but as I looked down at Daisy, she was fixed on the light as well, and I could see the curved reflection in her eyes. As we closed, I could see the slender figure was not quite an adult, and was wearing a hooded sweatshirt. The figure turned and looked at us as it struck a match and flung it out into the water with a hiss. It was expressionless with only depressions where its eyes must have been. Wisps of its long hair framed its porcelain face. The harder I looked at it to find any defining feature, the less I saw.

As we passed the spectral figure, I wiped the sweat from my brow and quickened my pace. Just another Davis teenager with nothing better to do, I thought.

"Annie would say something," I muttered to myself. "Even if it is wet, playing with matches is not a good thing to do behind all these houses."

I stopped and turned, but the figure was gone. It had vanished into the thickening fog. I listened for footsteps but heard nothing.

"What the hell are we doing, Daisy?" I massaged her head drawing her ears closer together. "Do we even belong here?"

We turned west and headed downtown. The fog began to lift as we ran by the soccer fields adjacent to Tremont Elementary.

"Charlie has a game at nine tomorrow," I said to myself.

As we ran over the Richards Boulevard overpass and down through the reflective cylindrical Richards bike tunnel into downtown, the pace that we had been keeping began to catch up with us. My legs felt deadened and heavy. Every step required much more effort than the last. I could feel my brain waves slowing as every footfall required a conscious effort.

"I don't think I've eaten since lunch," I said to Daisy as I pushed the crosswalk button where Richards met First and E streets. "Did we even remember to feed you dinner?"

Daisy flapped her ears and impulsively tried to pull ahead as we walked downtown. We zigzagged our way through the grid of streets, jaywalking and avoiding bicyclists. I could hear music drawing me toward the building that used to be the Davis Saloon. A bass drum was rumbling a familiar rhythm, like a heartbeat. Every time the door to the bar opened, the melody spilled out into the night and then suddenly muted when the door slammed shut.

The Brodys were playing inside, and they were playing "Anne Marie." I walked up to the window and peered through my reflection at the band bouncing and jumping around the corner stage. Surrounding the band were concentric circles of undergrads with pints in hand, grad students with pints in hand, and then people like me, well beyond school age standing and swaying back and forth with someone pressed up against their sides, hugging each other sideways, like the only way Magda will hug anyone.

I longed to be here with Annie, singing along, having fun, reliving what once was — a life free of worry. My eyes glazed over and Daisy wedged her head between my legs. As I refocused my vision, I could see a familiar man waving violently at me in the window. It was Frank. He pointed for me to stay put, and then he disappeared into the crowd.

"You came!" Frank exclaimed as he burst out the door.

"Sorry I didn't call you back. I didn't realize there was a show tonight. I was just going for a run with Daisy to try to unwind, and I thought I heard something familiar."

"Hi, Daisy!" Frank patted her haunches.

Her tail wagged rapidly, but she did not remove her head.

"Come in, you won't believe who is here. Do you remember those girls across the hall in the dorms, Sally and Lakshmi," Frank said, making googly eyes and sticking his tongue out of his mouth sideways.

I feigned shock and surprise. "What do you care about girls? Besides, we're both married." I said, pointing at Daisy. "And how am I supposed to take a dog into a bar?"

"It's Davis, you can take a dog anywhere," Frank replied with a smile. "I know the bouncer."

"I'm sure you do," I said. "Charlie has a soccer game in the morning, but why don't we try to meet up for lunch, or come over to our place for dinner and drinks tomorrow?"

"No, I want to hang out tonight. Go save us that bench across from Woodstock's," he directed, and ran back into the bar.

Daisy and I complied and sat down on the metal bench across from the pizza shop. The sweet smell of yeast and pizza sauce reminded me of how hungry I was. As I sat and waited for Frank to return I could see the figure of a woman working at her computer in the office above the adjacent skate shop.

I pulled my phone from my running belt and texted Annie: *Going to be late, ran into Frank downtown.*

My phone immediately buzzed with her reply. *Great, have fun. FYI she is now in our bed.*

"Of course," I mumbled.

"Here, take one of these." Frank handed me a low-ball glass.

"Where did you get these?"

"Behind the bar."

"And what are they for?"

"This." He pulled a bottle of scotch from a paper bag. "A student of mine gave me this today. Aged twenty years, single malt," he said reading the label. "It has to be good, right?"

"Where have you been keeping that?"

"My car – it's in the lot." He pointed back over our heads. "Neat, right?" He poured two fingers into my glass.

"Sure," I said.

"Cheers," he said.

"Cheers."

"Remember how we used to take shots of Southern Comfort at these shows?"

"We didn't know any better," I said. "They still sound good – the band, that is."

As I drank, the warmth started at my lips, struck the center of my chest, and exploded in my midsection. "You're like a Saint Bernard."

Notes of cream and oak frolicked behind my nose.

"We had to put Berdoo down yesterday," Frank said. His expression changed from jovial to flat.

"I had no idea, Frank. I'm so sorry. I feel like an awful friend. I've been so wrapped up in my own world, I have no idea what's going on in other people's lives."

"Dr. Clementine said it was heart failure. I guess it can happen in big dogs," he said with a soft shrug. He looked away, somewhere distant, swirled his glass then sipped. "He started coughing about three months ago. We thought it was pneumonia at first, but as it turns out…" Frank was unable to finish.

"I'm so sorry," I said again. "If there is anything Annie and I can do, please don't hesitate to call us."

"Angelo is actually taking this harder than I am. He hasn't been out of bed all day."

I reached down and stroked Daisy from the top of her head to the center of her back. "I can't even imagine."

Frank wiped his face and added a splash of scotch to both our glasses.

"To Berdoo." He lifted his glass.

"To Berdoo." I lifted mine.

We both drank.

"Annie wants to move," I said.

"Move where?" He asked.

"That's just it, we don't know. Things have been shit-God-awful at school for Magda."

"Not that it makes you feel any better, and I'm not just saying this to keep you here, but public education for spectrum kids, or kids with other disabilities for that matter, sucks just about anywhere you go," Frank said.

"I know. I'm sure it does. It's just that here it seems particularly bad." I sighed. "Skipping all the details, Magda is coming home with bruises and scratches. She cries inconsolably just about every night. She's even been talking about hating herself."

"Ugh," he groaned. "Look, I had to leave this town. I still don't know if coming back was the right thing to do. Every summer, Angelo moans about the heat and threatens to move back to the city. I know he hates more than just the weather."

"I don't blame him," I said.

Frank sipped his scotch. This place has a lot going for it. I don't know how many times I've forgotten to lock my car at night or lock my front door even, and guess what? Nothing happened. San Francisco, Oakland, Berkeley–" he waved his hand westward "–forget about it."

"A lot of my hesitation to move is for Charlie," I said. "I really don't know what it would do to him. He has so many friends here. He is comfortable here. I just don't know if it is fair to him, and if I'm being truthful about all of this, we moved here for him. But then again, I feel like we are doing real harm to Magda by keeping her here."

"Did you know that there are at least two EPA superfund sites in Davis?" Frank said.

"No."

"Most people don't." Frank shook his head in disgust. "There is the old fertilizer plant down by the Target, and there are all the beagle corpses they exposed to radiation during the cold war somewhere south of campus."

"I'm sure no one wants to advertise that," I said.

"No, of course not, would you?" He smirked. "But the problem is, these aren't just one-off events. Even if you heard about what they did to those dogs, you could compartmentalize it, put it in a box. You know it was something that happened a long time ago – ancient history. But what do you think they are doing right now at the primate center? If you want to hide behind advancing medical science as your rationale for torturing animals, where is the line that you think you shouldn't cross? Radiation is bad for beagles, but giving monkeys AIDS is supposed to be okay? I don't think so!" he exploded. He took a long swig of his drink.

"It's disgusting," I said, feeling languid and lightheaded from the scotch.

"This town is littered with issues no one wants to talk about. If it doesn't improve home values, then they don't want to hear about it," he ranted. "The only thing that gets press is if voters will approve the next housing development, or how many cell towers the city will allow, or what they are going to change the name of the gifted program to so the dumb kids and their parents will feel less shitty about being left out."

"I have to tell you, you're kind of making my point for me. Our priorities are wrong." I drained the last swallow from my glass.

"We are all self-preservationists," said Frank. "We don't want to believe we are flawed. The further you can push something that is uncomfortable to think about away from you, the less you have to care, and the less you feel obligated to do. But if you want to be a leader in this community – school board, city council, chancellor, whatever –you have to be willing to employ a little empathy from time to time, and use some balanced judgment."

"I think people only see what they want to see," I said.

"Or are capable of seeing," he amended.

"Right." The warmth of the alcohol was affecting my ability to form words. "You remember that *Dark Side of the Moon* poster you had in our dorm room? It took up the whole window."

"Vaguely."

"How mind-blowing must it have been to discover that sunlight was made up of all these different colors?" The effects of exhaustion, an empty stomach, and twenty-year-old scotch were making it difficult to paste together a coherent thought. "We were so smart, but then some-one came along and said there is light we still can't see – the infrared, the ultraviolet. That is where Magda exists – Daisy too." I set my glass down on the bench and leaned back. "It's all dark matter. You can't see it. You can only measure it by what it displaces. It's so easy for someone to be dismissive when you're willfully ignorant."

"I don't remember you being such a light weight," Frank said. "That scotch went straight to your head."

"I haven't been sleeping well, and I forgot to eat dinner tonight."

"Let me get you something from across the street." Frank stood up and gestured toward the pizza place.

"Don't worry about it." I attempted to sit upright.

"I don't need you passing out on me. I'll be back in a minute. Stay conscious!" Frank grinned, trotted across the street, and disappeared into the pizzeria.

Behind me, the saloon door opened up and people began to spill into the parking lot lighting cigarettes. The band was taking a beer and pee break halfway through their set.

I sat in a daze. Daisy was still wedged between my legs, which now felt distant and removed from my body. My hands had been tied down and my torso restrained to the back of the bench. My ears were the only functional part of my body left, and all I had been reduced to was an eavesdropper – which wasn't difficult since most of the patrons were yelling at each other as if the band were still playing.

"I teach that kid's Fisheries class," a distant voice said. "I feel old. Are we those creepy guys that hang out at bars with undergrads now?"

"Gross. Probably. But who cares," said the man he was with. "You want another beer?"

"I feel old," I said under my breath.

"Here you go," Frank said shoving a medium pizza box in my lap. "Are you ever going to look at me, Daisy?"

Daisy lifted her head as I opened the box.

"You've gotten gray, girl," Frank said as he rubbed her snout.

Daisy smiled back at Frank, flapped her ears, and wiggled herself deeper between my legs.

"Oh my god, this smells amazing," I said. "Thank you so much. Are you sure you don't want to go back inside?" I nodded to where the band had finished their break and was strumming the first slow chords of their anthemic "Beer Truck Driver."

"Nope," Frank said grabbing a slice of the Causeway Classic. "I could eat this every day. So good – tastes like college."

The building behind us began to reverberate as the crowd sang along with the band.

"When the kids were littler, Magda maybe two, if that, I was at my parents' house and ran into a friend of mine from high school." I paused to chew and swallow. "I hadn't seen him in years, and he had a daughter about the same age as Magda. We talked about this and that, and as we were parting ways, he said, 'You know, we really should get our girls together for a play date.'" I wiped my mouth with a paper napkin. "How do you say to somebody, 'You know, I really appreciate the offer, but I just don't think that is going to happen.' And that's not to say I wouldn't love for it to happen."

"Probably just like that," Frank said.

"You're probably right. I just didn't have it in me at the time. Now I feel like all I do is explain her to everyone."

As we ate, I began to sober up, and the fog dissipated. Frank and I caught up in a way we hadn't in months. We talked about everything from each other's jobs to the Proposition 8 legal fight and the aggressive flocks of turkeys that were taking over Davis. For a moment, I forgot where I was, what had happened in the last day, the last week, the last few months and years.

"I think they're finishing up," Frank said throwing his head off to the side.

I could hear their ever-changing 80s metal and pop medley cover crescendo with "Hungry Like the Wolf." Then the stage went silent and the house lights came on.

"I think you're right," I said.

"I'm taking the Tipsy Taxi home," Frank said. "You want to come?"

"I thought that was only for students. I think I need to walk off some of this pizza and scotch."

A trio of twenty-something women spilled onto the sidewalk. "OMG, puppy! I want a puppy!" shrieked the one wearing black stretch pants and a block letter UCD sweatshirt. She came running over to where Frank and I sat, the heels of her UGG boots scuffling the concrete with every stride. "OMG! Can I pet her?" She was an octave or two above sobriety.

"Sure," I said.

"What's wrong with her?" Her face became twisted and her voice popped and croaked. "Why won't she look at me? Is she like messed up or something?"

Before I could tell her to fuck off, one of her friends screamed as she crumbled into a ball after walking headlong into a tree.

"OMG! Are you okay?" said the girl in the UGGs as she got up and ran over to her friend.

"She's probably a human development major and wants to become a school psychologist because, OMG, she really enjoys working with kids," I said in my best impression of her.

Frank laughed. "Ah, you never know, she seems to really want to help people. She may pull her shit together and go to nursing school."

"Ouch," I said. "Touché."

"Can we meet tomorrow?" Frank asked.

"Charlie has a game at nine."

"Where?"

"Tremont," I said. "But it may be that Annie goes and not me."

Frank squinted at me.

"Magda," I said. "She can't make it through a game."

"I'll be there regardless."

"That would be great. Charlie loves his uncle Frank. Annie would be happy to see you too."

Frank reached down and rubbed Daisy's head then wrapped me in a bear hug.

"I'm really sorry about Berdoo," I said into his shoulder.

"Thanks," he said.

We parted, and I turned the block to follow the railroad tracks home.

Crossing Fifth Street, I could see that a single kitchen light had been left on underneath the wavy roof of the Dairy Queen. I tried my best to balance on the track. Daisy walked only on the ties, avoiding the rocky bed. She was unfazed by the plastic bag that bounced along next to us in the soft breeze. She had no clue that yesterday had already become tomorrow.

As we approached our front door, I couldn't help but wonder what was next for Magda. All I could hope was that it was in fact hope. I looked down at my dog knowing that at some point, sooner than any of us ever wanted, we would have to face what I knew was next for her now that she was getting older. Parting with Daisy was something I could not fathom yet, so I pushed it out of my mind.

Understanding

*"You have enemies? Good. That means you've stood
up for something, sometime in your life."*

— Winston Churchill

The *Delta Breeze's* calliope whistles through the arcade of branches
and leaves. I stand in my orchard of plenty looking up at clouds
painted into happy white expressions. I cannot and dare not crawl out
from that under which I am standing. There is an understanding, an
implicit agreement. I'm not under a rock. I'm under the giving tree that
very few can afford, and I'm afforded all its shade and community as I
hum along in lockstep.

Under here, what I want is handed out like candy on prescription
pads, so they say, to the tattooed carnies, the fat ladies, and their bearded
aunts. It's all fun and games. There are carnivals every Saturday in the
park. Ignorance and innocence blindly and blissfully throwing darts and

323

tossing rings are bound to win one of the swirling lollipops hanging from underneath every set of leaves. Here, under my tree, grown in a public garden and watered from deep wells, ubiquity is the new norm and the new passport. "Step right up! Everybody plays, everybody wins!"

Only something is wrong. I was blindfolded before I was given my turn, left with only a glimpse of the target, the point, or the reason I'm here. The game has been rigged. The baseballs are lopsided. The gun barrels crooked. Someone keeps bumping me out of line. An invisible hand pushes me out from the cool shade and into the mutating radiation of the sun.

Tossed from the midway, I search to understand.

Upset, I'm determined to quit playing and throw away the blinder from my eyes. I retreat to my tree only to find it blighted and dead. There is no low-hanging fruit. The only fruit in abundance belongs to someone else, forbidden to me. And all that my hands turn up is callous. I peel the thickened skin, looking for the softer part of me that I once wore. I'm met by peals of invisible laughter roaring like a lion through the grandstands and peanut galleries.

From the lowest limbs, under the jeering, the looks, the upturned noses, I understand that they think I'm a monkey banging cymbals – a novelty, a nuisance – but I think I'm the scapegoat. So I climb atop the crown, where there is only room for a lightning rod and a birds-eye view of the farm hidden in the trees. From there, I see the strings of disadvantaged marionettes clamoring for an advantage that they are told will only disadvantage those without a disadvantage. Fairness is handed out in the puppet theater without a handout, to those without outstretched hands – hands buried in someone's pocket.

Listening closely, I can hear the pitchmen whisper backstage readying the gifted dogs and talented ponies. Louder yet, criers and barkers boast as a chivaree of electric clown cars zip through fire drills in an Entrance of the Gladiators. Behind them, a bandwagon of performers spins wildly and without purpose, throwing bowling pins and flaming sticks into the crowd for the masses to juggle. The ringleaders arrive armed with pies to throw in the face of air polluters, and oversized shoes to stamp out climate changers, blowing their horns as they extinguish the autistic blaze in a shower of water squirted from a joke-shop lapel daisy.

At the top, it is clearer. These trunks are paper maché. The leaves are tissue paper. The sun is hung by fishing line, the clouds are pillow stuffing, and the canopy is a billowing striped tent held upright by packaging string. The tightrope is stretched and frayed.

The true stakeholders stand hidden in the shadows holding the stakes.

I refuse to crawl back under the big top, but the only way down is a suicidal dive into a miniature pool. My heart beats a thundering parade of elephants. I can hear the trumpeting of pomp and circumstance – the price of admission for a lie. The image of inclusion stands distorted in the fun house mirror.

I scream from the top, "The penny-wise should bear witness to the real spectacle – this sleight of hand, this three-ringed circus!" But blinded by snake oil, they cannot see me. Deafened by this illusion, they cannot listen.

How much does it cost to get my full ticket price refunded so I can step out from under this understanding? Oh, how I wish these trees were real. Logging takes so little skill – only a sharpened saw and the will. Or, as an arsonist with his tinder, I'd leave little but cinder. But then I'd be no better. And who do I go to for help when there is no one left in the spotlight who understands?

But then again, this façade – this paper, canvas, and string will burn. Maybe I will too. The *Delta Breeze* will bellow, and dormant chimneys will once again crackle and belch as it is finally okay to light tonight.

This community of heat will char the bunting, level the seating, melt the coffers, and line the public path to the city beyond the circus in gold.

KINGS PLAY CHESS ON FUNNY GREEN SQUARES

ACT III
(UNDER PRESSURE)

SETTING: The kitchen and dining area of Arthur and Annie's home in Davis. It's two in the morning.

AT RISE: Annie is sitting under dim light at the kitchen table reading a book. Arthur and Daisy enter through a red door at stage left.

ARTHUR

What are you still doing up?

ANNIE

Couldn't sleep.

ARTHUR

What are you reading?

ANNIE

(sets book down, removes glasses)

A book I started eight years ago and never finished. It's trash. Besides, Magda is in our bed, and she is fitty. How is Frank?

                         ARTHUR
              (places Daisy in her crate)

They had to put Berdoo down.

                         ANNIE
Oh no! What happened?

                         ARTHUR
Heart failure from what it sounds like. Angelo
is taking it pretty badly I guess.

                         ANNIE
Do they need anything?

                         ARTHUR
I don't think so. I asked.

                         ANNIE
Daisy is getting older.

                         ARTHUR
Mari is right. The pear trees are dead.

                         ANNIE
I saw that. Shame. I loved those trees. It's
going to make the front of the house look like
crap.

                         ARTHUR
Do you want to replace them?

                         ANNIE
I honestly don't care.

ARTHUR

(sits down across from Annie)

Neither do I. You remember seeing that picture
in the paper on the first day of school this
year? It was a father kissing his daughter on
the forehead, sending her off to her first day
of kindergarten.

ANNIE

Was that the paper that had the quiz about how
much of a Davisite you are?

(pauses)

You got more points if you owned a Prius or had
kids in the gifted program.

ARTHUR

Yeah, that's the one. It was an amazing
photograph, one of those you could frame. It
was rife with emotion: Elation. Depression.
Fear. Hope. Joy. I don't think we ever had
that with Magda in a photo-friendly moment, do
you?

ANNIE

Depression, yes! Fear, yes! Hope, joy, we will
one day. I have to believe that.

ARTHUR

I maybe remember having that with Charlie, but
it seems so distant.

                              ANNIE

It's been rough.

                              ARTHUR

                    (pauses)

I'm done here, but I just can't leave. We can't
leave. I wish we could just walk away. Quit
playing.

                    (Annie reaches across the table
                    and takes Arthur's hand)

                              ARTHUR

I just feel angry all the time. This whole
thing just feels like a slow steady march to
our funeral.

                              ANNIE

That's a bit of an overstatement. But we are
both different. We don't laugh as much. We
don't smile as much.

                              ARTHUR

You can see it in photographs. Just look at
pictures of us, all of us, before Magda started
kindergarten. We looked so happy. Even with all
the brain scans and therapy, we were happy. She
looked so happy.

                    (buries face in hands)

                              ANNIE

I know.

ARTHUR

What happens next? Are we just looking forward
to the end of our children's childhood so
we can get them out of these schools? How
miserable is a sentiment like that?

ANNIE

How do you get out of a game you never wanted
to play?

ARTHUR

Do we know what we are going to do?

ANNIE

I think we need to flesh it out a little more.

ARTHUR

Are we ready?

ANNIE

Have we ever been?

ARTHUR

Are you okay?

ANNIE

Are we okay?

ARTHUR

I think we are as okay as we can be.

ANNIE

How do we get back to where we wanted okay to
be?

ARTHUR

I honestly don't know. Remember when I reached
out to our state representative to try to get
them to put Sensory Processing Disorder on the
list of things the state would use to qualify
someone for special ed?

ANNIE

Yes.

ARTHUR

Is it bad that now I just don't even care? I
wouldn't even try today.

ANNIE

I think it's sad.

ARTHUR

I guess that's my point, if I even have one.

ANNIE

You know we aren't the only family this has
happened to.

ARTHUR

I know. The whole system is a conflict of
interest.

ANNIE

What is?

ARTHUR

Them – what they do. You shouldn't have
those responsible for deciding be the ones
delivering.

ANNIE

Okay, you lost me on that one.

ARTHUR

The person responsible for getting your food
shouldn't be the same person deciding if
you're hungry. (Pauses) If doctors were the
ones responsible for paying for blue paint and
wheelchair stencils, I guarantee there would be
a whole lot fewer handicap parking spots around
the country.

ANNIE

Principal Costa sent me an email while we were
meeting with Charlie's teacher. Didn't see it
until after you went out.

(pauses)

They are denying our request for a transfer to
Huynh Elementary.

ARTHUR

Of course they are. So they are making us
choose between fighting to keep her in Opal's
classroom versus homeschooling her.

ANNIE

Pretty much.

ARTHUR

You know the funny thing is, they are playing a
very dangerous game.

ANNIE

They play lots of games.

ARTHUR

They have made us out to be the villains.
They've done the same thing to all those other
families no doubt. But they are banking on us
being not completely crazy. They just tell
everyone we are crazy.

ANNIE

I don't get it.

ARTHUR

They want us to crack under pressure and give
up. But what if cracking meant more than just
folding under the weight of their relentless
onslaught? What if we weren't mentally stable
enough to handle this pressure? What if we
were deranged? Had a screw or two loose? Worse
yet, what if one of these kids that they don't
think needs special ed cracks under their
pressure?

ANNIE

They would find a way to side step that
responsibility. Hide behind a smokescreen of
privacy concerns.

ARTHUR

(speaking quietly)

You know that dream where you are trying to run and you can't? You know your legs are moving, but when you look down at the ground below you, your feet are going nowhere. Or it's like you are swimming upstream. You are working your ass off, and nothing moves. (Pauses) Even if we win this, it won't ever end. We aren't here to win. The only way I see us winning is by getting her in a safe place, in a safe school, with what she needs. What are we willing to pay for that?

ANNIE

I just don't see that happening here. The game is rigged. We are getting kicked out because she doesn't fit in.

ARTHUR

It's bigger than us.

ANNIE

Yes it is.

ARTHUR

I feel badly about Berdoo. I can't imagine what it's going to be like when we lose Daisy – what it will be like for the kids, for her.

ANNIE

I don't even want to think about it.

(BLACKOUT)

(CURTAIN)

Eject

"What we have once enjoyed deeply we can never lose.
All that we love deeply becomes a part of us."

— Helen Keller

Annie and I sat down with Magda's current therapist at our new kitchen table in Oakland.

"I'm sorry to spring this upon you here, but we need help with a letter of reference and a clear explanation of the support she requires for several of the high schools that we are applying to," Annie said as Magda bounded through our new house with her new dog in tow.

"Nutmeg! Let's go!" Magda screamed as she trotted her puppy out to the front yard, tennis ball in one hand and leash in the other.

I told everyone that Daisy had autism. I felt they needed to know, or at least I wanted them to know, especially Magda – not as an offhand comment or as a dismissive remark. Just as the truth that it was. Before

Magda was born, I had always hated labels. It was a teenager's stance. I never wanted to be measured by someone else's yardstick. And of course, as a parent, I felt forced to foist my own belief system upon my child.

I religiously held to my truths until I realized that once you identify something, you own it. Once you own it, if you don't do anything to help it, you are a dick. And you are an even bigger dick if you are doing nothing while saying you are doing something.

The skin of the parent of an autistic child has to grow thicker than the offhand remarks that can cut to the core, or the hurtful comments that can sink deep and take root. When their words do cut and make me bleed, the wound has to heal quickly. It has to; otherwise, it isn't tough enough to fight an entire system of people in positions of power whose only expertise and offerings appear to be false pretense or open hostility.

The ridiculous truth is that it was always easier for people to believe me when I talked about the dog than it was when I talked about my daughter, probably because there were no consequences associated with the dog.

The best thing about Daisy being autistic is that it gave Magda the opportunity to identify with someone like her. Daisy never judged her. Daisy loved her unconditionally. Daisy's autism gave Magda something to hold on to. The dog made it real. The dog made it okay. The dog expanded the definition beyond the silos of Magda's thoughts, her islands of capacity, and allowed her into the world of empathy, something the schools couldn't teach because they never believed.

The margins get pushed aside in the march toward progress. But what are we progressing to? American progress is nothing more than product placement, and autism is no cash crop – it is in fact what people do not want in their schools.

Everyone believed us when we told them that Daisy had cancer. She had melanoma in the back of her throat and was suffocating on her own blood and saliva. There were no under-their-breath comments. There were no doubts. Defining how she would end was somehow infinitely easier than defining how she lived.

For all of us, Daisy never did end. She will always be present. Whenever it feels like I have lost her, or I need her companionship, I know exactly where to go. She still runs free on the farmers' dirt roads of Yolo County. She always stops to admire the boxes of bees humming with activity where the Willow Slough and the old railroad trestle meet. I've seen her setting a solid pace across the Davis freeway pedestrian overpass on my commute to work. Regardless of where I see her, I will always know that she lives where I do, because she lives in Magda.

Mari had a melanoma removed the year we moved. Around the same time, the *Enterprise* published an article citing that an entire elementary school could be filled with the amount of special education students Davis wasn't identifying. That was the same year breast cancer attacked Feather. She had a radical double mastectomy and moved to Woodland to be closer to the only support system Quincy ever had. That was the same year she cracked, the year the burden became too burdensome.

"They build memorials to lost souls, souls purposefully put in harm's way," Feather said the day Annie and I helped her move. "From the National Mall to local parks they etch names, dates, and locations in granite. Museums put under glass artifacts of war," she said as we unloaded banker's boxes of educational records, doctor's reports, and legal documents. "When will they do that for us?"

Feather had a calling, like a preacher. The day she finally realized that her pulpit was made of indifference, she fell through the floor and raced her child to the bottom of their depression. The last time we saw her, she had aged twice as many years as we had known her.

What do labels mean? Are they simply just words with capital letters?

YUSD never gave disabled kids blankets infused with small pox, or shipped them off to internment camps. Feather's autism memorial will never be built because her battle never made it to the evening news; likewise, when a disabled child dies, the coroner never lists autism as the cause of death.

Anjou was certain there was no program for autistic children in Davis. I think that was only partially true. Not only was there no program, there was, and still is, no incentive to create a program. Autistic children and their families are labeled as troublemakers, systematically removed from civil society, and put on reservations of forced homeschooling or a life of disciplinary hearings.

It was easy to walk away from Daisy's trainer and never go back. We couldn't do the same with Magdalena and school. How do you tell a child to trust the adults that you yourself do not? How do you tell a lie to someone who only knows you to tell the truth? How do you say to your child "you are safe at school" when you know it's untrue? If I agree with the schools, then I'm putting my child in harm's way, and I'm forced to lie to my child so that she won't believe that we are complicit.

I realize now that Annie and I have our own form of PTSD. We want nothing more than for Magda to be successful. We want our daughter to be stretched beyond what has constrained her. Why then do I still find myself restrained by the facts of her past, our past? Why can't I let the weight of those burdens slip from my shoulders? Especially now that she has arrived in a place that cares for her and loves her, and only wants the best for her.

I see her smiling, say the demons.

Yes, but she still strains to make eye contact with those she is interacting with, I counter.

See, she is hugging people, one whispers.

Yes, but she only gives her body to them sideways, I note.

I know that it will take time to undo what has been done to all of us, but I am looking forward to that process.

In 2005, the epidemic of autism struck my house; it just wasn't the plague reported in the papers. We were never prepared to have an autistic daughter, but like most special needs parents, we learned. Ten years after a team of professionals had coaxed speech past Magda's lips, my daughter would tell me how much she hated the word epidemic because it made autism sound like a sickness. I told her the moniker was true, but that the epidemic in autism rested with people in positions of power passing corruption and deceit back and forth like a virus.

Words are weapons in the war against cruelty. And if they can't be used to destroy, at least they can be there to document the atrocity. In Emily Perl Kingsley's poem "Welcome to Holland," she offers consoling thoughts to new parents of disabled children saying they have not arrived in "a horrible, disgusting, filthy place, full of pestilence, famine and disease. It's just a different place." I struggle to believe her.

Daisy was real. She wasn't a metaphor. Magdalena is real, and her childhood educational experience unearthed a side of humanity full of pestilence and disease.

Annie and I consider ourselves among the rare few parents who clawed their way out. But unfortunately, for so many others, there is no way out. There are no other options.

I can tell you that today Magda's smile has made a comeback. I can tell you that she misses her old friend every day. I can tell you that she is relishing making a connection with her newest friend. I can tell you that she gets invited to birthday parties and that she has peers in her life that consider her a friend. And I can tell you that is a good start.

Author's Parting Thoughts

"Find out just what any people will quietly submit to, and you have found out the exact measure of injustice and wrong which will be imposed upon them."

— Frederick Douglass

When I completed the manuscript for *Daisy Has Autism*, the Centers for Disease Control (CDC) had just released a report detailing the prevalence of autism in the United States. Their Autism and Developmental Disabilities Monitoring (ADDM) Network estimated that one in fifty-nine children had an autism spectrum disorder (ASD) at the time of writing. The CDC also reaffirmed that boys are four-to-one more likely to be identified as having an ASD than girls. This finding is often misconstrued to mean that boys are much more likely to have autism than girls. In fact, the CDC's own website makes that claim.

After Leo Kanner published his groundbreaking work on autism in 1943, it took until 1980 before the American Psychiatric Association included ASD in the "bible" of psychiatric diagnoses, the Diagnostic and Statistical Manual of Mental Disorders (DSM-III). Seven years after finally acknowledging autism, that same group would finally remove homosexuality from the DSM.

In order to believe the underlying assumption that boys and girls are disproportionately affected, and there is some yet undiscovered fundamental reason for this disparity, one must have faith that the current definition of autism is equally applicable to boys and girls. If that is true, one must also have faith that the testing mechanisms and instruments are equally valid for every gender identity. But more to the point, one must believe that the current mechanism for autism identification is unbiased.

Digging deeper into the CDC report also reveals that there are racial disparities in the reported prevalence of autism, despite the fact that there is no science to support that skin color has any relationship to developmental disorders or intellectual abilities. The CDC does acknowledge that non-white children are less likely to be identified and tested.

Like most health care disparities today, autism should also be held as an exemplar when discussing access to services based on gender, ethnicity, and socioeconomic status.

Even though developmental concerns can be recognized by as early as sixth months of age, and an ASD diagnosis can reliably be obtained by a child's second birthday, the CDC showed that the average identified autistic isn't diagnosed until age four – and they are mostly white males. The lack of, or delay in, identification portends huge risks to the children and families affected by autism.

When a child turns three, the responsibility for identifying and providing intervention services to disabled children is transitioned to the public school system. Even if an autistic child qualified for government-based services prior to their third birthday, there is no guarantee that services, or even identification, will survive the transition to the school-based Individualized Educational Program (IEP) required by law.

There is also no guarantee that the public schools are actively seeking out and testing children for disabilities such as autism, as they are required to do by federal law. The CDC's estimated incidence of autism is heavily reliant upon the data captured during the special education testing of children in public schools. If we are to believe that only one in fifty-nine children has autism, and that the gender and racial disparities are legitimate, we also have to believe the source data to be true and accurate. *Daisy Has Autism* sheds light on why we should *not* believe this.

The special needs community needs a #metoo movement. The goal of *Daisy Has Autism* is to spark a national conversation. What your school district does is a matter of public record, and your local school boards are serving at the behest of the public. It is their responsibility to oversee how your schools provide access to your child's education.

Pressure from the top requires oversight because self-policing by school administrators and school boards is rarely effective. Pressure from the bottom requires you. The kind of change you and I want to see requires political pressure. If this book has moved you to action, here are a few things you can do:

- Write your state superintendent of education demanding change.
- Write the secretary of education demanding the same.
- Be visible and present at your local school board meetings, more than once. Ask to be put on the agenda.
- Make a public records requests of your district and ask how much money they are spending on legal fees fighting special needs families.
- Demand that your school district provide appropriate training to staff who interact with, provide services to, and are responsible for identifying disabled children – and demand proof that they've done it.
- Share your story publicly in as many venues as possible.

Tip O'Neill, the former Speaker of the House from 1977 to 1987, is credited as saying that "all politics are local." If you take away anything from *Daisy Has Autism*, remember that your voice in the operation of your public schools rests with the school board members and trustees that you elect. You are not alone. If they do not represent your voice or your values, the most powerful thing you can do is to either persuade them or vote them out!

Sources:

Baio J, Wiggins L, Christensen DL, et al. Prevalence of Autism Spectrum Disorder Among Children Aged 8 Years — Autism and Developmental Disabilities Monitoring Network, 11 Sites, United States, 2014. MMWR Surveill Summ 2018;67(No. SS-6):1–23. DOI: http://dx.doi.org/10.15585/mmwr.ss6706a1

https://www.cdc.gov/ncbddd/autism/data.html

Acknowledgments

Janet Angelo, for helping this bird take flight

Joyce Irvine, for helping me reframe the debate

Leo C. Jones, for always keeping things interesting

Scott Russell, for your stage presence

Matthew Deusans, for your detective skills and mastery of the public record

The Davis AYSO community, for giving all of us a safe haven

The Davis special needs community, for your support and tenacity

The Manks, for laying out the first few mile markers

Children's Therapy Center in Woodland, CA, for doing what you do

The STAR Center, for expanding our toolkit exponentially

Felix Battistella, for accepting nothing less than common sense and critical thinking

Lara Hoekstra, for being my favorite English teacher

Ian Marrow, for helping to keep me sane

The beta readers, for sharpening the edge

Our parents, for your unending support

The Guistinos, for laughing at the exact same things

The teachers and therapists who showed up wanting to make a difference, for being willing to see what everyone was so motivated to hide

Lisa Greenberg, for stretching what often appears unpliable

"L" de Milo, for the way you think

All the people who came into our home, because you became family

Bill Coate, for convincing a thirteen-year-old that someday this was possible

Yolo County Animal Shelter, for the gifts you've given us

Arthur Brito, for always keeping the laces out

Veronica "Kitty" Foley, for all of the listening and all of the scotch

Anyone willing to see this as a call to action

My bike, the lake, and a good pair of running shoes – for keeping the balance

Julia, for being tough as nails and sharp as a tack

Ryan, for being my first teacher, and for having to work twice as hard as a sibling (and for being the first one to know)

Lisa, for everything

And forever Daisy, for loving all of us

About the Author

Aaron J. Wright is the product of a public education and a member of a family deeply entrenched in public education. He is a Nurse Practitioner and the parent of two children, one with autism. Professionally he has worked with severely injured adults and children for nearly two decades. Outside of work, he has been a staunch advocate for disabled students in public education and youth sports. He firmly believes in the benefits of a public education and access. He lives in the San Francisco Bay Area with his family and three distinctly different dogs.

Aaron's contact information:

Follow me on Twitter at: @Aaron_J_Wright
Facebook: Daisy Has Autism
Email me at: daisyhasautism@gmail.com
www.daisyhasautism.com

Physical mail:

Aaron J. Wright
PO Box 3423
4900 Shattuck Ave.
Oakland, CA 94609-2031

Made in the USA
Coppell, TX
03 July 2020